"Matthias Küntzel's new work is a fascinating and important exploration of the influence of Nazi propaganda during a crucial period in the formation of the modern Middle East. Like all the best books, it challenges the reader to consider familiar terrain from a new perspective, with a fresh analysis rooted in archival sources and rigorous research. The story it tells is, as the title suggests, shocking in its implications."

Dr. Dave Rich, *Director of Policy at the Community Security Trust*

"This book is required reading for anyone wanting to discover the antisemitic roots of the Middle East conflict and its devastating consequences. Küntzel deftly transcends prevailing assumptions about the region to reveal how adept the Nazis were at exporting genocidal antisemitism to the region."

R. Amy Elman, *Kalamazoo College, USA*

"Making crucial connections between history and contemporary realities, this book is a must-read for anyone who seeks to fathom the complexities of today's Middle East and what they bode for tomorrow."

David Patterson, *Hillel H. Feinberg Distinguished Chair in Holocaust Studies, University of Texas at Dallas, USA*

T0384833

NAZIS, ISLAMIC ANTISEMITISM AND THE MIDDLE EAST

Nazis, Islamic Antisemitism and the Middle East demonstrates the impact on the Arab world of Nazi ideology and propaganda in the 1930s and beyond.

In 1937, with the brochure "Islam and Judaism," a new form of Jew-hatred came into the world: Islamic antisemitism. The Nazis did everything they could to anchor this new message of hate through their Arabic-language radio propaganda. The book sheds light on this hitherto unknown chapter of Germany's past. It presents new archive findings that show how the image of Jews in Islam changed between 1937 and 1948 under the influence of this propaganda and other Nazi activities. This fresh look at Middle East history allows for a more precise assessment of the present: What exactly is "Islamic antisemitism"? How is it currently manifesting itself in Germany and France? What makes it particularly dangerous? Only when we understand how strongly modern Middle East history is shaped by the aftermath of National Socialism will we be able to correctly interpret the hatred of Jews in this region and its echo among Muslims in Europe and develop adequate countermeasures.

This volume will be of interest to those researching antisemitism, Nazi foreign policy and the political history of the Middle East.

Matthias Küntzel is a German political scientist and historian. His previous books include *Jihad and Jew-Hatred: Islamism, Nazism and the Roots of 9/11* and *Germany and Iran: From the Aryan Axis to the Nuclear Threshold*.

Studies in Contemporary Antisemitism

Series editors

David Hirsh, *Senior Lecturer in Sociology, Goldsmiths, University of London and Academic Director of the London Centre for the Study of Contemporary Antisemitism* and Rosa Freedman, *Professor in the School of Law, University of Reading and Research Fellow at the London Centre for the Study of Contemporary Antisemitism.*

Published in conjunction with the London Centre for the Study of Contemporary Antisemitism, *Studies in Contemporary Antisemitism* is a timely, multidisciplinary book series, drawing primarily, but not exclusively, on the social sciences and the humanities. The series encourages academically rigorous and critical publications across several disciplines that are explicit in understanding and opposing the presence and ascendancy of contemporary antisemitism in both its theoretical and empirical manifestations. The series provides a unique opportunity to offer an intellectual home for a diversity of works that, taken together, crystallize around the study of contemporary antisemitism. The series consists of research monographs, edited collections and short form titles.

Nazis, Islamic Antisemitism and the Middle East
The 1948 Arab War against Israel and the Aftershocks of World War II
Matthias Küntzel

For more information about this series, please visit: www.routledge.com/studies-in-contemporary-antisemitism/ book-series/SICA

NAZIS, ISLAMIC ANTISEMITISM AND THE MIDDLE EAST

The 1948 Arab War against Israel and the Aftershocks of World War II

Matthias Küntzel

Translated by Colin Meade

Routledge
Taylor & Francis Group

LONDON AND NEW YORK

Designed cover image: Getty Images

First published in English 2024
by Routledge
4 Park Square, Milton Park, Abingdon, Oxon OX14 4RN

and by Routledge
605 Third Avenue, New York, NY 10158

Routledge is an imprint of the Taylor & Francis Group, an informa business

© 2024 Matthias Küntzel

Published in German by Hentrich & Hentrich 2019

British Library Cataloguing-in-Publication Data
A catalogue record for this book is available from the British Library

Library of Congress Cataloging-in-Publication Data
Names: Küntzel, Matthias, author.
Title: Nazis, Islamic antisemitism and the Middle East : the 1948 Arab War against Israel and the aftershocks of WW II / Matthias Küntzel.
Other titles: Nazis und der Nahe Osten. English. | 1948 Arab War against Israel and the aftershocks of WW II
Description: Abingdon, Oxon ; New York, NY : Routledge, 2024. |
Series: Studies in contemporary antisemitism | "Originally published 2019 as 'Nazis und der Nahe Osten: Wie der islamische Antisemitismus entstand'"—Foreword. | Includes bibliographical references and index. | In English, translated from the original German.
Identifiers: LCCN 2023007164 (print) | LCCN 2023007165 (ebook) | ISBN 9781032438504 (hardback) | ISBN 9781032437767 (paperback) | ISBN 9781003369110 (ebook)
Subjects: LCSH: Antisemitism—Arab countries. | Islam—Relations—Judaism. | Judaism—Relations—Islam. | National socialism—Influence. | Israel-Arab War, 1948–1949.
Classification: LCC DS146.A67 K86 2024 (print) | LCC DS146.A67 (ebook) | DDC 305.892/40174927—dc23/eng/20230510
LC record available at https://lccn.loc.gov/2023007164
LC ebook record available at https://lccn.loc.gov/2023007165

ISBN: 978-1-032-43850-4 (hbk)
ISBN: 978-1-032-43776-7 (pbk)
ISBN: 978-1-003-36911-0 (ebk)

DOI: 10.4324/9781003369110

Typeset in Times New Roman
by codeMantra

CONTENTS

FOREWORD

Nazis, Islamic Antisemitism and the Middle East makes available to English readers Küntzel's 2019 work *Nazis und der Nahe Osten: Wie der islamische Antisemitismus entstand* [Nazis and the Middle East: How Islamic Antisemitism Emerged], a work that examined the intertwining and the antisemitic aftereffects of Nazism and Islamism. Though it emerged from the intellectual and scholarly climate in Germany in recent decades, its arguments are of direct relevance to discussions of these issues in Britain and the English-speaking world in general. *Nazis, Islamic Antisemitism and the Middle East* offers a bold and compelling interpretation of the origins of the Arab–Israel war of 1948 that challenges a great deal of liberal and certainly leftist conventional wisdom. It offers essential historical background to the study of contemporary antisemitism.

Matthias Küntzel is a leading figure among liberals in Germany who have examined the historical connections between Nazi Germany and Islamist ideologues and organizations during World War II and the Holocaust as well as their political aftereffects in the immediate postwar years. In that context, the German political tradition of frank reckoning with crimes of the Nazi past, including the Holocaust, includes scholars and writers who examine contemporary antisemitism in all of its three variations on the right, on the left and from Islamists. In 2003, *ca ira*, a small, left-liberal publisher in Freiburg, Germany, published Matthias Küntzel's *Djihad und Judenhass: Über die neuen antijüdischen Krieg* (Jihad and Jew-Hatred: On the New Anti-JewishWar).

In that work, Küntzel traced the ideological lineage of the Al Qaeda terrorists of the 9/11 attacks from the Arab collaborators with Nazi Germany, the Muslim Brotherhood from the 1940s to the 1960s, to the Hamas Charter of 1988, and then to Osama bin Laden and Al Qaeda. In 2007, Telos Press in the United States published a revised and expanded English translation entitled *Jihad and Jew-Hatred:*

Islamism, Nazism, and the Roots of 9/11. As I was working on the anti-Jewish propaganda of the Nazi regime and shared Küntzel's views of the reactionary character of Islamist ideology, I agreed to write the foreword to the American edition. *Jihad and Jew-Hatred* was one of the most important works published in Europe and the United States that examined Islamism and terror in the decade following the 9/11 attacks.

Nazis, Islamic Antisemitism and the Middle East examines how the Nazis could anchor Islamist antisemitism in the Arab world and how the image of the Jews in Islam changed under the influence of Nazi Germany's Arabic language propaganda. Islamism emerged as a distinctive interpretation of the religion of Islam evident in key texts by Haj Amin el-Husseini, Hassan Al-Banna and Sayyid Qutb. The result was to justify "a religious war" which fostered a cult of martyrdom, fanaticism and justification of terror aimed at the Jews. Antisemitism in the Arab societies was not primarily a response to the establishment of the state of Israel. Rather "admiration for Hitler and Rommel and hatred of the Jews was strong before Israel was established. After 1945, the Arab area was the only region of the world in which a pro-National Socialist past was a source of pride, not shame." One of Küntzel's key arguments is that the reason for that anomaly was not the establishment of Israel but "the influence of the Nazis on events in the Middle East between 1937 and 1948 and the impact of years of antisemitic Nazi propaganda in the Arabic language... Only when we understand how strong modern Middle Eastern history was influenced by the aftereffects (*Nachwirkungen*) of National Socialism will we be able to properly understand and adequately counter Jew-hatred (*Judenhass*) in this region and its echo among Muslims in Europe" (23–24).

Nazis, Islamic Antisemitism and the Middle East attributes agency to the Arabs, in particular to Husseini, and his text of 1937, "Islam and the Jews." Küntzel calls it "the founding document of Islamic antisemitism" (34), one that presented "the first comprehensive statement that constructed a continuous line connecting Mohammed's confrontation with the Jews in Medina and the contemporary conflict in Palestine, and that linked the seventh to the twentieth century"(34). Husseini contributed to transforming "a limited and secular conflict over Palestinian territory into an unlimited religious war that was a matter of life and death" (64) at whose core what an antagonism to the Jews which Husseini claimed was at the core of Islam. Part of the historical import of "Islam and the Jews" was that Husseini wrote it four years before he went to Berlin in 1941 and began his most intense collaboration with Nazi Germany, and 11 years before the state of Israel was founded in 1948. Küntzel draws attention to this temporal sequence to reject the argument that postwar antisemitism in the Middle East was a consequence of Zionism and the establishment of the state of Israel.

Küntzel argues that "this early moment in time suggests that it was not the later intensification of the Middle East conflict that fostered antisemitism. Rather it was the antisemitism that was previously fanned and inflamed [in 1937] that produced the subsequent conflict and its intensification" (35–36). In other words, Islamic antisemitism was not the result of the Zionist goals before 1948 or of the actions of the state of Israel during the war of 1948 and after. Rather, it was the cause first of the rejection of the compromise partition plans and then of the war itself.

Küntzel interprets the war of 1948 as an "aftershock of National Socialism" (84). It took place "because Nazi Germany's antisemitic Arabic language propaganda shaped the political climate of the postwar years and because in this heated climate no one was able to put limits on the politics of the Mufti and the Moslem Brotherhood." The Arab war against Israel of 1948 was "a kind of aftershock of the previous Nazi war against the Jews. Amin el-Husseini, the Mufti of Jerusalem, embodied the continuity between both events" (84).

He concludes that fighting antisemitism today requires a rethinking of the Israeli–Arab–Palestinian conflict. "If it is the case that Nazi propaganda made an important contribution to antisemitism in the Arab world, then our view of the Middle East conflict needs to change. It is not Israel's settlement blocks but rather the Palestinian ideological blockade that constitutes the biggest barrier to peaceful arrangements. The Jew-hatred in this region must no longer be played down as a kind of local custom. For when we are looking at the antisemitic manifestations that take place from the Middle East to Europe, we are looking directly at the face of our own past" (123). Küntzel's argument thus asserts that the meaning of coming to terms with the Nazi past includes understanding the causal importance that Nazism had for fostering and strengthening antisemitism in the Middle East.

The arguments and evidence in *Nazis, Islamic Antisemitism and the Middle East* recall the years immediately following the Holocaust when liberals and leftists in the late 1940s in Britain, Western Europe, the United States all viewed the Zionist project as a continuation of World War II anti-Nazism. The Soviet Union also supported the Zionists with a mixture of shared wartime antifascism and hopes of driving the "Western imperialists" out of the Middle East.

With the benefit of decades of published research and his own original work in the archives, Küntzel can offer a deeper understanding of Islamic antisemitism than was possible at the time. To those liberals and leftists who have not followed the scholarship of recent decades, *Nazis, Islamic Antisemitism and the Middle East* will indeed come as a bit of a shock, but it is a necessary and long overdue jolt to conventional wisdom. It comprises an original and again path-breaking contribution to the scholarship and intellectual discussion of the origins, nature and consequences of both the indigenous and international sources of Islamic antisemitism from 1937 to the present.

It is most welcome that it should appear in a series sponsored by the London Centre for the Study of Contemporary Antisemitism. Tragically, the not-so-very-distant past is apparent in strains contemporary antisemitism. The English edition comprises valuable contribution both to scholarship and to public discussion.

Jeffrey Herf
University of Maryland, College Park
December 2022

ABBREVIATIONS

ADAP	Akten zur Deutschen Auswärtigen Politik
ADL	Anti-Defamation League
AdG	Keesing's Archiv der Gegenwart
BAB	Bundesarchiv Berlin
BA-MA	Bundesarchiv Militärarchiv Freiburg
BDS	Boycott, Divestment, Sanctions
BESA	Begin-Sadat Center for Strategic Studies
BNA	British National Archive
CDU	Christliche Demokratische Union Deutschlands
CSU	Christlich Soziale Union in Bayern
DGK	Deutsches Generalkonsulat
Ditip	Türkisch-Islamische Union der Anstalt für Religion
DS	Drucksache (printed matter)
FAZ	Frankfurter Allgemeine Zeitung
FDP	Freie Demokratische Partei
IGS	Islamische Gemeinschaft der Schiitischen Gemeinden in Deutschland
IS	Islamic State
ISIS	Islamic State in Iraq and Syria
IZH	Islamisches Zentrum Hamburg
JTA	Jewish Telegraphic Agency
MEMRI	Middle East Media Research Institute
NACP	National Archive College Park (USA)
NATO	North Atlantic Treaty Organization
NSDAP	Nationalsozialistische Deutsche Arbeiterpartei
OIC	Organization of Islamic Cooperation
PAAA	Politisches Archiv des Auswärtige Amts

PMW	Palestinian Media Watch
POW	Prisoner of War
SPD	Sozialdemokratische Partei Deutschlands
SS	Schutzstaffel
ToI	Times of Israel
UNESCO	United Nations Educational, Scientific and Cultural Organization
UNSCOP	United Nations Special Committee on Palestine
ZfA	Zentrum für Antisemitismusforschung
ZMO	Zentrum Moderner Orient

INTRODUCTION

According to my Webster's New World dictionary, an "aftershock" is "a minor earthquake that follows a larger earthquake and originates at or near the same place."

In this book, I refer to the 1948 Arab war against Israel as an aftershock. Here I show for the first time how that "minor" war was connected to the "larger" Nazi war against the Jews that ended in 1945.

The central role of Nazi antisemitism in the planning and implementation of the Shoah is well known. The impact of that same Nazi antisemitism on the Middle East, on the other hand, remains gravely under-researched.

My book aims to fill this gap to the extent currently possible. It sets forth the methods used by Nazi Germany from 1937 onward to disseminate its antisemitism in the Middle East in the Arabic language and the role that this antisemitism would play 11 years later, when the Arab armies fell upon the newly founded Jewish state of Israel. This fateful war triggered the refugee catastrophe that has marked the Middle East conflict ever since.

I am not the only person to have noticed the similarities between Middle Eastern antisemitism and that of the Nazis. Thus, 30-years ago, Bernard Lewis, the doyen of Middle East research, stated that "Since 1945, certain Arab countries have been the only places in the world where hard-core, Nazi-style anti-Semitism is publicly and officially endorsed and propagated."[1]

His finding has subsequently been confirmed by many studies detailing the denial or even justification of the Holocaust in this part of the world,[2] the striking similarities between Arab anti-Jewish caricatures and those of the Nazis,[3] the many Arabic editions of Hitler's *Mein Kampf*[4] and *The Protocols of the Elders of Zion*[5] and the pro-Hitler sentiments of Arab youth.[6]

At the same time, however, this "hard-core Nazi-style antisemitism" is usually attributed to a single cause: Zionism and Israel's role in the region.

DOI: 10.4324/9781003369110-1

This argument is, first, methodologically false. One of the main results of antisemitism research is the understanding that antisemitism does not originate with the Jews so that reference back to alleged Jewish behavior cannot explain it. Second, however reprehensible Israel's behavior might conceivably be, it can neither explain nor justify the glorification of National Socialism. Third, only in recent years has the significance of the Nazis' Arabic-language propaganda as a means for exerting influence in the Arab world been brought to light, notably through the pioneering work of Jeffrey Herf. In 2009 he introduced us to the content of the manuscripts of the Nazis' Arabic-language broadcasts in his book *Nazi Propaganda for the Arab World*. Five years later, David Motadel published further important findings in his study *Islam and Nazi Germany's War*.[7]

Building on these studies, the current book shows that it was the Nazis themselves who initially brought genocidal antisemitism to the Arab world. At the same time, it presents a series of new facts that have the potential to change our view of the past and present of the Middle East conflict.

First of all, I set out what is currently known about the origin and dissemination of the pamphlet *Judaism and Islam*, which was first published in 1937 in Cairo. It is a shocking text that uses religion for the sole purpose of inciting Jew-hatred. The Nazis distributed large numbers of copies of this text in several languages in Muslim-inhabited regions. A translation of the German version, published in 1938 in Berlin, appears as an appendix to this book.

This piece is significant because it represents the first attempt to link the Jew-hatred of early Islam to Christian-inspired antisemitism of European origin and thus create a new expression of Jew-hatred – Islamic antisemitism. The very date of its publication and dissemination – 11 years before the foundation of Israel and 30 years before Israel's assumption of control in Gaza and the West Bank – is revealing, since it shows genocidal Jew-hatred to be a cause, not a consequence of later crises in the Middle East conflict.

Second, I present new archival discoveries relating to the collaboration between German Nazi agents and the Muslim Brotherhood in Egypt – activity in which Goebbels took a close personal interest. In 1938–1939, the focus of this collaboration was Palestine. The Nazi operation paid off after 1945, when that very same Muslim Brotherhood, now grown into a mass movement, pushed the Arab rulers into war against Israel.

Third, I analyze – building on the previously mentioned study by Jeffrey Herf – the nature and impact of the Nazis' Arabic-language radio propaganda broadcasts that disseminated and exacerbated Jew-hatred in this part of the world between 1939 and 1945. One of the consequences of this propaganda was that by 1947 large swathes of the Arab public viewed a Jewish state as a mortal threat that had to be violently destroyed.

Fourth, I describe the measures taken by the Nazis in 1944/1945 to prepare for the forthcoming war against Israel. With their own defeat looming, they wished to preserve their antisemitic legacy by taking steps to prevent the future establishment of a Jewish state.

Fifth, I for the first time substantiate in detail my assumption that the Nazis' antisemitic propaganda was one of the decisive factors that led to the Arab states going to war against Israel in May 1948. I show that there is an ideological link between the Nazi war against the Jews and the Arab war against Israel three years later so that the latter can be interpreted as a kind of aftershock of the great catastrophe of 1939–1945. With this thesis I break new ground. I am well aware that my interpretation does not amount to a definitive judgment and that the topic requires further research, in particular by scholars who read Arabic.

My book lays a particular emphasis on the years 1937 and 1947. In 1937 the British Peel Commission brought forward the first proposal for a two-state solution for Palestine. In 1947 a resolution setting out a two-state plan for Palestine was adopted by the General Assembly of the United Nations by a two-thirds majority and with the support of both the United States and the Soviet Union. Moreover, on both occasions there were Arabs who favored the path of moderation and compromise. Why then did both efforts at compromise fail?

The answer is of the greatest contemporary relevance, at a time when the "Abraham Accords" of 2020 – peace agreements between Israel and the United Arab Emirates and Bahrain – have offered a new prospect of compromise between Jewish and Arab interests.

In 1937, in order to defeat the Peel Commission proposal, the pseudo-religious pamphlet *Judaism and Islam* was conceived; in 1947, in order to block the implementation of the UN decision, Zionism was denounced as an alleged "danger to all the Islamic nations." In subsequent years, an Islamized antisemitism was repeatedly mobilized to block compromise and normalization.

Today the religion of Islam is again being used as an instrument to prevent reconciliation. Today once more, the rulers in Ankara and Tehran, in Ramallah and Gaza, are resorting to their special interpretation of Islam in order to undermine the Abraham Accords. "Normalization means that you agree … to natural relations with the enemies of Prophet Muhammad," Mahmoud Al-Habbash, the Palestinian Authority's top sharia judge, has threatened,[8] while in May 2021 Hamas used the religious symbol of the Al-Aqsa Mosque to justify its attacks on Jerusalem and Israel. The declared aim of the hail of missiles was to torpedo the cautious process of reconciliation between Israel and the Arab world currently under way.[9] Whether, with the Abraham Accords, the forces of peace will finally prevail, is in no way certain, but it is certainly a hope.

Islamic Antisemitism

A second hope that I place in this book is that of overcoming the resistance to discussion of the topic of Muslim antisemitism.

Many observers prefer to avoid mention of antisemitism among Muslims out of fear of being labeled "racist" or "Islamophobic." They feel "motivated to deny the problem, to minimize it, to excuse it, to explain it away, and to attack or ridicule those who see it as important."[10]

It is true that not only are there some people who try to whitewash Islam and deny any connection between it and Jew-hatred, but also others who no less sweepingly wish to besmirch the name of Islam and make the religion the sole reason for Muslim antisemitism. I reject both generalizations. In dealing with this topic careful distinctions, semantic and historic analysis and a lack of ideological prejudice are all requirements. The book's first chapter therefore is devoted to establishing for the first time a precise definition of the term "Islamic antisemitism."

In the final chapter, I return to this matter. Here I consider the intra-Islamic arguments regarding Jew-hatred among Muslims, the role of Islamic antisemitism in Europe and the question of how this hatred can be combated in Germany and beyond.

New Debates in the Arab World

The ideas put forward in this book may help to provide an answer to a question now being posed by increasing numbers of people in the region as they contemplate Israel's successful development and the depressing condition of many Arab societies: what went wrong? Thus, in Chapter 5 I document a series of statements from Arab sources that deal self-critically with their governments' traditional rejectionist approach towards Israel.

They lament the fact that in 1937 and 1947, possibilities for compromise were rejected, retrospectively declare the various Israel boycotts of recent decades to be mistaken and examine the antisemitism and Israel-hatred of the Arab world.

Certain Arab media have also dealt with the destructive role of Hajj Amin al-Husseini, the former Mufti of Jerusalem, and his alliances with the Nazis and the Islamist Muslim Brotherhood.

Thus, in April 2019 a film festival in Ismailia in Egypt featured a documentary about the Nazi ties of the Muslim Brotherhood's founder, Hassan al-Banna.[11] Then in February 2020 the popular Saudi daily newspaper *Okaz* published a lengthy article entitled "The Nazi Brotherhood," which dealt with the relations between Hitler, Al-Husseini and the Muslim Brotherhood. The cover picture showed Hassan al-Banna wearing a fez with a swastika on it.[12]

The new discussions about these connections are most welcome. However, the photomontage of Al-Banna with the swastika reveals a propagandistic intent: to damage a political opponent, in this case the Muslim Brotherhood, by using inaccurate accusations. While my book rejects such simplifications, I nonetheless hope that the incipient discussion of previous Arab mistakes will lead to an increased interest in verifiable historical facts.

New Debates in the USA?

It is my impression as an outside observer that anti-Zionist propaganda is making inroads in the USA. For example, when in February 2020 the renowned historian

Deborah Lipstadt spoke on antisemitism at the University of California's Berkeley Law School, three young people displayed placards in protest. The first placard advocated BDS, the second asserted that "anti-Zionism" was not antisemitism and the third referred to the 1948 Middle East war in these terms: "The crimes of 1948: 800,000 refugees, 13,000 killed, 531 villages destroyed, 11 urban neighborhoods emptied."[13]

The 1948 war was, of course, a war in which not only Jews but also Arabs suffered terribly. The problem with the placard is that it stands historical reality on its head by holding Israel responsible for the war. The three young people seem ignorant of the fact that the Jewish side supported the UN partition resolution, while the Arab rulers not only rejected it but launched their war with the explicit aim of destroying Israel. Moreover, the protestors, who presumably belong to the progressive part of American society, seem unaware that in 1948 the Soviet Union explicitly praised Israel for its pro-UN behavior and deemed the Arab world responsible for the outflow of refugees.

The placard display followed an age-old antisemitic pattern in which historical facts are twisted as much as is necessary to make the Jews appear solely responsible for war and misery. This pattern was repeated during the Gaza war of May 2021. This time it was not some ignorant youths but the prestigious *New York Times* that shocked its readers with half-truths designed to channel their anger towards Israel.

On 28 May 2021, the *Times* published on its front page, under the headline "They Were Just Children," portraits of 64 children alleged to have been killed as a result of Israeli attacks on Gaza. The paper glossed over the fact that it was Hamas – the Palestinian branch of the Muslim Brotherhood – that had unleashed this latest war. In addition, there was not a word about the fact that Hamas deliberately places its launch pads in residential areas, abusing those living there as human shields whose sufferings can then be used to further whip up hatred against the Israeli "child-murderers."[14] Instead of providing this crucial information, the influential paper played Hamas's game: it one-sidedly condemned Israel using a picture that lent itself to interpretation in terms of the venerable clichés about Jewish child-murder.

This book aims to correct such distortions of reality. For they are not without consequences: according to a poll conducted by the ADL in June 2021, 60% of American Jews surveyed had been subject to online and offline antisemitic attacks in the context of the May 2021 war. Over three-quarters expressed their growing concern over rising Jew-hatred and a similarly large majority called for stronger political countermeasures.[15]

It was not Israel or Zionism that provoked the May 2021 war but the anti-Zionism and antisemitism in the Arab world. And it is not Israel and Zionism that have created the exceptional state of affairs we have become accustomed to calling the Middle East conflict: the only exceptional thing that places the Jewish state in an exceptional situation is the 75-year-old anti-Zionist and Islamist call to destroy it. No other state in the world is confronted with this kind of campaign.

At the source of this flood of hate lies the Nazis' desire to transform the political conflict over Palestine into an antisemitic war of life and death. They wanted to destroy not only the Jews but any prospect of Jewish statehood. After 1945 the antisemitic part of Arab society – led by Amin al-Husseini and the Muslim Brotherhood – continued this war. They caused the aftershock – the 1948 war – that further strengthened the "hard-core, Nazi-style antisemitism" and continues to shape the Middle East conflict this day.

My Approach

My book is written from the point of view of a non-Jewish author who is interested in the effects of antisemitism on the development of the Middle Eastern conflict. This point of view implies a certain degree of partisanship. First, the study of Jew-hatred and racism is never a neutral activity, but, especially since 1945, has been bound up with the moral imperative of repressing and opposing anti-Jewish and racist resentment. Second, my view of the Middle East conflict is not totally neutral. Anyone who has studied racism and is therefore conscious of the sufferings of Black people can scarcely fail to rejoice in the disappearance of apartheid in South Africa whatever reservations they may have about South Africa's current policies.

Applying the same position to Jew-hatred means: because I study antisemitism, I am also conscious of Jewish suffering and cannot do otherwise than welcome the exercise of the Jewish right to self-determination and the resulting existence of a Jewish state, even though I may not always be pleased with Israeli government policies.

Arab nationalists write about the Middle Eastern conflict in other terms. They view the Balfour Declaration of 1917 in which Britain promised "the establishment in Palestine of a national home for the Jewish people" as a mistake. They criticize the fact that in 1922 the League of Nations, the predecessor of the United Nations, recognized not only the Balfour Declaration but also a "historical connection of the Jewish people with Palestine." Both represented major victories for the Zionist movement due to both its negotiating skills and specific historical circumstances. In neither case were Palestine's Arabs consulted. To that extent, I can well understand and respect the alternative interpretation of the facts. I do not, however, feel the same about the accusation advanced by many Arab writers that after 1945 the Arabs in Palestine were made to pay for the Nazis' Jewish policies – so for the sins of others. Because the Palestinian Arabs too bear at least an indirect responsibility for the Holocaust. It was their anti-Zionist campaigns that caused Britain to restrict Jewish immigration to Palestine. Many Jews were murdered because they had no place to flee to. By ensuring that the doors of Palestine were also closed to them, a large proportion of the Arabs living in Palestine bore some responsibility for the impending tragedy.[16]

This book would not have come about without the help of Professor Alvin Rosenfeld, who has followed and supported my work for many years. I would also like to express my profound gratitude to Indiana University's Institute for the Study of Contemporary Antisemitism, which Professor Rosenfeld leads, for financing the translation.

Special thanks must also go to my colleague and friend of many years, Professor Jeffrey Herf, who provided me with a substantial selection of program manuscripts from Radio Zeesen for the purposes of this book, and to Dr Edy Cohen, who translated Arabic texts for me.

There are many more colleagues and friends from different countries who have encouraged me in my work over the years and made it better through their findings and comments. Among them are Amr Bargisi, Yehuda Bauer, Ulrike Becker, Bastiaan Belder, Russell A. Berman, Pascal Bruckner, Catherine Chatterley, Ben Cohen, Irvin Cotler, R. Amy Elman, Hassan Eltaher, Rolf Fader, Niram Ferretti, Martin Finkenberger, Joel Fishman, Monika Gödecke, Stephan Grigat, Marc Grimm, Gabi Gumbel, Friedhelm Hoffmann, David Ipsen, Günther Jikeli, Alan Johnson, Lesley Klaff, David Labude, Armin Langer, Meir Litvak, Florian Markl, Faryar Nikbakht, Nora Pester, Karl Pfeifer, Mary Piccone, Dina Porat, Yehoshua Porath, Doron Rabinovici, Alexander Ritzmann, Shimon Samuels, Eric Sanders, Boualem Sansal, Kay Schweigmann-Greve, Michael Spaney, Joseph S. Spoerl, Pierre-André Taguieff, Bassam Tibi, Laurence Weinbaum, Michael Whine and Robert S. Wistrich, who sadly left us in 2015.

Last but not least I would like to thank my friend Dr. Colin Meade for his excellent translation and my beloved wife, interlocutor and editor, Rosi Wittenhagen, whose unsparing criticism contributed so much to this work.

Matthias Küntzel, 1 September 2021.

Notes

1 Bernard Lewis, "The Arab World Discovers Anti-Semitism", Sander L. Gilman and Steven T. Katz (eds.), *Anti-Semitism in Times of Crises*, New York and London 1991, 343–352, here 343.
2 Meir Litvak and Esther Webman, *From Empathy to Denial. Arab Responses to the Holocaust*, London 2009, 195.
3 Arieh Stav, *Peace: The Arabian Caricature. A Study of Anti-Semitic Imagery*, New York 1999.
4 Stefan Wild, "'Mein Kampf' in arabischer Übersetzung", *Welt des Islam*, Vol. 9, 1964, 207–211.
5 Stefan Wild, "Importierter Antisemitismus? Die Religion des Islam und die Rezeption der 'Protokolle der Weisen von Zion' in der arabischen Welt", Dirk Ansorge (ed.), *Antisemitismus in Europa und in der arabischen Welt*, Paderborn 2006, 201–216.
6 Bahraini Writer, "I Was Shocked to Discover How Many Young Arabs Idolize Adolf Hitler", *MEMRI*, Special Dispatch No. 6624, 22 September 2016; see this book, Chapter 5.
7 Jeffrey Herf, *Nazi Propaganda for the Arab World*, New Haven, CT 2009; David Motadel, *Islam And Nazi Germany's War*, London 2014.
8 Jacques Zilberdik, "Israel Is 'The Enemy of Prophet Muhammad' – PA Seeks Religious War over UAE-Israel Peace Agreement", *PMW Bulletin*, 19 August 2020.
9 "Hamas Leader in Gaza Yahya Al-Sinwar Salutes Al-Jazeera TV, Iran, and Yasser Arafat, Adds: We have 10.000 'Martyrdom-Seekers' within Israel", *MEMRI*, Special Dispatch No. 9364, 27 May 2021.

10 Neil J. Kressel, *'The Sons of Pigs and Apes'. Muslim Antisemitism and the Conspiracy of Silence*, Washington, D.C. 2012, 97.
11 Hannah Wettig, "Aber die Israelis greifen doch immer an", *Welt*, 28 June 2019.
12 "Saudi Arabia Escalates the Conflict with the Muslim Brotherhood (MB): Saudi Government Daily Claims MB Founder Hassan Al-Banna Worked for the Nazis", *MEMRI*, Special Dispatch No. 8567, 18 February 2020.
13 The photo with the placard-wavers can be found at Stephen M. Flatow, "American Jews Know Antisemitism When They See It", *Algemeiner*, 24 June 2021.
14 Robert Satloff, "What's Wrong with the NY Times' Report on Children's Death? So Much", *Times of Israel*, 31 May 2021.
15 https://www.adl.org/resources/blog/survey-american-jews-recent-violence-israel.
16 Benny Morris, "Dann schickte Allah Adolf Hitler", *Welt*, 30 January 2010.

1

ISLAMIC ANTISEMITISM

We begin with Mohammed Ali, a friend of Iranian origin. He was so named after his dead uncle, an atheist and member of the Iranian Communist Tudeh Party, who had been murdered by agents of the Shah in the 1950. Once in Germany, my friend found that everyone thought he was a Muslim because of his name despite the fact that, while not a member of the Tudeh Party, he still considered himself an atheist. Finally he had had enough. In frustration, he changed his first name from Mohammed Ali to Michael.

This goes to show how an alleged Muslim identity may be falsely attributed and people thereby insulted. Moreover, even among the observant, there is no such thing as the typical Muslim: Muslims differ widely in the practice of their faith. For example, as a teacher in a technical college, I have witnessed "Muslims" openly stating in front of the class that in their hearts they have abandoned Islam. On one occasion – during the fasting month of Ramadan – three Muslim students formed a working group. One of them openly ate ham rolls in the morning, another retreated to the restroom to eat and the third fasted according to the rules without condemning the others.

On the other hand, some of my Muslim students – although by no means all – have bluntly stated that they hate Jews. This comes as no surprise. Every survey in recent years has revealed higher levels of antisemitism among Muslims than non-Muslims.

In 2006, in Great Britain, 47% of Muslims and 7% of the total population had a "negative opinion" of Jews; in France this was true for 28% of Muslims and 13% of the total population, while the corresponding figures for Germany were 44% and 22% respectively. A study conducted by the Berlin Social Science Center revealed a sharp difference between Christians and Muslims ... 7.1% of

DOI: 10.4324/9781003369110-2

Christians and 43.4% of Muslims in France held that Jews could not be trusted. In Germany, the figures were 10.5% of Christians and 28% of Muslims; the corresponding figures in Belgium were 7% and 56.7% respectively.[1]

This shows, according to antisemitism expert Günther Jikeli, "that among Europe's 15 to 22 million Muslims antisemitism, rather than being an exceptional occurrence, is so widespread that Jew-hatred is often the norm."[2]

As with the general population, aversion to Jews by Muslims expresses itself in the most diverse forms: classical conspiracy theories that attribute to "The Jews" an imaginary power over the world economy and media; notions derived from Christian sources such as the ritual blood libel, nationalist constructions that view the Jews as "The Other," denial or relativization of the Holocaust or antisemitism directed at Israel.

However, in addition to all of the above, there is a special type of Jew-hatred that can be found only among Muslims: Islamic antisemitism. Many object to this terminology, claiming that it represents a covert attempt to stigmatize all Muslims. In fact, however, the opposite is the case: linguistic clarity aids the drawing of distinctions. When we talk, for example, of "Christian anti-Judaism," we are not pointing the finger at all Christians but naming a specific and clearly defined ideology. And it has to be named if it is to be combated, above all within Christianity itself.

The same applies to the concept of "Islamic antisemitism." How can we combat this delusion if, in order to avoid upsetting anyone, we dare not name it? The term is aimed neither at Islam in general, whose texts also contain pro-Jewish passages, nor in a blanket fashion at all Muslims, not a few of whom reject antisemitism. Nonetheless, we are dealing here with an ideological doctrine, a specific type of antisemitism, with specific characteristics and specific effects, which must therefore be specifically combated – especially within the Muslim world.

So, what is Islamic antisemitism?

Islamic Anti-Judaism

The roots of enmity towards Jews in Islamic societies lie in the formative period of Islam. The Koran does indeed contain verses in which the *banu Isra'il* ("children of Israel") are praised. "There is guidance, and there is light, in the Torah which We have revealed," states Sura 5, Verse 44, for example. Other verses can be read as legitimating the State of Israel. "We gave the persecuted people dominion over the eastern and western lands which We had blessed. Thus your Lord's gracious words were fulfilled; for the Israelites because they had endured with fortitude," thus Sura 7, Verse 137.

Anti-Jewish statements are, however, considerably more frequent, for example:

Ignominy will attend them wherever they are found.

(Sura 3, Verse 112)

Then your Lord declared that He would raise against them others who would oppress them cruelly till the Day of Resurrection.

(Sura 7, Verse 167)

And he has been angry, changing them into apes and swine.

(Sura 5, Verse 60)

And the most notorious of all, Sura 5, Verse 82: "You will find that the most implacable in their enmity to the faithful are the Jews and pagans."[3]

The Tunisian philosopher, Mezri Haddad, himself a Muslim, has described these verses as "antisemitic dross" and demanded that, since the Koran cannot be amended, they should be reinterpreted with "intellectual audacity" and "hermeneutic reasoning."[4]

The contradictory nature of the image of the Jew in the Koran – sometimes pro-Jewish, sometimes anti-Jewish – is related to Muhammad's prophetic career. This begins in 610 in Mecca. During this period, Muhammad appears as an admirer of Jewish traditions and beliefs. However, his monotheism made no headway in a polytheistic Mecca. As a result, in 622 he moved north from Mecca to the town of Yathrib, later known as Medina, and home to some 10,000 Jews. They were divided into three feuding tribes: the Qurayza, the Nadir and the Qaynuqa. In a place where Jewish monotheism had put down roots, Muhammad's new teaching could hope for a better reception than in Mecca.

Initially, Muhammad anticipated that the Jews of Medina would convert to Islam and support him in winning over the Arab pagans. He therefore adopted many of their rituals and ordered his supporters to pray towards Jerusalem. However, the strictly orthodox Jews were skeptical about and contemptuous of Muhammad's teaching, and their doubts threatened to undermine the faith of Muhammad's own adherents. In response, Muhammad's initial sympathy for the Jews switched over into hostility. This was a watershed development that would take the new religion in a new direction.

In 624, Muhammad found a pretext to force the Qaynuqa to leave Medina; the Nadir had to depart the following year. His treatment of the remaining Jewish tribe, the Qurayza, was especially harsh. In 628, according to Johan Bouman,

Muhammad went to the market in Medina and caused graves to be dug. Then the Jews were brought to him and beheaded by the graves – some 600 to 900 men in total. The executions lasted the whole day. Despite what awaited them, the Jews remained true to their beliefs, with only four converting to Islam to save their lives. The women and children were for the most part sold into slavery in Medina.[5]

It was through this break with the Jews of Medina that Islam developed into an independent religion. After these events, Muhammad's followers would pray towards

Mecca rather than Jerusalem, while the day of prayer was moved from Saturday to Friday. At the same time, the language used of Jews in the Koran changed – no longer are they described as the *banu isra'il*, but as *al-yahud*. And henceforth they would be reproached not only for falsifying the true doctrine but also as a people accursed by Allah whose members no Muslim should befriend.[6]

In 629, a year after the massacre of the Qurayza, Muhammad resumed his triumphal progress. The next step was the Battle of Khaybar, an oasis to the north of Medina. To this day, Muslims recall this battle, chanting: *Khaybar, Khaybar, ya yahud, dschaisch Mohammed saya'ud*! – "Khaybar, Khaybar, oh Jews, Muhammad's army will soon return."

This Jewish-populated oasis was the first place that Muhammad conquered and brought under his sway. He attacked it with an army of 1,400 foot soldiers and 300 horsemen. The siege and bloody fighting lasted a month and a half. Nine hundred Jews were killed. Finally, the surviving Jews surrendered on the condition that, while they could remain in the oasis, they would have to give half of their agricultural yield to the Muslims. This agreement – the Pact of Dhimma ("protection") – set a precedent for the agreements that Christians too would later be compelled to make with their Muslim conquerors.

According to this pact, *dhimmis* ("protected persons") were tolerated and as a rule protected by the authorities as long as they allowed themselves to be humiliated by Muslims and accepted their lower rank and legal status. They were obliged to pay a poll tax, wear degrading clothes and ride donkeys rather than horses. They were forbidden to attend Muslim schools. Their testimony before a court was worth less than that of a Muslim, and Muslims who committed crimes against *dhimmis* only had to pay half the penalty for similar deeds against fellow Muslims.

It is true that, overall, the Muslims offered the Jews of the medieval Orient more tolerance and legal security than did the Christians in Europe. However, this does not justify talking about some kind of "golden age" for Jews living under Islamic rule. They were systematically oppressed and humiliated and also from time to time fell victim to pogroms and massacres.[7] Unlike in Christian tradition, the image of the Jew in Islam was characterized not by fear or envy but by permanent degradation, humiliation and subordination.

An example of how things stood is provided by an account written by the Muslim sheikh Al-Maghili (born 1440). In his view, the *jizya* ("poll tax") "must be paid in a public ceremony in which the *dhimmi* at the moment of payment is given a tap on the neck and pushed forward to show him he has thus escaped the sword. This abasement is more important than the sum paid."[8] The practice is based on Sura 9, Verse 29, of the Koran, according to which Christians and Jews should be "utterly subdued" when they make the payment. "All-pervading fear dominates the history of all Jewish communities in Arab lands," writes historian George Bensoussan. He quotes French Islam expert Eliezer Cherki to prove the point:

> The Jew lives in daily fear, because at any moment he can, on the basis of various pretexts, be summarily arrested, imprisoned, beaten, mortally wounded,

mutilated, etc., on the grounds that he had raised his head or looked directly at a Muslim, not to mention the grave accusations of blasphemy against the Prophet and his companions in violation of the pact of *dhimma* which alone allows him life and protection in return for his subjection and humiliation. This humiliation is his fate, because Allah himself has decreed it in Sura 9/29.[9]

This imperative to humiliate has remained a characteristic of Muslim Jew-hatred to this day. The impulse was clearly on display when in summer 2014 Arab youths in Berlin shouted the slogan "Jew, Jew, cowardly pig, come outside and fight alone." When, in April 2018, an Arab in Berlin took off his belt in order to beat a Kippa wearer with it, he was also following an archaic pattern that expressed more than just a lust for violence: like spitting at or slapping a Jew, a blow from a belt serves to belittle the victim – humiliation was more important here than inflicting actual physical harm.

But let us return to the Middle Ages. While in Medina the issue was still Muhammad's self-assertion against particular Jewish tribes, the victory at Khaybar settled the status of the Jews as such. Henceforth, the Jewish presence would be a secondary problem for Muslim societies. As long as Jews accepted their inferior status, they no longer required any particular attention. The Christians were a different matter. With the onset of the Crusades, they became the main adversaries of Islam.

Of course, Jews were also downtrodden in Christian realms. Here, however, doctrine stated not that, as in Medina, the Prophet killed the Jews, but that the Jews killed the Prophet, in the person of Jesus, the Son of God. In the medieval Mystery Plays that recounted the Passion of Jesus, this myth was permanently reenacted. The difference between the claimed "success" of the Jews against Christ and their "failure" against Muhammad was reflected in the differing images of the Jew in the two religions.

"For the Muslim, he might be hostile, cunning and vindicative, but he was weak and ineffectual – an object of ridicule, not fear," writes Bernard Lewis. "For the Christian, he represented a dark and deadly power, capable of deeds of cosmic evil."[10] Only on Christian soil, therefore, could the propaganda about the Jewish world conspiracy arise and flourish. Only here do we find as long ago as the first quarter of the thirteenth century the charge that "Jewry has united in a conspiracy to totally destroy the whole of Christendom."[11]

When, a few decades later, the Black Death struck, a scapegoat was ready at hand: in league with the Devil, the Jews had inflicted the epidemic on Christendom. Only in a Christian context could religious anti-Judaism grow over into antisemitism.

European Antisemitism

The term "antisemitism" first appeared in the 1870s in Germany at a time when the last remaining restrictions on Jewish civil rights had finally been removed. Jews now enjoyed equal civil and political rights and began to assume influential positions in politics, art, journalism and science and as attorneys, bankers, businessmen and writers. These achievements correlated with the liberalization of capitalism and an unprecedented economic expansion. When, following victory over France in the war of 1870/1871, an additional five billion French gold francs in war reparations flowed into Germany, economic optimism knew no bounds and free enterprise boomed. Thus, in Prussia, in the single year of 1872, "twice as many joint-stock companies were established as in the entire period from 1790 to 1867, among them 49 banks and 61 chemical firms."

Then it all came crashing down. "The world economic crisis of 1873 struck this optimistic, forward-striving and wildly speculating Empire like a flash of lightning," writes Paul W. Massing. "A stock-market crash that wiped out many rapidly acquired fortunes and a vast quantity of hard-won small savings alike inaugurated an economic collapse. It ushered in one of the longest and most serious economic crises in German history."[12]

A scapegoat for the catastrophe was sought and found. In the chaos of the next few years, liberalism, henceforth identified as "Jewish," became the chosen culprit.

The journalist Wilhelm Marr (1819–1904), a man of the Left who had never hidden his loathing of liberalism, saw the signs of the times. His achievement consisted in transferring Jew-hatred from its religious roots "onto a post-religious foundation."[13]

In February 1879, he published a pamphlet that sold like hot cakes, running through twelve editions in its first year, entitled *The Victory of Judaism over Germanism – Considered from a Non-Religious Perspective*. In his very title, Marr distanced himself from traditional anti-Judaism. For him, the opposite of Jewry was no longer Christendom but "Germandom." "Race" replaced religion. According to Marr, owing to their "innate" characteristics and "ethnic nature," the Jews cannot be integrated through either baptism or educational improvement. By designating them as "Semites" (and himself later as an "anti-Semite"), he attempted to provide his racism with a scientific veneer.

It was, of course, nonsense, since there are no Semites, only Semitic languages that differ from other linguistic groups such as the Indo-European. Marr's racist construct of "Semites" would, however, be adopted by the Nazis as the opposite of their equally racist construct of "Aryans."

At the same time, with his paradigm of "the victory of Judaism over Germanism," Marr created a cliché that remains effective to this day, in which the fantasy of Jewish omnipotence is contrasted with the allegedly helpless impotence of non-Jews. Here he skillfully appealed to the feelings of impotence engendered by the economic crisis, creating an outlet for the pressure of ever-growing discontent by casting all the guilt and responsibility onto the Jews. "The 'Jewish question' is a socio-political question," he asserted in his tract: "Who was ... in the vanguard of the destabilizing and socially corrupting boom that followed the [Franco-German] war? The Jews."[14]

Marr and the Anti-Semitic League that he founded would henceforth proceed to attribute any and every unwelcome event to the Jews. It was the Jews who were allegedly responsible for the collapse of traditional social structures, for exploitation and economic crises, and for disunity and periods of national weakness.

While some aspects of this antisemitism were already present in Christian anti-Judaism, the differences are of crucial importance. Anti-Judaism appears in religious guise: the Jew who converts to Christianity or Islam can survive. In contrast, racial antisemitism, by attributing immutable characteristics to Jews, closes this escape route. Second, the aversion in anti-Judaism is restricted to everything specifically Jewish. In contrast, antisemites "know" not only that everything Jewish is evil but that all evil is Jewish – Communism and Wall Street, materialism and destructive criticism.

The key text of antisemitism is a forgery created by Jew-haters that was first published in 1903 known as *The Protocols of the Elders of Zion*, which attributes the responsibility for everything bad that happens in the world to international Jewry. A few decades later, this text would provide the motive for the Nazi Holocaust: if Jews were responsible for all the misery in the world, their annihilation was the only way to redeem that world.

Let us return to Islamic antisemitism. Having first distinguished Islamic from Christian anti-Judaism and, second, anti-Judaism from antisemitism, we can now recognize what distinguishes Islamic antisemitism from all other forms of Jew-hatred: only here are the degrading anti-Judaism of early Islam and the conspiratorial antisemitism of modern times fused together.

So long as under premodern conditions Islam continued to adhere to traditional anti-Judaism, it was not antisemitic. This changed, however, in the course of the twentieth century. Now Muslims begin to adopt the European Christian idea of the Jews as a "cosmic evil." Henceforth, the most negative images of Jews from both Christianity and Islam were brought together, and the twentieth century combined with the seventh. The traditional Islamic images of Jewish weakness and cowardice are linked with the Western conspiracy paranoia about Jews secretly pulling the strings. Here are two examples of this combination at work.

Sayyid Qutb: "Our Struggle with the Jews"

Sayyid Qutb (1906–1966) was the most important ideologist of the Muslim Brotherhood and, in the second half of the twentieth century, one of the most famous figures of the Muslim world. I have described his importance for the development of Islamism elsewhere.[15] Here we will concern ourselves solely with an essay he wrote at the start of the 1950s entitled *Our Struggle with the Jews*. In 1970 this key text of Islamic antisemitism was republished by the government of Saudi Arabia and disseminated throughout the Muslim world.

"The Jews ... plotted against the Muslim Community from the first day it became a community," Qutb writes here. "This bitter war which the Jews launched against Islam," he continues, "is a war which has not been extinguished, even for one moment, for close on fourteen centuries." "The struggle between Islam and the

Jews continues in force and will thus continue, because the Jews will be satisfied only with the destruction of this religion (Islam)."[16]

Here Qutb has revised the Koran and rewritten the traditional history of Islam. While the Jews of Medina in reality had no chance against Muhammad and his companions, Qutb presents the Muslims as the victims and the Jews as the aggressors against Islam. In his mind, the particular local events in Medina become part of a global and bitterly conducted war that can end only with the destruction of one side or the other. The basic structure of this paranoid fantasy is the same as in National Socialism, with the difference that in the latter case it was Germany rather than Islam that the Jews were alleged to be bent on destroying. Hitler projected his own lust for destruction onto the Jews in order to legitimize it. Qutb took the same path ten years later.

Qutb makes only fleeting mention of Hitler in his text. He considers the Nazi efforts to destroy the Jews as a well-deserved and Allah-approved punishment that should now, with the creation of Israel, be followed by "the worst kind of punishment."[17] Unlike in the Koran, moreover, Qutb's image of the Jew is marked by racism. He treats the Jews as a totalized collective marked by characteristics that have remained permanent for thousands of years.

What matters to Qutb is the religious dimension of the dispute. Just as the Jews in Medina allegedly sought to disturb the Muslims and lead them astray, so now, he claims, the Jews are undermining the adherence of Muslims to their faith. Qutb identifies such promoters of modernity as Karl Marx, Sigmund Freud and Emile Durkheim as the most important opponents of Islam, and then "reveals" them to be Jews: "Behind the doctrine of atheistic materialism was a Jew; behind the doctrine of animalistic sexuality was a Jew; and behind the destruction of the family and the shattering of sacred relationships in society, ... was a Jew."[18] Qutb's Jew-hatred thus turns out to be a war cry against the intellectual achievements of modernity. This is also evident from his redefinition of the concept of "the Jew."

While in the past the boundaries between Jews and Muslims had been clear-cut and Jews who converted to Islam could be reasonably confident of their security, Qutb systematically erased these boundaries. "Anyone who leads this Community away from its Religion and its Qur'an can only be a Jewish agent," he writes referring to reform-minded Muslims.[19] "The Jews have instilled men and regimes (in the Islamic world)," he insists. There is

> a massive army of agents in the form of professors, philosophers, doctors and researchers – sometimes also writers, poets, scientists and journalists – carrying Muslim names because they are of Muslim descent!! And some of them are from the ranks of the "Muslim religious authorities"!![20]

So we see that Qutb considers every Muslim who sympathizes with modernity, even if they are a religious authority, to be a crypto-Jew who will destroy Islam from within. This shows the role antisemitism plays in his thinking. The traditional

Islamic image of the "Jew" has been revitalized and vastly magnified in order to resist the march of modernity in Islamic societies.

The Charter of Hamas

A further central document of Islamic antisemitism is the Hamas Charter published in August 1988 against the background of the First Intifada. In May 2017, Hamas published a more moderate program. Hamas representatives, however, have made it clear that the 1988 version has not been repudiated.[21]

As with Qutb's text, the Charter too accuses the Jews of wanting to destroy Islam. Here too, behind the hatred of Jews and Israel lies a call to arms against the spread of liberal ideas in the Islamic world. Once again, the Jews are viewed as pulling the strings. Thus, we read that "the Zionist invasion ... relies greatly in its infiltration and espionage operations on the secret organizations it gave rise to, such as the Freemasons, The Rotary and Lions clubs, and other sabotage groups." "They aim at undermining societies, destroying values, corrupting consciences, deteriorating character and annihilating Islam."[22] (Article 28)

A reference to the formative period of Islam appears in almost every one of the document's 36 paragraphs. The Koran is quoted 33 times along with six hadiths – instructions by the Prophet to his companions whose transmission is traced back to the latter. Article 7, for example, cites a well-known hadith to which we will have occasion to return:

> The prophet, Allah bless him and grant him salvation, has said: "The Day of Judgement will not come about until Muslims fight the Jews (killing the Jews), when the Jew will hide behind stones and trees. Then stones and trees will say: O Muslims, O Abdulla, there is a Jew behind me, come and kill him. Only the Gharkad tree would not do that because it is one of the trees of the Jews." (related by al-Bukhari and Muslim).

This is an especially cruel hadith. First, allegedly from the mouth of Muhammad, the resurrection or salvation of the Muslims is here made dependent on the murder of Jews. But that is not all. As if not only the Muslims but the whole universe have conspired against the Jews, even the stone (symbol of inanimate nature) and the tree (symbol of animate nature) demand that the last terrified hidden Jew be dragged from his hiding place and killed. This saying reproduces the stereotype of the helpless Jew that permeates the early Islamic writings. However, only a few lines later, in Article 22 of the Hamas Charter, the Jews are presented as the rulers of the world:

> They were behind the French Revolution, the Communist revolution and most of the revolutions we heard and hear about, here and there. ... They were behind World War I, when they were able to destroy the Islamic Caliphate. ... They

were behind World War II, through which they made huge financial gains by trading in armaments. ... There is no war going on anywhere, without having their finger in it.[23]

In Article 32, Hamas names the source of these fantasies: "Their plan is embodied in the 'Protocols of the Elders of Zion' and their present conduct is the best proof of what we are saying."[24]

This text portrays the Jews in one and the same breath as both weaklings who flee and have to hide behind trees and stones and at the same time the secret and real rulers of the world. The combination is admittedly absurd – but so is antisemitism in general. In Islamic antisemitism, both components come together and mutually reinforce one another. European antisemitism is radicalized through connection with the fanatical aspects of Islam. Antisemitically minded Muslims in Germany frequently display their hatred in more direct, aggressive and violent forms than other actors. And while the stated aim of killing Jews had seemed to be totally discredited after the fall of Nazi Germany, it has been revived by Islamic antisemitism – with Muhammad now the alleged model.

At the same time, the traditional image of the Jew derived from the Koran has gained a new eliminatory dimension through the admixture of world-conspiracy theories. Thus, the warning cry that Jews strive for the "destruction of Islam" is one of the hallmarks of Islamic antisemitism.

But how can the reproach that Jews have wished to destroy Islam be illustrated? How can religious fanatics mobilize people to fight this alleged danger? One of the crucial protagonists of Islamic antisemitism had an idea. We are talking about Amin el-Husseini, appointed Mufti of Jerusalem by the British Mandate authorities in Palestine in 1921.

"Al-Aqsa in Danger!"

Amin el-Husseini was the first Arab leader of modern times to justify his Jew-hatred on religious grounds and so succeed in reactivating a force that had long been in abeyance in the Arab world: religious mobilization. In the 1920s, he attempted to turn the Temple Mount in Jerusalem, with its Muslim holy sites – the Al-Aqsa Mosque and the Dome of the Rock – into an emblem of the struggle against Zionism. To this end, he promoted a complete fabrication: the Jews want to destroy these sites in order to erect their Third Temple on the ruins. In this way, he endeavored "to arouse the religious susceptibilities of the masses [in Palestine], who remained indifferent to nationalistic slogans which were more difficult to understand."[25]

At the same time, he benefited from the fact that – after Mecca and Medina – the Temple Mount is Islam's third most holy site. With the battle cry "Al-Aqsa in danger," he hoped to mobilize the entire Islamic world against Zionism.

This was the aim of the General Islamic Conference that the Mufti organized in December 1931 in Jerusalem in partnership with the President of the Indian

Caliphate Movement, Shaukat Ali. The Mufti's goal was to highlight both the global significance of Jerusalem for Muslims and his own importance. While Shaukat Ali did not share El-Husseini's hatred of Jews, it was not he but the Mufti who was named President of the Conference. Instead of an anticipated 2,000 delegates, only some 150 Muslims from about 20 countries attended, and the Conference made no immediate impact. It, nonetheless, contributed to the spread of anti-Zionism to the wider Islamic world.[26]

The Temple Mount, however, is holy for Jews too. This is the place where in 950 BCE the Temple of Solomon and 400 years later the Second Temple that was destroyed in the year 70 in the Roman-Jewish War had been built. The Wailing Wall, Judaism's most important place of prayer, is a remnant of the walls that supported the Temple. Following the Islamic conquest of Palestine, around 690 the famous Dome of the Rock – with its dome, later gilded – was erected on this plaza to be followed a few years later by the Al-Aqsa Mosque. The close proximity here of Jewish and Muslim places of prayer offers great scope for provocations.

In an open letter of 1928, the leadership of the Palestinian Jews pledged never to disrespect the religious rights of Muslims on the Temple Mount but to no avail.[27] In 1929 the Mufti circulated forged photos of an arson attack on the Al-Aqsa Mosque.[28] His call to defend the holy places led to the Hebron massacre in which 133 Jews were killed and 339 wounded.

In the following years the Egyptian Brotherhood took up the cry. "Oh you young men! The English soldiers and Jewish police are defiling the Dome of the Rock," claims a leaflet distributed in Cairo in October 1938. "They are destroying its dome and walls. As a result of this terrible torture and mutilation the Arabs in the Holy Land are in danger of destruction (…) the jihad for Palestine has become a holy and God-desired duty."[29]

During World War II, El-Husseini continued to spread rumors about the Al-Aqsa Mosque in his radio talks in Arabic on the Nazis' shortwave radio station: in 1943, for example, he fulminated about "the greed of the Jews for the Islamic holy places and their wish to build a Jewish temple in the place of the blessed Al-Aqsa Mosque."[30]

However, after Jordan took control of East Jerusalem, which includes the Old Town and Temple Mount, in the 1948 war, Jerusalem suddenly lost its allure; there was no more interest in the Al-Aqsa Mosque. From 1948 to 1967, when the Temple Mount (*Haram al-Sharif*) was under full Arab control, the only Arab leader to visit was the Moroccan King. For Jews, this was a difficult time. During the nearly 20 years of Jordanian occupation, they were forbidden from praying at the Wailing Wall. All Jewish synagogues, schools and cemeteries were destroyed.[31]

And then in July 1967, in the course of the 6-Day War, Israel won possession of the Old City including the Temple Mount. Now the Jews could have paid the Arabs back in their own coin: destruction of religious objects and a ban on Muslims praying on the Temple Mount. However, that is not what happened. Instead, at that time the Israeli Defense Minister, Moshe Dayan, laid down the rules that have remained in force ever since: first, the Temple Mount was to remain under Jordanian administration and serve as a place of prayer for Muslims; second, Israel's sole responsibility would pertain to the safety of the Mount's access points and, third, while Jews would be guaranteed entry to the sites, they would be forbidden to pray there.

So this most important of Jewish holy places is the only one where Jews are forbidden to pray. Today only a small group of ultra-orthodox Jews refuses to accept this restriction, calling for the Temple Mount to be reclaimed by the Jews and a third Jewish temple constructed. They are a marginal force in Israeli society. Dayan's *ad hoc* arrangements have become set in legal stone.

Nevertheless, Muslim and Arab authorities launched a new religious campaign, this time denying the connection between Judaism and Jerusalem. Of course, no serious historian or archeologist doubts the close relationship between the people and the place. This did not, however, stop Yasser Arafat, asserting in 2000 that there had never been a Jewish temple in Jerusalem, proclaiming that "I myself visited Yemen and was shown the site where the Temple of Solomon existed."[32]

Countless Arab sources show the extent to which the notion that Jews have no connection with Jerusalem has taken root.[33] So, Mahmoud al-Habbash, a senior advisor to Palestinian President Mahmoud Abbas, talked in 2018 of the "Arab, Muslim and Christian identity of Jerusalem," stating that the Jews are

… claiming territory based on a false Jewish or Biblical pretext whose sole purpose is to take over the land. The Al-Burak Wall [i.e., the Western Wall] has nothing to do with a [Jewish] temple, and [the Jews] have no right over its stones. This is an imperialist myth.[34]

Abbas himself repeated this lie at the end of 2017 in a speech to the Organization of Islamic Cooperation (OIC) where he described Jerusalem as a "Palestinian Arab Muslim Christian city" – that is, with no connection to the Jews.[35] His view was supported by a Jordanian professor of archaeology Mohammad Waheeb Al-Husseini: "The [Israelites] … are unable to convince anyone anywhere in the world that they have a historic right to this blessed land. They did not have any existence in history in Palestine, and especially not in Jerusalem."[36]

Behind this denial of Jewish history lies a new dimension of Jew-hatred expressed through the falsification of historical facts, in the spirit of Holocaust denial. One would be inclined to laugh at such nonsense, but those who promote it are in earnest. Here a new front in the religious war has been opened, and new fuel poured on the fire of Islamic antisemitism. For, just like Holocaust denial, Temple denial requires acceptance of the existence of a vast Jewish conspiracy, in which the Jews, using their power over politics and media, effectively suppress the "real truth" about Jerusalem.

But let us return to the alarm cry: "Al-Aqsa in danger." To this day throughout the Arab world, one finds cartoons in which loathsome serpents and squid-like creatures, all bearing the Star of David, cling onto the Al-Aqsa Mosque or Dome of the Rock, or in which we see Jews in the form of rats undermining the shrines, or grossly obese figures devouring the Dome of the Rock.[37]

In July 2017, it became apparent how effective this agitation has been. On 14 July 2017, three Israeli Arabs succeeded in smuggling weapons onto Temple Mount and shooting two Israeli policemen at one of the Mount's crossing points.

Thereafter, Israel set about installing metal detectors, a process which entailed a two-day ban on entry to the Temple Mount. The Palestinian propaganda machine then went into overdrive to create the false impression that the metal detectors were part of a secret plan to wage a religious war against the Muslims and destroy the mosques. 19 July 2017 was designated a "day of rage." "On this day we must come out on great demonstrations in all Arab towns," demanded Abbas Zaki, a member of the Fatah Central Committee.

The Turkish government denounced the two-day closure of the Temple Mount as a "crime against humanity." Turkish President Recep Tayyip Erdogan summoned the world's Muslims to play an active part in the defense of the Al-Aqsa Mosque, while in Istanbul demonstrators besieged the Neve Shalom synagogue and pelted it with various objects. Al-Qaida called for armed resistance. The Iranian regime did not want to miss the party. It supplied the tens of thousands of demonstrators in Jerusalem with food and drink and a message of support from its Supreme Guide, Ali Khamenei.[38]

The hysteria over the imaginary destruction of the Al-Aqsa Mosque inspired a 19-year-old Palestinian to break into the house of a Jewish family and stab three people to death. Meanwhile, four Arabs were killed in clashes with Israeli security forces. Only after Israel backed down and dismantled the metal detectors did this nightmare reach a temporary end.

When a few months later US President Donald Trump recognized Jerusalem as the capital of Israel,[39] the show resumed. The Palestinian authorities once again played the religious card, condemning Trump's decision as "aggression against Islam, … aggression against the Koran, … aggression against the Muslims, … aggression against the Al-Aqsa Mosque … and aggression against humanity."[40]

With a nod towards the Christian blood libel, Recep Tayyip Erdogan again poured fuel on the fire. "The fate of Jerusalem cannot be left in the hands of a country that nourishes itself on blood." In his capacity as Chairman of the OIC, he organized a special OIC summit in Istanbul in order to set "the whole Islamic world in motion."[41]

To no effect. The protests against the recognition of Jerusalem amounted to a storm in a teacup. However, while the Arab Street in Cairo and Riyadh remained quiet, radicalized Muslims in cities such as London and Berlin erupted in fury. "Jerusalem belongs to all Muslims of the *umma* of this world. To no one else," proclaimed one of the slogans at a demonstration at Berlin's Brandenburg Gate. The US President, with this decision, "had declared war not only on the Palestinians, but on all Muslims." In addition, according to the *Frankfurter Allgemeine Zeitung*, the demonstrators yelled in Arabic:

> "Death to Israel! Death to Israel", "Khaybar, Khaybar, ya yahud, dschaisch Mohammed saya'du" ("Khaybar, Khaybar, oh you Jews, Muhammed's army will soon return"). ... In addition, Hamas headbands, flags of Islamic Hezbollah, a burning cloth decorated with a Star of David. ... Similar rallies took place throughout Germany ... In Düsseldorf the Israeli flag was spat and trampled on amid calls for an Intifada. The Khaybar rhyme was also heard in Koblenz. In Mainz maps from which Israel had been erased were shown.[42]

Of course, the few thousand participants in these events comprised only a tiny minority of Germany's Muslim population, and, of those participants, only a minority shouted antisemitic slogans. Nonetheless, the anti-Jewish frenzy of this minority was sufficiently vehement to elicit a response from politicians and the media in Germany. A motion proposed by all major parties of the Bundestag condemned the "anti-Israeli rallies in December 2017 at the Brandenburg Gate" as "unacceptable." According to the statement, freedom of expression and demonstration in Germany leaves "no room for antisemitic incitement and violence."

On the one hand, the statement does not downplay the threat of "an antisemitism reinforced by immigration." On the contrary, it emphasizes that "the unrestricted acceptance of Jewish life" is "a measure of successful integration" and deems "antisemitic hate calls" a behavior that justifies an "especially serious interest in deportation."[43] On the other hand, words such as "Muslim" or "Islam" or "Islamic antisemitism" are nowhere to be found in this lengthy document. Nor do we find any mention of the encouragement of Jew-hatred by Turkish, Iranian or other Middle Eastern mass media. Indeed, use of the term "Islamic antisemitism" was shunned not only by the political class but also by professional antisemitism experts.

This attitude was expressed in the most radical fashion by Wolfgang Benz, the former longstanding head of the Berlin Center for Research on Antisemitism. He doubts whether there is such a thing as Islamic antisemitism at all. The widespread antisemitism among Muslims has absolutely nothing to do with religion, he declared in 2018. "The enmity of Muslims towards Jews is not based on the Koran ... religion-based Jew-hatred characterized Christianity for two thousand years, but not Islam." And he then readies himself for a counterattack on those who disagree with him: dangerous "fanatics ... who stir up the public with the construct of a genuine Muslim antisemitism, that is, hostility to Jews derived from the theological premises of Islam."[44]

A more sophisticated argument is that of Islam scholar Michael Kiefer. He proposes the term "Islamized antisemitism" on the grounds that what we have here is "antisemitism with an Islamic veneer" that "in all important structural elements is identical with modern European antisemitism."[45] In this version, the radicalizing and mobilizing contribution of religion is downplayed and depicted as providing no more than a form of concealment. Another term on offer is "Islamist antisemitism," which suggests that this form of Jew-hatred is only found among Islamists.

Here too, however, the dogma that in this case Islamic beliefs are merely being instrumentalized for political ends misses the mark. For conservative Muslims religion is not a means but an end. By taking particular stipulations from the Koran and hadiths literally, they feel themselves to be the most faithful followers of Allah. It is hard to talk about "instrumentalization" in this context. The problem therefore is those stipulations themselves that "antisemitic dross" to which Mezri Haddad referred.

Scholarly work begins with terminological precision. The term "Islamic antisemitism" defines a specific variant of antisemitism whose reach extends far beyond the Islamist camp and mobilizes the religious potential for Jew-hatred present in Islam. In fact, we are dealing here with a religious war, a form of war that, apart from the Troubles in Northern Ireland, has not been seen in our climes since the end of the 30 years' war in 1648.

In the first place, we have the transcendental aspect: only in religious wars do the martyrdom ideology and belief in Paradise find expression. "Each drop of blood that was spilled in Jerusalem is pure blood as long as it's for the sake of Allah. Every *shahid* (martyr) will be in heaven and every wounded person will be rewarded, by Allah's will," as even the reputedly moderate leader of the Palestinian Authority, Mahmoud Abbas, once put it.[46]

Here too we find the second, mass-mobilizing, aspect: religion is seen as the only means capable of moving the world's 1.7 billion Muslims as a united "Muslim nation" into action against the 14 million Jews.

And finally there is the totalitarian aspect: in the final battle between the Party of God and the Party of Satan, "humanity will be relieved of their [the Jew's] presence, since subsequently, not one Jew will remain alive," as Islamist writings put it.[47]

Why do so many Muslims in Europe support this war? The conventional answer is that it is because they or their ancestors have come from countries where antisemitism is commonplace. This contains an important truth: we cannot begin to understand Islamic antisemitism if we restrict our attention to Germany or the European Union. It is essential that we take into account the Arab-Islamic world, with which many European Muslims are connected in multiple ways – through family ties, access to Arabic or Turkish mass media or a sense of solidarity with Israel's Middle Eastern adversaries.

The broader view, however, simply raises the same question on a larger scale: why is antisemitism rampant in these regions? How is it that only a few years after the Holocaust extreme Jew-hatred was so widespread? There is a well-established answer: because of Israel. In fact, however, admiration for Hitler and Rommel and hatred of Jews were already strong *before* the founding of the Jewish state in 1948. Indeed, after 1945 the Arab world was the only region in the world in which a pro-Nazi past remained a source of pride rather than shame. But why?

To explain this phenomenon, we need to take a new look at a specific facet of recent history: the influence of the Nazis on events in the Middle East in the period between 1937 and 1948 and notably the impact of the Nazis' Arabic-language anti-semitic propaganda effort during those years.

Therefore, in order to explain Islamic antisemitism adequately, we must take into account not only its geographical but also its historical context. That is what we will attempt to do in the next three chapters. They illuminate an aspect of the German past that is commonly overlooked and show, drawing on new archival discoveries, how the Nazis succeeded in embedding Islamic antisemitism in the Arab world. This new view of Middle Eastern history gives us a clearer picture of the present. Only if we realize how strongly modern Middle Eastern history has been shaped by the impact of National Socialism can we correctly interpret the Jew-hatred in this region and its resonance among Muslims in Europe and develop effective countermeasures.

Notes

1 Günther Jikeli, "Muslimischer Antisemitismus in Europa. Aktuelle Ergebnisse der empirischen Forschung", Marc Grimm and Bodo Kahmann (eds.), *Antisemitismus im 21. Jahrhundert. Virulenz einer alten Feindschaft in Zeiten von Islamismus und Terror*, Berlin 2018, 113–133; here, 120.
2 Ibid., 113.
3 *The Koran*, translated with notes by N. J. Dawood, Penguin, Harmondsworth, 1974. I have followed Dawood in using "Allah" rather than "God" throughout the main text. I have used this translation throughout the book, except for the document, *Islam–Judaism*, where I have translated the Koranic passages directly from the German – translator's note.
4 *Middle East Media Research Institute* (MEMRI), "Tunisian Philosopher Mezri Haddad: Islamists Have Reduced the Koran to a Nauseating Antisemitic Lampoon", Special Dispatch Series No. 1362, 21 November 2006.
5 Johan Bouman, *Der Koran und die Juden*, Darmstadt 1990, 86 and Norman A. Stillman, *The Jews of Arab Lands. A History and Source Book*, Philadelphia 1979, 3–21.
6 Hamed Abdel-Samad, *Mohamed. Eine Abrechnung*, Munich 2015, 188f.
7 See the account of crimes committed against the Jews in the Orient in Andrew G. Bostom (ed.), *The Legacy of Islamic Antisemitism*, New York 2008; George Bensoussan, *Die Juden in der arabischen Welt. Die verbotene Frage*, Berlin-Leipzig 2019.
8 Bostom, *Legacy*, 50.
9 Bensoussan, *Die Juden*, 79.
10 Bernard Lewis, *Semites & Antisemites. An Inquiry into Conflict and Prejudice*, New York and London 1986, 129.
11 Léon Poliakov, *Geschichte des Antisemitismus, Band II. Das Zeitalter der Verteufelung und des Ghettos*, Worms 1978, 7.
12 Paul W. Massing, *Vorgeschichte des politischen Antisemitismus*, Frankfurt/M. 1959, 4.
13 Johannes Heil, "'Antijudaismus' und 'Antisemitismus' – Begriffe als Bedeutungsträger", Wolfgang Benz (ed.), *Jahrbuch für Antisemitismusforschung 6*, Frankfurt/M. 1997, 92–114, here 99.
14 Wilhelm Marr, *Der Sieg des Judenthums über das Germanenthum. Vom nicht confessionellen Standpunkt aus betrachtet*, Bern 1879, 41, 30.
15 Matthias Küntzel, *Jihad and Jew-Hatred. Islamism, Nazism and the Roots of 9/11*, New York 2007, 80–85.

16 Ronald L. Nettler, *Past Trials & Present Tribulations. A Muslim Fundamentalist's View of the Jews*, Oxford 1987, 81f., 85.
17 Ibid., 86f.
18 Ibid., 83.
19 Ibid., 72.
20 Ibid., 77.
21 "Dieser Prozess wird scheitern", Spiegel interview with Hamas leader Khaled Meshal, *Spiegel* 22/2017, 91. The 2017 document can be found at: https://www.middleeasteye. net/news/hamas-charter-1637794876.
22 Hamas Convenant of 1988, https://avalon.law.yale.edu/20th_century/hamas.asp.
23 Ibid.
24 Ibid.
25 Uri M Kupferschmidt, *The Supreme Muslim Council. Islam under the British Mandate for Palestine*, Leiden and New York 1987, 238.
26 Kupferschmidt, *Supreme*, 187–220; Thomas Mayer, "Egypt and the General Islamic Conference of Jerusalem in 1931", *Middle Eastern Studies*, Vol. 18, No. 3, July 1982, 311–322.
27 Nadav Shragai, *The 'Al-Aksa Is in Danger' Libel: The History of a Lie*, Jerusalem 2012, 27.
28 Jennie Lebel, *The Mufti of Jerusalem Haj-Amin el-Husseini and National-Socialism*, Belgrade 2007, 25.
29 Gudrun Krämer, *Minderheit, Millet, Nation? Die Juden in Ägypten 1914–1952*, Wiesbaden 1982, 293.
30 Gerhard Höpp (ed.), *Mufti-Papiere. Briefe, Memoranden, Reden und Aufrufe Amin al-Husainis aus dem Exil, 1940–1945*, Berlin 2001, 172.
31 David Klein, "Die heilige Stadt der Juden", *Basler Zeitung*, 13 December 2017.
32 Shragai, *Libel*, 39.
33 Ibid., 40f.
34 *MEMRI*, "Palestinian Authority Supreme Shari'a Judge and Abbas' Advisor Mahmoud Al-Habbash: The Jews Have No Connection to Jerusalem; This Is an Imperialist Myth and Distortion of History", Special Dispatch No. 7511, 7 June 2018.
35 *WAFA Info*, "Abbas at the OIC: Israel's Violations Absolve Us from Our Commitments", 13 December 2017.
36 *MEMRI*, "Jordanian Archaeologist Mohammad Waheeb Al-Husseini: The Jews Have No Historic Right to the Land, the Zionist Movement Wants to Rule the World", Clip No. 6769, 2 September 2018.
37 Shragai, *Libel*, 10.
38 "Harte Worte aus Teheran", *tachles*, 26 July 2017; Alexander Fulbright, "Iran Accused of Helping Fund Temple Mount Unrest", *Times of Israel* (ToI), 1 August 2017.
39 Trump also declared in his statement of 6 December 2017 that this step did not affect the legal status of the divided city, whose final settlement depended on an agreement between Israel and the Palestinian Authority.
40 *Palestinian Media Watch* (PMW), "Abbas' Advisor Incites Religious War", *Bulletin*, 13 December 2017.
41 "Islamische Staaten erkennen Ost-Jerusalem als Hauptstadt Palästinas an", *Die Welt*, 13 December 2017.
42 Justus Bender, "Nichts gegen Juden, aber...", *FAZ*, 14 December 2017.
43 "Deutscher Bundestag, Antisemitismus entschlossen bekämpfen", Antrag der Frak-tionen CDU/CSU, SPD, FDP und BÜNDNIS 90/DIE GRÜNEN, *Drucksache 19/444*, 17 January 2018.
44 Wolfgang Benz, "Woher der muslimische Antisemitismus kommt", *Tagesspiegel*, 17 January 2018.

45 Michael Kiefer, "Islamischer oder islamisierter Antisemitismus", Wolfgang Benz and Juliane Wetzel (eds.), *Antisemitismus und radikaler Islamismus*, Essen 2007, 71–84, here 80, 84.
46 Khaled Abu Toameh, "Abbas: 'Israelis Have No Right to Desecrate Our Holy Sites with Their Filthy Feet'", *Jerusalem Post*, 16 September 2015.
47 Esther Webman, "From the Damascus Blood Libel to the 'Arab Spring': The Evolution of Arab Antisemitism", *Antisemitism Studies*, Vol. I, No. 1, Spring 2017, 157–206, here 170.

2

1937

The Watershed

European antisemitism made slow headway in the Arab world. The transformation of the Jewish adversaries of Muhammad from a minor annoyance into the incarnation of evil took time. The process was pioneered by members of the Christian minorities in the Ottoman Empire and European priests and diplomats who brought the ritual murder blood libel of the Christian Middle Ages to the Middle East. In 1840, the Damascus Affair attracted international attention. Franciscan monks and the French consul accused Jews of murdering a member of the order and his attendant to obtain their blood for use in the forthcoming Passover Feast. The anti-Jewish riots that followed spread throughout the Ottoman Empire, always incited by Christians.[1]

Some decades later, the upsurge of antisemitism that accompanied the guilty verdict against the French army officer Alfred Dreyfus in 1894 was reflected in the French sphere of influence in the Maghreb. Thus, in 1898, French colonists in Tunis organized an antisemitic demonstration under the slogans "Down with Zola" and "Down with the Jews."[2]

However, in the Maghreb, the Jews had to contend not only with excited Christian settlers from France but also with Muslims who interpreted the Jews' progressive liberation from *dhimmi* status as a plot against Islam and despised them as profiteers from colonialism. Algerian Jews – unlike Muslims – were allowed to become French citizens and were therefore viewed as agents of the colonial power and hated as such by sections of the Muslim population.

In addition, antisemitic works of European provenance were now translated into Arabic, among them an Arabic edition published in Cairo in 1899 of August Rohling's agitational pamphlet *The Talmud-Jew*.

Then, in 1918, in Palestine the first Arabic edition of the *Protocols of the Elders of Zion* appeared.[3] Shortly thereafter, in March 1921, the Palestine Arab Congress

DOI: 10.4324/9781003369110-3

in Jerusalem sent the British colonial minister, Winston Churchill, a memorandum that clearly drew on this source. "Jews have been among the most active promoters of destruction in many countries," it asserts. "The Jew is a Jew everywhere in the world. He supports wars whenever his own interests dictate and thus uses the armies of the nations to do what he wishes."[4]

However, this type of antisemitism could not reach more than a tiny minority of Muslims, let alone convince them. Other means were needed in order to drum the idea of a Jewish world conspiracy into the heads of the illiterate mass of Muslims. "The propagation of anti-Semitic themes," emphasizes Bernard Lewis,

> was not left to chance, nor was it entirely entrusted to Middle Eastern enterprise. Anti-Semitism has been energetically propagated by various European groups. The most important in this century were the Nazis, who, from the early 1930s until the defeat of Germany in 1945 devoted great efforts to the spread of anti-Semitic doctrines among the Arabs.[5]

In 1933 Hitler had met with an Egyptian journalist who in 1936 would agree to translate *Mein Kampf* into Arabic. This project came to nothing, although in the same year Hitler himself had stated his agreement with "refraining from a translation of those passages of which… in the light of the sensitivities of the Arab peoples a translation does not seem suitable."[6] This comment refers to a decidedly anti-Arab passage in the book in which Hitler talked about the "racial inferiority of these so-called 'oppressed nations'" and mocked the "holy war" of the Muslims.[7]

It was only in June 1937 that Berlin first began to take a serious interest in the Arabs of Palestine. According to Elie Kedourie, "The period 1937–9 may be considered a watershed in the somber, disaster-strewn history of the Palestinians."[8] It was therefore no accident that the first document of Islamic antisemitism, a pamphlet entitled *Islam and Judaism*, appeared in 1937 in Cairo against the background of events in Palestine in the summer of that year.

Terror against the Partition Plan

At the start of July 1937, a report by a British government commission headed by Lord William Robert Peel recommended the partition of Palestine into a small Jewish and a larger Arab state, with Jerusalem being placed under international administration. This was the first partition plan for Palestine. Although the proposed Jewish state would comprise only some 20% of the territory, the majority of the Zionist movement was prepared to accept it in principle. But how did the Arab side react? "It appears that partition was at first accepted by a considerable section of the Arab Governments," writes historian Lukasz Hirszowicz.[9]

However, in Palestine itself opinion was divided. On one side were the radical forces of the Husseinis, the Mufti at their head, on the other side were some groups that publicly expressed support for the Peel Commission Plan (parts of the National Liberation League and the Palestinian Communist Party) and others, such as the Nashashibi family, who preferred not to proclaim their supportive views in public.[10]

At first, when in early summer 1937 rumors of the envisaged partition began to spread, the Nashashibis and their National Defense Party

did not conceal their support for the principle of partition and even organized meetings and used other propaganda means to win public support for it. This positive attitude also prevailed immediately upon the publication of the Commission's report. In private, two leaders of the Party, Raghib al-Nashashibi and Ya'qub Farraj told the HC [High Commissioner, M.K.] that they were in favor of the principle of partition.[11]

Then, however, the Nashashibis pulled back from this position. According to Israeli historican Yehoshua Porath,

First of all strong pressure was exerted on the Nashashibis to identify themselves with the HAC's [Higher Arab Committee – M.K.] reaction. Threats were made on their lives, and indeed during the summer of 1937 various moderates and Nashashibi-supporting notables were assaulted or murdered.[12]

According to historian Mustafa Khaba,

contrary to what has been written in the texts dealing with the partition plan, this [pro-partition] camp did not include a small minority. The feeling that it was a minority resulted from the fact that the vast majority of this camp chose not express its positions publicly.[13]

A crucial reason for this choice was that the Mufti and his acolytes not only opposed the plan but also caused its Arab supporters to fear for their lives. On 14 July 1937, the Jerusalem correspondent of the *London Times* summed up the prevailing mood in Palestine thus:

There seems to be little chance that anyone who sees the advantages in it [the partition plan – M.K.] will raise his voice as long as the Mufti of Jerusalem retains his present influential position. ...If the partition scheme goes through the Mufti's position must inevitably be liquidated. ... Any Arab who makes a conciliatory move or does anything short of rejecting the partition scheme as impossible may expect to find himself denounced as a traitor and exposed to terrorism. ... Thus from both the Arab and the Jewish side we see that the Mufti's maintenance in his present position is an obstacle to any consideration of the [Peel – M.K.] Report on its merits.[14]

The picture given in *The Times* is supported by numerous documents found in the British National Archives. In September 1937, Bernard Joseph complained in a letter to Chaim Weizmann, President of the World Zionist Organization, about

> the almost complete terrorization of the Arab section of the community by the Mufti and his entourage ... One by one Arab notables who were not of his supporters and who dared express opposition to his wishes ... have been murdered in cold blood by his terrorist gangsters ... The situation has by now become so dreadful that the entire Arab community lives in constant dread of these terrorists. ...Unless the all-powerful Mufti is deposed there is no possible hope of the evolution of an Arab moderate view towards partition.[15]

On 19 September, a report from an Arab informant stated that

> terrorism in the country was in full swing. It operated on people's minds not so much through its toll of life, but through the very existence of the terrorist bands, and the fear to which they subjected large sections of the Arab people. There was no one left who would dare to raise his head and put up a fight. Nowadays, one did not wait till one received a threatening letter. One roamed the streets to try and find out where a band leader could be found so that one could pay him a ransom, even without being called upon to do so, and thus ensure one's life.[16]

One thing was clear: for the partition plan and so the possibility of a peaceful compromise solution to succeed, Amin el-Husseini had to be deposed. And indeed the *Times* article quoted above did not remain without effect. On 16 July 1937, Sir Arthur Wauchope, High Commissioner for Palestine, admitted in a letter to the British government that "I do consider that there is some truth that moderate Arabs fear to express their real feeling for fear of reprisals." Therefore, "I consider that the situation is such that the interests of Palestine as well as of the Government demand the deportation of the Mufti and [his associate] Ouni Bey without delay."[17]

After getting the green light from London, on 17 July 1937 the High Commissioner took action. On that day the Mufti's Arab Higher Committee was due to meet at its Jerusalem headquarters at 5.00 p.m. Two hours earlier, an order was issued for the arrest of the Mufti before he could enter the building. He was then to be taken to Haifa by plane where the British cruiser *Repulse* would be waiting to transport him to the Seychelles, a group of islands located to the north of Madagascar. The "ship will anchor outside breakwater so as to obviate possibility of demonstration on wharf," reported the captain John H. Godfrey in a top secret telegram. The prisoners were to be conveyed from the quayside to the ship in a dinghy.[18]

However, El-Husseini was tipped off and the plan failed. He entered his headquarters that afternoon through a back entrance that the British police in Palestine – according to their own self-justificatory account – knew nothing about. While both of the main entrances to the building remained under constant police observation, this back door remained unmonitored, allowing the Mufti to leave the way he had come in.[19] He fled directly to the Mosque quarter of the Temple Mount where he remained in hiding in the coming months. Now London had to explain away this embarrassing failure. The arrest attempt had not been directed against the Mufti, was the new official version by the British government, but against one of his colleagues, whom they had in fact succeeded in arresting.

If the Mufti had been arrested on 14 July 1937 and held in the Seychelles until 1945, the Middle East might today be a different place. Instead of confrontation there might have been compromise and instead of religious fanaticism interest-based political agreements. In any case, the Mufti succeeded in defeating the first attempt at a two-state solution through the use of antisemitism and terrorism. And it would be the very same Mufti who from 1941 onward would export Goebbels's Nazi antisemitism into the Arab world and then, in 1947, incite the Arabs to go to war against the newly proclaimed State of Israel, thereby torpedoing the second attempt too.

Berlin Steps In

1937 was also the year when the Nazi leadership began to give active support to the Mufti's policy. At the beginning of that year, two of the Mufti's emissaries met Fritz Grobba, the German envoy in Baghdad. They explained to him that Britain could only be forced to abandon the partition plan by a "major uprising." Grobba's report goes on to note that, according to the emissaries, "Arabs are already preparing this struggle. The only great power that is interested in Arab victory over Palestine's Jews and in which Arabs have complete confidence is Germany. Supreme Arab Council counts therefore on German help."[20]

In January 1937, Grobba responded evasively to this appeal for help. This changed, however, when the Peel Commission Plan became known. At no price would Berlin accept a Jewish state. There is "a German interest in strengthening the Arabs as a counterweight to any such increase in the power of the Jews," insists a circular of 1 June 1937 from the Nazi Foreign Minister, Konstantin von Neurath. "The Jewish question is one of the most important problems of German foreign policy," confirmed a Foreign Office note of 22 June 1937. "That means that there is also a huge German interest in developments in Palestine."[21]

It is only partially possible to reconstruct the precise scale and type of German support for the "major uprising" that began in April 1936 and then flared up again in summer 1937. The Arab archives remain unavailable, and most of the relevant German records went up in flames in 1945, including the bulk of the records of the Propaganda Ministry and those of the German Embassy in Cairo from 1933 to 1939. In the German Foreign Office archives, I came upon the following handwritten note: "The report of 4.9.37 [4 September 1937] no. 1669 regarding Syrian support for a new Arab uprising in Palestine and telegram concerning this of 4.9.37 are located in the records marked 'Geheim' ['secret']."[22] The secret records themselves, however, were not to be found.

In the prewar years, contacts between Nazi agents and the Muslim Brotherhood in Egypt, the most important country in the region, were also top secret. Egypt was the birthplace of Hitler's henchman, Rudolf Hess, whose family had resided in Alexandria since 1865. In 1926, his brother Alfred had begun to organize an Egyptian section of the Nazi foreign organization, numbering several hundred members. Until the beginning of the war in September 1939, the Brotherhood's propaganda efforts were supported by the German Embassy in Cairo and the Deutsche Nachrichtenbüro (DNB), a department of the Nazi propaganda ministry with a broad remit. The DNB furnished the Brotherhood with funds, according to records found in the home of Wilhelm Stellbogen, the head of the DNB office in Egypt.

It was no accident that the Nazis considered the Muslim Brotherhood founded by Hassan al-Banna in 1928 a natural partner: Al-Banna had already in 1927 established ties with Amin al-Husseini and given unreserved support in Egypt to his antisemitic campaigns. In 1936, the Muslim Brotherhood had called for a boycott of the businesses of Egyptian Jews; between 1936 and 1938, as a result of their Palestine campaign, membership of the Brotherhood had risen from 800 to 200,000.[23] By 1945 it had become the most influential mass movement and most important purveyor of Islamic antisemitism in the Arab world.

The Brotherhood's collaboration with Nazi agents came to light by chance. Immediately before the outbreak of World War II, the Cairo Nazis had had to make a hasty departure from their premises in the city, leaving behind papers that fell into the hands of the British secret services. Even the few clues retrieved from the search of the premises revealed cooperation on a level previously unsuspected by the British. They showed that the Brotherhood had received funds from Nazi sources, "which were considerably larger than the subsidies offered to other anti-British activists," writes Islam scholar Brynjar Lia. "These transfers appear to have been coordinated by Hajj Amin al-Husayni and some of his Palestinian contacts in Cairo."[24]

The 30-page report *Note on German Suspects – Egypt* which I discovered in March 2016 in the British National Archives reveals that Nazi agents attended conferences of the Muslim Brotherhood, that German officials held "Palestine meetings" with the Brotherhood and that they also discussed the issue directly with Hassan al-Banna. The fact that the collaboration with the Brotherhood was known about at the highest levels in Germany is clear from the following note, dated 16 August, found by the British secret services in Wilhelm Stellbogen's Cairo residence:

Further advance payments to the Moslem Brothers are, in my opinion, very necessary, because these people can do very much. An immediate connection with Berlin through the Legation should be started and more funds asked for. The conversation with H.B. [Hassan al-Banna] about the P. [Palestine] question is very satisfactory and likewise GOEB. [Goebbels] has spoken about it with much praise.

The British source adds: "(Note: Year not stated but possibly 1938.)."[25]

A certain Dr Walter Uppenkamp, described as "Training Officer" of the local branch of the Nazi party in Cairo, invited Egyptians and especially Brotherhood members to lectures on "the Jewish question," while Ernst Engelen, deputy chairman of the branch, in notes on German–Egyptian cooperation in the preparation of bomb attacks in Palestine, reported that

> The last 200 Kilos of chlorate have been delivered to Helwan [a surburb of Cairo – M.K.]. We have ourselves advised that, instead of making explosives here, young chemists should be trained for such manufacture and should be sent to Palestine. So far several have left already. The expenses have been paid by the Arabs. We have been asked to assist regularly at the meetings of the Moslem Brethren.[26]

In Palestine itself, the Nazis also sought to fan the flames of anti-Jewish and anti-British revolt. German assistance was not confined to advice and encouragement; it also involved supplies of arms and large-scale funding. "The Mufti has asked me to convey his sincere thanks for the support so far provided," we read in speakers' notes for Admiral Wilhelm Canaris of June 1939. "Only through the funds we provided was he able to go ahead with the uprising in Palestine." Canaris was head of the German military intelligence organization, the Abwehr. The note was written by a subordinate officer, Oberst Hans Pieckenbrock, head of Military Foreign Espionage. A remark to the effect that "funds have been provided for the victims of the uprising" shows how deeply the Abwehr, which reported directly to the Wehrmacht's High Command, was involved in prewar Palestine.[27]

In a British War Office file entitled *German Nazi Activities in Palestine. Oct '38- Oct '39*, there is a reference to German assistance in the production of explosive devices. Apparently a firm run by "Palestinian Germans" – members of the German minority in Palestine – was used for bomb-making. In March 1939, the premature ignition of a bomb on the firm's premises had killed an Arab employee and seriously wounded another. In May 1939, the British authorities expelled a certain Oscar Dietrich from the territory. He was accused of having joined the insurgents and served as their specialist in the manufacture of landmines.[28]

Ferdinand Seiler, the German Consul General in Beirut, was among those Nazi functionaries who in these prewar days sought to promote terrorism against Jews and Britons. In September 1937, he wrote in relation to thwarting the Peel Plan: "The only way to achieve this seemed and seems to me to lie in the effort by the Arabs to use terrorism to intimidate the Jews and at the same time put pressure on the English."[29] How close the ties between German officialdom and the leadership of the uprising were is shown by a telegram from Seiler of October 1937: "Agent gives notice terror action Amman Transjordan Friday aim relief Palestine front."[30] Here the German Consul General is being informed in advance about a terrorist action.

In retrospect the disastrous consequences of the frustration of the Peel plan are clear: "For had a Jewish state been created in 1937, even in a small part of Palestine, it could have saved the lives of hundreds of thousands, possibly millions, of those unfortunate Jews who later perished in the Holocaust."[31]

Although by the start of 1938 the Peel Plan was a lost cause, the Nazis still sought to sustain the unrest. The reason for this was provided by Alfred Rosenberg, head of the NSDAP's Foreign Policy Office: "The longer the fire burns in Palestine," he prophesied in December 1938, "the stronger becomes the opposition to the Jewish regime of violence in all the Arab states and, moreover, also in the other Muslim countries."[32]

As later events were to show, not only the Nazis but also Amin el-Husseini attached great importance to the internationalization of antisemitism. In the evening of 16 July 1937 – the eve of the failed attempt to arrest him – he had a conversation with Walter Doehle, German Consul General in Jerusalem.[33] It is not known whether it was the Consul General who tipped the Mufti off about the arrest attempt. However, we do know that the Mufti remained in contact with Doehle through intermediaries while in hiding in the Mosque quarter of the Temple Mount.[34] Moreover, it was in this period, when El-Husseini was directing operations from his refuge, that a pamphlet entitled *Islam and Judaism* was published. This document might well be considered the founding text of Islamic antisemitism.

"Islam and Judaism"

This text, first published in Arabic on 18 August 1937 in Cairo, is the first full presentation of the construct of a direct connection between Muhammad's clashes with the Jews in Medina and the contemporary conflict in Palestine and of a link between the seventh and twentieth centuries. "A distinguished Arab [probably a reference to El-Husseini – M.K.] wrote this book about the profound hostility of the Jews to Islam and their actions against Allah's prophet," states the Foreword. The very next sentence links the Prophet with the present day.

> The Palestinian-Arab Information Office in Egypt is publishing this investigation because it is important for Muslims and Arabs to be clear about the Jews. This is of special importance in these days, in which they are obtaining a state in Palestine and wish with the help of the British to drive out the Muslims and Arabs.[35]

Since his appointment as Mufti of Jerusalem in May 1921, the aim of El-Husseini's policy had been to turn the limited territorial conflict in Palestine into an unlimited religious life-or-death war. From 1922 to 1936, he concentrated his campaigning on the alleged threat to the Islamic holy places. With the aim of mobilizing the religious peasantry, who were little impressed by nationalist slogans, and focusing the attention of the world's Muslims on Jerusalem, he elevated the Temple Mount into the symbol of the anti-Zionist struggle and declared defense of the Al-Aqsa

Mosque a religious duty.[36] In early summer 1936, he sent agents to Egypt to win support for his cause there. "The core of their argument consisted as before in the alleged intention of the Jews to destroy the Islamic holy places."[37]

The publication of *Islam and Judaism* in summer 1937 marks the beginning of the second stage of the process of turning the territorial conflict in Palestine into a religious war. What made it different from the previous efforts?

In the first place, the subject is no longer the Jews in Palestine, but global Jewry as a closed collective with immutable characteristics. Its hostility to Islam is depicted as "age-old and rooted in Jewish souls since the advent of Muhammad." This "eternal hatred" is not confined to the Palestine conflict. "Whoever believes that, if the Palestine problem is solved or if the Jews are defeated in this conflict everything will be fine, are wrong," states the Arabic original. "Even then nothing will change as regards their hostility to Islam and the Arabs. Allah will therefore see to it that the Jews are humiliated and their backbone broken."

Secondly, here the Koran and Muhammad's complex biography are reduced to a single theme: the alleged enmity of the Jews. In order to demonstrate the "eternal" nature of the Jews' malicious character, over a dozen incidents from Medina are recounted. Their alleged attempts to kill the Prophet or lure the faithful into error are treated not as time-and-place-bound episodes but as proof of the need to pursue the war against the Jews allegedly started by Muhammad in the here and now. In this respect, *Islam and Judaism* is the direct antecedent of Sayyid Qutb's polemic *Our Struggle with the Jews*, which appeared some 15 years later.

Third, a new medium for this antisemitism was created: a type of pamphlet that uses simple words to promote a form of Jew-hatred based on religion and integrating aspects of European antisemitism. Some individual Muslim leaders, such as Abd al-Aziz ibn Saud (1875–1953), King of Saudi Arabia, Rashid Rida (1865–1935), editor of the monthly magazine *Al-Manar*, and Amin el-Husseini (1897–1974) himself, had already started to espouse Islamic antisemitism before 1937. For Ibn Saud, however, it was something of a "personal idiosyncrasy" expressed only in private, and for Rida it remained confined to articles in his elite magazine, while the Mufti had previously expressed his antisemitism only in speeches at mass rallies.[38] The format of a written pamphlet aimed at a wider audience was new. It pioneered the use of a medium that would henceforth also be adopted by the Muslim Brotherhood in Egypt.[39]

Moreover, even the timing of the publication – eleven years before the foundation of the State of Israel – is significant. The premise of previous research has been that "Islamistically-dressed antisemitism," to use Muhammad Sameer Murtaza's expression, begins in the 1950s with Qutb's pamphlet, so as a result of the establishment of the State of Israel in 1948.[40] *Islam and Judaism*, however, proves that Islamic antisemitism as a new form of expression of Jew-hatred was being promoted at a time when the flight and expulsion of the Palestinian Arabs (1948) and the Israeli occupation of Gaza and the West Bank (1967) lay many years in the future. The emergence of Islamic antisemitism not in the 1950s but 20 years earlier indicates that, rather than antisemitism resulting from the exacerbation of the Middle Eastern conflict, it was the other way round: antisemitism exacerbated the conflict.

It is true that the Arab Revolt had already taken place in 1936, after the Nazis' Jewish policy had led to a sharp increase in Jewish immigration into Palestine, but the Revolt was not provoked by any provocative action by the Jews. In the actual disturbances, we read in the Peel Commission report, "one side put itself, not for the first time, in the wrong by resorting to force, whereas the other side patiently kept the law."[41]

The publication of *Islam and Judaism* was not inspired by the behavior of Palestine's Jews, but by the fact that summer 1937 saw the first attempt to get agreement on a two-state solution. While the proposal for a partition of Palestine "offers neither party all it wants, it offers each what it wants most, namely freedom and security", states the Peel Commission report. The Mufti and his supporters, however, wanted neither "freedom" for the Muslims nor "security" for the Jews. A new form of Jew-hatred was stirred up in order to thwart plans for a peaceful sharing of the territory. This is underlined further by *Islam and Judaism*'s mode of dissemination.

The Bloudan Congress

Three weeks after the publication of *Islam and Judaism*, from 8 to 10 September 1937, the first ever Pan-Arab conference took place in the Syrian town of Bloudan, located some 50 km to the north of Damascus. It was attended by over 400 participants from Syria, Palestine, Lebanon, Transjordan, Iraq, Egypt and Saudi Arabia. Among them were such prominent Arab figures as the former Iraqi Prime Minister, Naji al-Suwaidi. Current members of Arab governments, however, kept away from this anti-British event. The discussions took place behind closed doors and journalists were excluded.

The British Consul General in Damascus, Colonel Gilbert MacKereth, nevertheless succeeded in infiltrating an agent. In his *Memorandum Bludan Congress* of 14 September 1937, MacKereth, drawing on his informant's report, defined the gathering as "a manifestation of Judaeophobia." He referred in this respect to "a startlingly inflammatory pamphlet entitled 'The Jews and Islam'. ... It had been printed in Egypt."[42]

An appendix to MacKereth's report bears the title "Description of a violently anti-Jewish pamphlet printed in Cairo for the Palestine Defence Committee there which was given to each of the persons attending the Bludan Congress." It explains that "the pamphlet has 31 pages and is entitled 'The Jews and Islam'. The information it imparts is stated to have been obtained from the Qoran and the 'Traditions'." There follows a list of the pamphlet's main points:

> An account of the unceasing struggle that has ever gone on between the Jews and the Moslems and of the hatred always shown by the Jews for Moslems.
> An account of an attempt of the Jews to assassinate the prophet Mahomet.
> All traitors are brothers to the Jews.
> An account of an attempt of the Jews to poison the Prophet.

As a result of this attempt the Prophet always had bad health.

An account of how the Jews seek to engender a spirit of hatred and rivalry among the Moslems.

An attempt by the Jews to make the Prophet change his faith.

An account of Jews disguising themselves as Moslems for the purpose of bringing doubt to the Believers.

The rumour spread by the Jews that the Prophet was slain in the battle of Badr.

The Jews send messengers to the Kurdish tribes.

The Jews prefer agnosticism to Islam.

Quotations from the Prophet's sayings (the unfavourable ones) about the Jews.

The Jews are the servants of Satan.[43]

"This pamphlet," the report concludes,

is said to have been written by the Ulema of Palestine and is of a highly inflammatory nature and is intended to stir up (and doubtless will do so) passions not only against the Jews but also against the British Authorities called the tyrants.

There can be no doubt that the text given to the Congress's participants that MacKereth refers to is identical to the Cairo text. Perhaps the latter had even been produced specifically for distribution at Bloudan. In any case, it is certain that the initiator of the conference was Amin el-Husseini, the pamphlet's presumed author.

In June 1937, shortly before the bid to arrest him, the Mufti had held talks in Damascus about the holding and organization of the event and assigned people to this task.[44] He had moreover "put up the money needed to book both the grand hotels in Damascus and Bloudan and provide a large number of penniless participants with free places," according to a report from the German Consul General in Beirut.[45] The Mufti was not able personally to attend, since until October 1937 he remained in hiding. The participants in Bloudan nonetheless appointed him Honorary President of their gathering.

In the following years, Berlin took on the task of distributing *Islam and Judaism*. The Nazis' efforts to mobilize Arabs against Jews had shown them that Muslims did not understand and rejected their racial antisemitism. They therefore laid new stress on promoting an Islam-related variant of Jew-hatred. During World War II, the Arabic edition of the pamphlet was disseminated in the Middle East and North Africa and slightly modified editions in German and Serbo-Croat were also produced and distributed.

Archival documents reveal that in 1942 Berlin's Foreign Office sent the German Consul in Tangiers 1,500 copies of a "German propaganda text written in Arabic, *Islam and the Jews*," for "discreet distribution." The Spanish authorities in Tangiers, however, took the view that "the distribution of such a pamphlet which is directed against the Jewish element in Spanish Morocco cannot be allowed" and ordered all copies to be seized and destroyed.[46]

In 1943, in Zagreb a further 10,000 copies of a Serbo-Croat translation of *Islam and Judaism* (*Islam i Židovstvo*) were printed and distributed in Bosnia and Croatia.[47] In his groundbreaking study *Islam and Nazi Germany's War*, David Motadel refers to *Islam and Judaism* as "One of the most significant examples of this kind of religiously charged anti-Jewish propaganda among Muslims,"[48] while historian Jeffrey Herf has characterized it as "one of the founding texts of the Islamist tradition, one that defined the religion of Islam as a source of hatred of the Jews."[49] So who in fact wrote and who in fact originally published *Islam and Judaism*?

Was It the Mufti?

The publisher of *Islam and Judaism* was Mohamad Ali al-Taher, Director of the Palestinian-Arab Information Office in Cairo. Al-Taher was a prominent journalist from Palestine who had lived for a long time in Cairo and was close to the Muslim Brotherhood. He attended the Jerusalem Islamic Conference in 1931 and was one of the better-known participants in the Bloudan event of 1937, where he joined a Propaganda Committee established there.[50]

The information regarding his relations with Nazi agents is contradictory. On the one hand, his son, Hassan Eltaher, asserts that while his father was indeed urged to make contact with the Nazis, he refused to do so and never had any such contacts.[51] On the other hand, the British secret service considered him to be a "prominent Egyptian under German influence."[52] The French embassy in Cairo also suspected the Office headed by Al-Taher of cooperating with Nazis.[53] According to Brynjar Lia, Al-Taher was one of El-Husseini's "Palestinian contacts in Cairo" who organized the transfer of Nazi funds to the Muslim Brotherhood.[54] On 30 July 1942, as Rommel's forces approached Cairo, Al-Taher was arrested. According to a report by the American ambassador in Cairo, Alexander Kirk, of 3 October 1942, referencing Radio Bari, "The arrest of … Mohamed Taher Pasha had been received with 'a general feeling of horror' in Germany." Radio Bari had further reported

> that Taher Pasha had in fact been arrested two month before at the time of the closing of the Royal Automobile Club in Cairo of which he was reported to be the President. Bari added that sixty members of the Club had been arrested at the same time and thrown into concentration camps.[55]

But who was this "distinguished" Arab to whom authorship of *Islam and Judaism* is attributed? Although this secret was revealed neither in Cairo in August 1937 nor a month later in Bloudan, people in Berlin believed they knew who it was. In 1938, the Berlin-based publishing house, Junker and Dünnhaupt Verlag, published the whole pamphlet under the title *Islam-Judentum. Aufruf des Großmufti an die islamische Welt im Jahre 1937* ("Islam-Judaism – Appeal of the Grand Mufti to the Islamic World in 1937"). Presumably in order to avoid causing friction with London, the document was inserted, with no mention of either an appeal or an author on the cover, in a booklet by Dr Mohamed Sabry entitled

Islam-Judentum-Bolschewismus.[56] Moreover, in subsequent editions of *Islam and Judaism* distributed by the Nazis during World War II, the Mufti is named as the author.

However, it remains unclear whether El-Husseini was in fact its moving spirit or sole author. What is clear, however, is that the Nazis used the pamphlet attributed to the Mufti for their own propaganda purposes. Did they contribute to its preparation? On the one hand, the Arabic text displays a poetic style characteristic of other writings by the Mufti.[57] On the other hand, the Mufti never acknowledged authorship.

In summer 1937, while he was in hiding in the Mosque quarter of the Temple Mount and had ample opportunity to write *Islam and Judaism*, El-Husseini was in contact with the German Consul General through intermediaries.[58] By then serious attention had already begun to be paid in Germany to Islam's antisemitic potential. In April 1935, the Nazi periodical *Weltkampf* ran a report on the "antisemitic movement in Islam."[59] Subsequently, Johann von Leers, one of a number of prominent Nazi activists who converted to Islam after the war, penned several articles on the theme of "Judaism and Islam as opposites" in which he quotes *Islam and Judaism*.[60] "According to his own account, from 1933 onwards Von Leers associated in Berlin with circles of Arab students some of whom were in contact with El-Husseini. Around 1936 Von Leers claims to have made personal contact with the Mufti," explains historian Martin Finkenberger, who has conducted an in-depth study of Von Leers's career.[61]

However, such allusions do not amount to proof that Von Leers wrote *Islam and Judaism*. To this day, we do not know for certain how and by whom *Islam and Judaism* came to be conceived and published and what role the Nazis played in the process. The same is true of the German translation. It is, moreover, puzzling that Ferdinand Seiler, the German Consul General in Beirut, does not mention the pamphlet in his four-page report on the Bloudan Congress.[62] Germany had been in a privileged position at that event: as an exception to the ban on journalists, a correspondent of the *Deutsche Nachrichtenbüro* (German press agency) had been allowed to attend the conference and the *Völkische Beobachter* even to include a photo in its report.[63] This much, however, is certain: the publication of *Islam and Judaism* opened a new chapter in the history of antisemitism. The lasting impression this text made on the attitude of religious elites to Jews and the State of Israel can be shown by the following example.

Prophesies of the Final Battle

In *Islam and Judaism*, the hadith of the tree and stone that we previously encountered in connection with the Hamas Charter is quoted:

> The Hour (the Resurrection) will only come when the Muslims have inflicted a crushing defeat on the Jews. When every stone and every tree behind which a Jew has hidden says to the Muslim: 'There is a Jew hiding behind me, come and kill him'.

According to antisemitism expert Yehoshafat Harkabi, this is a call for an "eschatological 'final solution'." The resurrection and salvation of the Muslims is made dependent on a prior massacre of Jews. "Such expressions cannot be said to be an essential part of Islam; they are dormant, even unknown to its adherents, and have no influence or significance … so long as they are not repeated with some frequency."[64]

It is precisely this repetition, however, that has happened. For long periods, this hadith was hardly ever mentioned in the mosques.[65] Then, in August 1937, it was retrieved from oblivion and for the first time presented to a mass audience. Subsequently – and especially after the Six-Day War – it has gone on to become one of the most frequently cited hadiths of all.

Particular responsibility for this development lies with an article published in October 1968 in *Majallat al-Azhar*, the monthly magazine of the Al-Azhar Mosque in Cairo, one of the oldest and most prestigious Sunni universities in the world. Its author was the Lebanese scholar Sheikh Nadim al-Jisr, an employee of Al-Azhar's Islamic Research Academy. Under the title "The Prophecies About the Battle of Destiny Between the Muslims and Israel," he argued for the special importance – and also at that point in time the great topicality – of this hadith for Muslims. For 14 centuries, he writes, the meaning of this hadith had remained unclear. For so long as the Jews lived dispersed across the world and remained locked in their *dhimmi* status, it was not possible to kill them. Then, however, Allah decreed that the Jews would gain power and establish a state. This happened to enable the prophecy of the stone and the tree to be realized. Now the killing of Jews is not only possible but also righteous.[66]

At this point, we must pause. For people who live in secularized societies, it is hard to understand how such a brutal passage can be accepted as divine revelation and taken seriously as an imperative. This is less of a problem for orthodox Muslims. For them religion is not a part of life but life is a part of Islam. For them Islamic history is nothing other than the fulfillment of the goal of human history under divine guidance. That this proves the superiority of Islam, even if it involves a massacre of Jews, is not for them open to question.

This is the only explanation for the fact that Muhammad Sayyid Tantawi, Sunni Islam's highest religious authority, now also stepped up to express the opinion that the destruction of Israel was preordained by God. For Tantawi, who headed Al-Azhar University from 1996 to 2010 as its Grand Imam, the main purpose of the ingathering of the Jews from exile into Israel was clear. The Jewish state had been created by the will of Allah in order to permit the prophesy expressed in the hadith to become reality.[67]

Hassan Nasrallah, leader of the Shiite Hezbollah, was following the same reasoning when in 2002 he explained the advantages of the concentration of the Jews in Israel in this way:

Among the signs … and signals which guide us, in the Islamic prophecies … is that this State [of Israel] will be established, and … that Allah the Glorified and

Most High wants to save you from having to go to the ends of the world, for they have gathered in one place ... and there the final and decisive battle will take place.[68]

Turkey's President Erdogan also let himself be guided by these "Islamic prophecies" in December 2017, when in a speech to the Organization of Islamic Cooperation he threatened the Jews of Israel that when the time came, they would find "no tree to hide behind."[69] This was an unmistakable allusion to the hadith about the death of even such Jews who sought to hide, at least for those who are acquainted with and know how to interpret the codes of Islamic antisemitism.

Let us return to the 1930s, when Islamic antisemitism was born in the context of the conflicts over Palestine. *Islam and Judaism* reached the literate elites of the Arab world. Nazi Germany, however, also wanted to arouse the Jew-hatred of the "Arab Street". For this purpose, an Arabic short-range radio was the perfect instrument.

Notes

1 Yossef Bodansky, *Islamic Anti-Semitism as a Political Instrument*, Houston 1999, 23.
2 Mohsen Hamli, *Anti-Semitism in Tunisia 1881–1961*, Tunesia 2018, 24–25.
3 Boris Havel, "Haj Amin al-Husseini: Herald of a Religious Anti-Judaism in the Contemporary Islamic World", *The Journal of the Middle East and Africa*, Vol. 5, No. 3, September–December 2014, 221–243, here 226.
4 The Memorandum is available in Martin Gilbert, *Winston S. Churchill, Vol. IV, Companion Part 2 (Documents July 1919–March 1921)*, London 1977, 1386–1388.
5 Bernard Lewis, *The Jews of Islam*, Princeton, NJ 1984, 188.
6 Quoted from Klaus-Michael Mallmann and Martin Cüppers, *Halbmond und Hakenkreuz. Das Dritte Reich, die Araber und Palästina*, Darmstadt 2006, 44.
7 Adolf Hitler, Mein Kampf, Zweiter Band, München 1934, 747.
8 Elie Kedourie, *Arabic Political Memoirs and Other Studies*, London 1974, 223.
9 Lukasz Hirszowicz, *The Third Reich and the Arab East*, London 1966, 24.
10 Mustafa Kabha, "Palestinians and the Partition Plan", Ruth Gavison (ed.), *The Two-State Solution. The UN Partition Resolution of Mandatory Palestine: Analysis and Sources*, New York and London 2013, 29–37, here 33.
11 Yehoshua Porath, *The Palestinian Arab National Movement. From Riots to Rebellion, Volume Two 1929–1939*, London 1977, 229.
12 Ibid.
13 Khaba, "Palestinians", 34.
14 British National Archive (BNA), CO 733/326/5, Partition of Palestine, *Times*, 14 July 1937.
15 BNA, CO733/332/11, Letter to the Jewish Agency for Palestine, 22 September 1937.
16 BNA, CO733/332/11, Extract from Letter, Haifa, 16 September 1937.
17 BNA, CO733/352/3, Cypher Telegram from the High Commissioner for Palestine to the Secretary of State for the Colonies. Dated 16th July 1937.
18 BNA, CO 773/352/3, Report of Proceedings – Haifa. From: The Commanding Officer, H.M.S. Repulse.
19 BNA, CO733/352/3, High Commissioner for Palestine to His Majesty's Principal Secretary of State for the Colonies, 16th August, 1937, with attached police reports and brief

description; Matthias Küntzel, "Terror und Verrat. Wie der Mufti von Jerusalem seiner Verhaftung entging", http://www.matthiaskuentzel.de/contents/terror-und-verrat.

20 Politisches Archiv des Auswärtigen Amts (PAAA), Pol. VII, R 104 791, Akten betreffend Judenfragen, Blatt 373169, Grobba, Bagdad, 5 January 1937.

21 Akten zur Deutschen Auswärtigen Politik (ADAP) 1918–1945, Serie D, Band V, Dok. 569, 629, 564, 633.

22 PAAA, Beirut 59, undated memorandum.

23 Abd al-Fattah M. El-Awaisi, *The Muslim Brothers and the Palestine Question, 1928–1947*, London 1996, 98; Matthias Küntzel, *Jihad and Jew-Hatred. Islamism, Nazism and the Roots of 9/11*, New York 2007, 20–25.

24 Brynjar Lia, *The Society of the Muslim Brothers in Egypt*, Reading 1988, 179.

25 BNA, FO 371/23343, 10.09.1939, Note on German Suspects – Egypt, 21.

26 BNA, FO 371/23343, 10.09.1939, Note on German Suspects – Egypt, 20, 24, 26.

27 Institut für Zeitgeschichte, Nbg. Dok., PS-792, Vortragsnotiz OKW/Ausl/Abw I v. 18.6.1939, cited after Klaus-Michael Mallmann and Martin Cüppers, *Halbmond und Hakenkreuz. Das Dritte Reich, die Araber und Palästina*, Darmstadt 2006, 61f.

28 BNA, WO 208/1701, CInC's Weekly Situation Reviews, Appreciations of German Nazi Activities Palestine and Transjordan – Period March, 1939, 3. – Period May, 1939, 5. (CInC = Combined Intelligence Centre in the Middle East).

29 PAAA, R 104 788, DGK Beirut, 22.09.1937.

30 PAAA, R 104 788, DGK Beirut, 28.10.1937.

31 Avi Shlaim, *The Politics of Partition. King Abdullah, the Zionists and Palestine 1921–1951*, Oxford 1998, 59.

32 Alfred Rosenberg, "Die Judenfrage im Weltkampf", A. Rosenberg (eds.), *Tradition und Gegenwart, Reden und Aufsätze 1936–1940, Blut und Ehre, IV. Band*, München 1943, 208.

33 Hirszowicz, *Third Reich*, 34.

34 BNA, GFM 33/611, Serial 1526, DGK Jerusalem, Politik des Mufti von Jerusalem und des arabischen Nationalkomitees, 10 August 1937.

35 I am grateful to the Israeli historian, Dr Edy Cohen, who discovered an Arabic original of the first edition, for making the text available to me and translating the foreword.

36 Yehoshua Porath, *The Emergence of the Palestinian-Arab National Movement 1918–1929*, London 1974, 262–273.

37 Gudrun Krämer, *Minderheit, Millet, Nation? Die Juden in Ägypten 1914–1952*, Wiesbaden 1982, 290.

38 As regards Ibn Saud, see Barry Rubin, *The Arab States and the Palestinian Conflict*, Syracuse, NY 1981, 88–89 and 153. For Rashid Rida, see Gilbert Achcar, *The Arabs and the Holocaust. The Arab-Israeli War of Narratives*, New York 2009, 113–120.

39 El-Awaisi, *Muslim Brothers*, 64.

40 "Muhammad Sameer Murtaza im Gespräch mit Deutschlandfunk Kultur", 8 July 2018.

41 *Königliche Palästina-Kommission: Bericht über Palästina*, Berlin 1937, 2.

42 Elie Kedourie, "The Bloudan Congress on Palestine, September 1937", *Middle Eastern Studies*, Vol. 17, No. 1, January 1981, 111.

43 Ibid., 124.

44 Yehuda Taggar, *The Mufti of Jerusalem and Palestine Arab Politics, 1930–1937*, New York 1986, 454.

45 BNA, GFM 33/611, Serial 1525, Bericht des deutschen Generalkonsuls über die Konferenz vom 16. September 1937.

46 Höpp-Archiv, 01.10.015, Zentrum Moderner Orient Berlin (ZMO), Deutsches Konsulat, Tanger, den 8. Mai 1942, "Beschlagnahme einer deutschen Propagandaschrift 'Der Islam und die Juden' (in arabischer Sprache)".

47 David Motadel, *Islam and Nazi Germany's War*, Cambridge, MA 2014, 196. The historian Jennie Lebel has translated the Croat version into English at Lebel, *Mufti*, 311–319.

48 David Motadel, *Für Prophet und Führer. Die Islamische Welt und das Dritte Reich*, Stuttgart 2017, 196.

49 Jeffrey Herf, "Haj Amin al-Husseini, the Nazis and the Holocaust: The Origins, Nature and Aftereffects of Collaboration", *Jewish Political Studies Review*, Vol. 26, No. 3 & 4, 2016, 15.

50 Kedourie, "Bloudan", 122.

51 I am grateful to Hassan Eltaher, who lives in Canada, for providing me with this information in January 2017.

52 BNA, FO 371/23343, Note on German Suspects – Egypt, 10.9.1939, 29.

53 Krämer, *Minderheit*, 291.

54 Lia, *Society*, 175.

55 National Archives College Park (NACP), Record Group (RG) 84, Kirk to Secretary of State, No. 640 Cairo, 3 October 1942, "Comment on Axis Broadcasts in Arabic with Particular Reference to Items Concerning Egypt", Egypt: Cairo Embassy General Records 1936–1955, 19f.

56 Mohamed Sabry, *Islam-Judentum-Bolschewismus*, Berlin 1938, 22–32.

57 Verbal communication by Edy Cohen.

58 Fritz Grobba, *Männer und Mächte im Orient*, Göttingen 1967, 184.

59 Kureshi, "Antisemitische Bewegung im Islam", *Der Weltkampf*, Munich, Vol. 12, No. 136, April 1935, 113–115.

60 Johann von Leers, "Judentum und Islam als Gegensätze", *Die Judenfrage in Politik, Recht, Kultur und Wirtschaft*, Nr. 24, Jahrgang VI, 15 December 1942, 275–277; see on Von Leers: Martin Finkenberger, "'Während meines ganzen Lebens habe ich die Juden erforscht, wie ein Bakteriologe einen gefährlichen Bazillus studiert' – Johann von Leers (1902-1965) als antisemitischer Propagandaexperte bis 1945", *Bulletin Nr. 2 des Deutschen Historischen Instituts*, Moscow 2008, 88–99; Joel Fishman, "The Postwar Career of Nazi Ideologue Johann von Leers, aka Omar Amin, the 'First-Ranking German' in Nasser's Egypt", *Jewish Political Studies Review*, Vol. 26, No. 3 & 4, Fall 2016, 54–72.

61 I am grateful to Martin Finkenberger for this information, which he gave me in October 2016.

62 BNA GFM 33/611, Serial 1525: Deutsches Generalkonsulat, Panarabischer Kongress in Bloudan, Beirut, 16 September 1937.

63 Kairo Pas, "Nach dem Panarabischen Kongreß von Bloudan", *Völkischer Beobachter*, 19 September 1937.

64 Yehoshafat Harkabi, *Arab Attitudes to Israel*, Jerusalem 1972, 269. The Hebrew original of this book appeared in 1967.

65 As communicated to the author by Yehoshua Porath in March 2006.

66 D. F. Green (a pseudonym of David Littmann) published Al-Jisr's article in David Fati Green (ed.), *Arab Theologians on Jews and Israel*, Geneva 1971, 42–47; Harkabi, *Attitudes*, 269.

67 Shaul Bartal, "Reading the Qur'an: How Hamas and the Islamic Jihad Explain Sura al-Isra", *Politics, Religion & Ideology*, 14 December 2016, http://doi.org/10.1080/215676 89.2016.1265514. Wolfgang Driesch, *Islam, Judentum und Israel*, Hamburg 2003, 88.

68 Yair Rosenberg, "Did Netanyahu Put Anti-Semitic Words in Hezbollah's Mouth?", *Tablet*, 9 March 2015.

69 Boris Kálnoky, "Was wirklich hinter Erdogans Jerusalem-Rhetorik steckt", *Welt*, 12 December 2017.

3

1939–1945

Goebbels in Arabic

In Nazi propaganda, the spoken word ranked higher than the written. In Germany itself, the human voice was given pride of place at mass rallies, while to arouse the Arabs the Nazis used their second most important propaganda instrument: the shortwave radio transmitter. With top-quality presenters and polished programming, Islamic antisemitism was disseminated to the Muslim world in Arabic, Farsi, Turkish and Hindi. Technically advanced shortwave radio offered an entertainment and information medium with a great power of attraction. In his memoirs, Grand Ayatollah Husain Ali Montazeri recalls the installation of a radio in an Isfahan coffee house at the end of the 1930s: "Thousands of people" had come to see and hear the radio including Montazeri himself, who was wondering, "what is a radio?"[1] On 25 April 1939, the Nazis' first Arabic-language broadcast came on air; the last would be on 26 April 1945. This six-year barrage of sound embedded Islamic antisemitism in the consciousness of the "Arab Street" and continued to exert its influence even in the postwar period.

The use of radio was pioneered by the Italian leader, Benito Mussolini, who understood that the mass of Muslims could only be reached in this way. In 1945, the illiteracy rate in Egypt was almost 80% and in Libya 85%. In Palestine, in 1931 75% and in 1947 67% of Muslim men could not read.[2]

In March 1934, *Radio Bari* went on air with Arabic speakers and music. In those days, listening to the radio was a public occasion. People did so in coffee houses and bazaars. Sometimes the radio would be placed on a pedestal in the town square around which the information hungry would gather, sometimes a set located in the mayor's garden would provide a meeting point for the village elders. What had been heard would immediately then be talked about, further extending the reach of the programs' message. It has been estimated that by the start of the 1940s, "about

DOI: 10.4324/9781003369110-4

a million people were regularly listening to the radio in the Middle East and North Africa."[3] In addition, Mussolini hit on a ruse for entrenching *Radio Bari's* position. He sent "to Arab cafés as the centers of social life free receivers built in such a way that they could only pick up a very narrow frequency range that corresponded to the relevant Italian wavelengths." In this way, he ensured that Arab cafe audiences "sipped their coffee and swallowed Italian propaganda with every mouthful," as one observer remarked.[4]

It was Said Imam, an associate of the Mufti, who at the end of 1937 first urged the German Nazis to set up their own Arabic-language radio operation. The German Foreign Office supported the proposal after some hesitation, and in light of the fact that by 1938 not only France, Japan and the Soviet Union but also the British BBC had begun to broadcast in Arabic.[5] The first trial broadcasts directed at the Middle East took place in March 1939, and the official program began at the end of April.

In World War II, in addition to the land, sea and air wars, there was also a radio war. By October 1939, German shortwave transmitters were broadcasting in 15 different foreign languages. However, of all the foreign-language broadcasting units, the "Orient Zone" was given "absolute priority."[6] It broadcast to Arabs, Turks, Persians and Indians, and employed about 80 people, including some 20 presenters and translators.

Editorial control was in the hands of the Foreign Office Radio Policy Department, and the program content was determined in cooperation with the Propaganda Ministry and the Wehrmacht High Command's Foreign Propaganda Department.[7] The broadcasts were recorded in no. 77 Kaiserdamm in Berlin and then transferred by a special telephone line to Zeesen, a small village 40 km south of Berlin.

The transmitter systems in Zeesen were equipped with state-of-the-art directional antennae. In 1938 American radio expert César Searchinger described the "huge" shortwave radio complex in Zeesen as "the biggest and most powerful propaganda machine in the world" and its "supremely cunning technology of mass influence" as "the most formidable institution for the dissemination of a political doctrine that the world has ever seen."[8]

While exaggerated, the assessment is not wholly false. The "cunning technology of mass influence" included so-called *Geheimsender* ("secret stations") directed from Berlin under the code name "Concordia A." One of them was known as The Voice of the Free Arabs (*Saud El-urubah Alhurrah*) which masqueraded as the mouthpiece of an Egyptian Pan-Arab liberation movement. The fact that it was broadcasting from Berlin was concealed. The official Nazi stations – *Berlin auf Arabisch* ("Berlin in Arabic"), *Bari auf Arabisch* and from 1941 onward *Athen auf Arabisch* – could be held responsible for what they broadcast. The Voice of the Free Arabs, on the other hand, could spread the crudest propaganda and the most outrageous fabrications so long as the speakers took sufficient care to provide local "Egyptian" color. German press agencies could then take up the disinformation and pass it on as if it were authentic. Another secret station (The Arab Nation) started broadcasting in November 1941 from Greece and a third (The Free Voice of Egypt) did so from Italy.

By the start of 1940, Zeesen was broadcasting two programs in standard Arabic each day. From late summer onwards, this was increased to three a day with a combined duration of 95 minutes. There was, in addition, a Moroccan program lasting about an hour. In May 1941, The Voice of the Free Arabs began a daily 30-minute broadcast. By mid-1942, colloquial Arabic was increasingly being used in the broadcasts. As the military action moved to North Africa, Zeesen started broadcasting in the North African Arab and Berber dialects. Two Moroccan programs purporting to be of French origin were for a time broadcast over the *Paris Mondial* transmitter.[9]

The timing of the broadcasts was carefully staggered. For example, on 4 July 1942, Berlin in Arabic ran at 19.30, followed by Bari in Arabic at 20.00. At 20.15, it was the turn of the first run of The Voice of the Free Arabs, followed by a repeat at 21.15.[10]

The Zeesen Shortwave Radio Station

While all the combatant powers in World War II used secret stations, the Zeesen operation had some special features. First, the overhaul of the Zeesen equipment carried out in preparation for the 1936 Berlin Olympics had greatly improved its long-range sound quality. No other station provided a better listening experience than Zeesen.

Second, The Orient Zone editors succeeded in recruiting Younis Bahri, formerly of Iraqi Radio, as their announcer.[11] With his incisive voice, the ability to modulate the volume of his voice and aggressive speeches that sometimes spilled over into rants, his programs soon became a trade mark.[12]

Bahri opened all his programs with verses from the Koran and peppered his presentations with witty-cynical remarks. "Among highly cultivated listeners he has even been named 'Prince of Speakers'," a "cultured Arab" whose report on "Arabic announcers on Radio Berlin" rests in the records of the Wehrmacht High Command wrote in 1942. "The enemy press criticizes him, describing him as an 'exact copy of his master', i.e. the Führer."[13]

Third, the Zeesen broadcasts employed a crude and folksy antisemitism. Jew-hatred was the core of Nazi doctrine, but in this context it was also a tactical ploy to win over the audience. On this topic, facts were irrelevant and incitement everything. Thus, the United Nations, already in the making from the start of 1942, was derided as the "United Jewish Nations," and Emir Abdullah of Transjordan was mocked as "Rabbi Abdullah" for his moderate stance.[14] With regard to Fakhri Nashashibi, a prominent opponent of the Mufti in Palestine, the station claimed that "The Jews provide him with all the money he desires … Fakhri and his people visit Jewish houses at night … hatching plots and conspiring before returning home before daylight with rich pickings in the form of young Jewesses."[15]

A report dated 13 October 1939 on the impact of German radio propaganda prepared in Palestine for the British War Office describes the style.

> In general it may be said that the middle, lower middle and lower classes listen to the Arabic broadcasts from Berlin with a good deal of enjoyment. They like the racy, "juicy" stuff which is put over. … But not even the credulous Arab of the humbler strata of society can swallow everything the Germans put over the air. … What the average Palestine Arab does imbibe, however, is the anti-Jew material. This he wants to hear and to believe; and he does both. To that extent German propaganda is definitely effective.[16]

In Muslim Garb

The fourth distinguishing feature of this radio propaganda, its Islamic orientation, was tactically motivated. The Nazis were initially divided as to whether they should play the Islamic or the nationalist card to mobilize Muslims. One of their early idols was Mustafa Kemal Atatürk who had cast off the shackles of Islam and banned "'Dervishness' from Turkey," as Hitler remarked admiringly in April 1942.[17] In 1936 the Nazi newspaper, *Der Völkische Beobachter*, summarized the nationalist approach thus:

> The opposition between the modern state model, which is coming ever closer to breaking through, and the immobile and timeless beliefs of Islam is irreconcilable and constantly intensifying. Nationalism, with its right to totality, must purposefully seek to kill off certain political excrescences of religion and restrict it to its proper sphere. True to its leadership role, Kemalist Turkey has taken the first, decisive and trend-setting step in this regard.[18]

A totalitarian nationalism that kills off religion – that would correspond to the program of the Nazi party NSDAP. The promotion of strict Islam evidently contradicts it. So why did the Nazis choose to engage in the latter?

The crucial impulse was provided by the Zionist project in Palestine and the religion-fueled Arab opposition to it. In light of the success of the Mufti's mobilization effort, Berlin began to reconsider its previous reticence towards Islam. "Precisely in the Palestinian case," wrote the *Rheinisch-Westfälische Zeitung* in 1937,

> it has been repeatedly shown how militant Islamic nationalism has drawn its strength from the traditional intolerance of the Islamic religion. In every disturbance that has engulfed Palestine, Friday, the Islamic day of prayer, has always been the crucial moment.[19]

Giselher Wirsing, a leading Nazi publicist, had also been greatly impressed on an SS-commissioned trip to Palestine and Egypt. He had noted "a pronounced return to

the religious traditions of Islam" and a "fierce opposition to Western liberalism …
The latest developments in Egypt … show how strongly this theocracy can revive
after the defeat of the initial liberal onslaught."[20]

The Islamic tactic now prevailed. The "traditional intolerance" of nascent
Islamism and the "return to religious traditions" observed by Wirsing were not only
welcomed in Berlin but also promoted, as we have seen from the Nazis' financial
support for the Muslim Brotherhood and the Islamic tenor of their Arabic-language
radio broadcasting.

However, the incompatibility with the Turkish model remained. Radio Zeesen's
initial attempts to use Islamic messaging in its Turkish-language programs aroused
a storm of criticism in Ankara. Turkish media made fun of this attempt at deceit
and recalled Kaiser Wilhelm II's futile efforts in World War I to instrumentalize
Islam for secular ends. Religion should not be a means of political propaganda, the
Turkish press insisted.[21]

Berlin was not swayed by the general point but did decide to treat Turkey henceforth as a special case and ensure that the content of each broadcast was tailored
to the specific audience. Thus, on the scripts for the broadcasts of 8 January 1940,
we find a variety of comments. Some scripts are marked "for all," some "for all
except Turkey," some "for Iran/Turkey" and still others "for Arabia." On the scripts
for 25 January, we also find racial sorting; an intellectually demanding script is
marked "India Arabic Turkey," while a banal anti-Jewish tirade carries the indica-
tion, "Arabic only."[22]

In the programming for the Arab world, Islam was central: Radio Zeesen
addressed this audience not as Arabs but as Muslims. Every news report would
begin with the recitation of verses from the Koran. For this purpose, Berlin had
obtained special permission from the Al-Azhar Mosque in Cairo. A great deal of
the available time was devoted to Islamic religious holidays (Feast of Sacrifice;
birthday of the Prophet; 1,000th anniversary of the Al-Azhar Mosque). In addition, a regular weekly religious talk dealt with topics such as "Islam, the religion
of work" or the "prohibition of pride and selfishness." At all times, the return
of Muslims to their roots was advocated. For example, on 18 September 1942,
at 18.00 one of the secret stations, The Arab Nation, broadcast the following
message:

> Democracy has nothing in common with Islam which has no connection with
> any European principles. … The Arabs and Muslims have their own traditions
> and customs. It is our duty to adhere to these traditions and not to follow Euro-
> pean customs and principles which have nothing to do with Islam.[23]

After Amin el-Husseini arrived in Berlin in November 1941, the tone of the programs became more radical, especially as regards antisemitism.

Jew-Hatred by Radio

The style and wording of the incitement broadcast by the Nazis to the Arab world are well documented. In the German Federal Archives, in Berlin there is an almost complete set of copies of the German-language program scripts for the period from 8 January 1940 to 31 August 1941.[24] In addition, due to the efforts of the American Ambassador to Egypt, Alexander C. Kirk, we also have access to the content of most of the subsequent broadcasts. For the period between September 1941 and April 1942, Kirk sent regular detailed reports of the Nazis' Arabic-language radio propaganda to his superiors in Washington. The process was refined for the period between April 1942 and February 1945 when excerpts from the Zeesen broadcasts in Arabic were recorded in shorthand and translated word for word. Each week Kirk sent a compilation of these records – 10–30 pages long – to the US State Department where the documents were stored. Historian Jeffrey Herf was the first to discover this trove in the USA's National Archives and present an analysis of it in his pioneering study, *Nazi Propaganda for the Arab World.*[25]

For the Nazis, the "final solution of the Jewish question" was not meant to be restricted to Europe. "This war will end with an antisemitic world revolution and the destruction of the Jews throughout the world," states a Nazi party directive from May 1943. "Both are the prerequisite for perpetual peace."[26] It was Hitler's declared will to expand the mass murder program known as the "final solution" to the approximately 700,000 Jews of North Africa and the Middle East. This objective was part of the promise that he made to the Mufti at their meeting on 28 November 1941 in Berlin. When the German armies reached the southern exit from the Caucasus, Hitler told his interlocutor, the German goal would be "the annihilation of the Jews living under the protection of British power in the Arab region."[27]

What was involved here, therefore, was more than just propaganda in the service of further territorial expansion. Nor was it only a matter of driving Zionism from Palestine. The goal of this radio-disseminated antisemitism was to prepare Muslim societies for the commission of all-out mass murder. And it almost happened: as Rommel's *Panzerarmee Afrika* embarked on its apparently unstoppable march towards Cairo in summer 1942, a special SS unit of seven senior officers and 17 lower-ranking officers was sent to join it. This unit was entrusted with implementing the murder of Jews, with the help, so it was believed, of a sufficient number of local Arabs.[28] So how was this Arab Jew-hatred whipped up?

An answer is provided in one of Kirk's reports to Washington on German radio propaganda of April 1942:

> The following themes are being repeated ad nauseam: 1.THE JEWS: The Jews, backed by Britain and the U.S.A., are the arch-enemies of Islam. They control American finance and have forced Roosevelt to pursue a policy of aggression. Roosevelt "the war-monger" and Churchill "the grave-digger of the British

Empire", though criminal in themselves, are playthings in the hands of the Jewish fiends who are destroying civilization.[29]

The above extract gives rise to an initial observation: to some extent, the traditional European antisemitic conspiracy ideology was retailed to Arabic audiences in original form. This also applies to the stations' repeated claims that the Jews instigated both World Wars I and II – a claim that 45 years later would find its way into the Hamas Charter. Here is an excerpt from a Voice of the Free Arabs program broadcast at 20.15 on 3 November 1943:

> Should we not curse the time that has allowed this low race to realize their desires from such countries as Britain, America and Russia? The Jews kindled this war in the interests of Zionism. The Jews are responsible for the blood that has been shed. … The world will never be at peace until the Jewish race is exterminated. Otherwise wars will always exist. The Jews are the germs which have caused all the trouble in the world.[30]

In addition, the full repertoire of racial antisemitism was translated into Arabic. "The Jews are microbes. Like leeches they cling to a country, sucking its blood, plundering, stealing and carrying on their subversive activities, which they style commerce," stated Radio Zeesen in August 1942.[31]

However, neither racial antisemitism nor conspiracy theories dominate the Nazis' radio programs, as Jeffrey Herf notes, emphasizing,

> the centrality … of the teachings of the Koran and of Islam in Nazism's Arabic programming: It was its reading of this work and this tradition – not citations from *Mein Kampf*, *The Protocols of the Elders of Zion*, or speeches by Hitler or Goebbels – that served as the most important entry point to Arab and Muslim listeners.[32]

And in fact from 1939 to 1945 the Islamic antisemitism that in 1937 could only be disseminated in written form was brought to the masses over the radio waves.

> Berlin made explicit use of religious rhetoric, terminology, and imagery and sought to engage with and reinterpret religious doctrine and concepts to manipulate Muslims for political and military purposes. … German propaganda combined Islam with anti-Jewish agitation to an extent that had not hitherto been known in the modern Muslim world,

writes David Motadel.[33]

Thus, on 23 December 1942, The Arab Nation broadcast a speech given by Amin el-Husseini on 18 December on the occasion of the opening of the Islamic Central Institute in Berlin. The similarity to the content of *Islam and Judaism* is striking.

Every Muslim knows that Jewish animosity towards the Arabs dates back to the dawn of Islam. Every Muslim knows how they opposed and hurt the Prophet as well as creating endless difficulties for him ... so that the Koran says: "You shall find that the most hostile people to the faithful are the Jews."

After this reference back to the seventh century, we get the link to the present:

The Jews are the same whether during the era of the Prophets or in succeeding eras. They never waver from their policy of intrigue and evil doing. They spread their venom in the Islamic countries for their ambitions and of late these ambitions have been clear in Palestine, the Holy Land, which they want to make a center for the extension of their domination. ... The Koran says that they heat the cauldron of war and bring corruption on the earth and God does not like those who corrupt. Such are their ways. Even in this war, they have brought about the clash between different opinions and as [Chaim] Weizmann said, this war is a Jewish war and in point of fact world Jewry dictates the war as was the case during the days of Mohammed. The Jews have spread their influence over Britain. They dominate America. The Jews are behind destructive and atheist communism. They have brought people against each other and the catastrophes and tragedies which are happening now are caused by the Jews.[34]

Again and again, the program makers of the Orient Zone repeated only those verses from the Koran that are suitable for presenting the Jews as "enemies of Islam." Day after day, the Age of Muhammad was combined with the twentieth century, and the alleged irreconcilability of the two religions stressed. Thus, on 28 January 1944, Berlin in Arabic stated

that this enmity and this struggle between Arabs and Jews will always continue until one side or the other is destroyed. The struggle and war between Arabs and Jews relates to religious beliefs and such conflicts can end only through the destruction of one side. ... Between Arabs and Jews enmity has always prevailed, from the olden times. But since the appearance of Islam it has become sharper.[35]

Seven years later, Sayyid Qutb's pamphlet *Our Struggle with the Jews* would seamlessly pick up the threads of this propaganda. As Jeffrey Herf writes, Qutb's tirade "displays a striking continuity with the themes of Nazism's wartime broadcasts."[36]

The Call to Pogrom

The Zeesen broadcasts did not only propagate antisemitic words; they also encouraged antisemitic deeds. The incitement to action was further stepped up when Rommel advanced on Egypt in summer 1942. After having captured the Libyan port of Tobruk near the Egyptian border in June 1942, in early July the German–Italian army launched an attack on the British positions near El-Alamein, 100 km from Alexandria. Cairo suddenly seemed within reach. While Mussolini flew to Libya so as not to miss the opportunity to enter Cairo at the head of the troops on a white horse, in the first weeks of July an unbroken line of trains left Cairo for Palestine to enable Jews – free of charge and with no passport controls – to flee Egypt in time. Then the British 8th Army succeeded in halting Rommel's advance.[37]

In these decisive weeks, Zeesen's propaganda shed all restraint. The victory of the Axis Powers was at hand, suggested The Voice of the Free Arabs at 21.15 on 25 June 1942. "Everywhere people are asking what part they can play in wiping out the British and the Jews." The broadcasters had an idea:

> All over the country, the Jews should be watched. Every Jew's name must be written down, together with his address and his business. The Jews must be watched carefully so that they may be wiped out at the earliest opportunity.[38]

Twelve days later, the station stepped up the rhetoric, demanding that "the Egyptians rise as one man to kill the Jews before they have a chance of betraying the Egyptian people." This appeal followed:

> Arabs of Syria, Iraq and Palestine, what are you waiting for? The Jews are planning to violate your women, to kill your children and to destroy you. According to the Muslim religion, the defense of your life is a duty which can only be fulfilled by annihilating the Jews. This is your best opportunity to get rid of this dirty race, which has usurped your rights and brought misfortune and destruction on your countries. Kill the Jews, burn their property, destroy their stores, annihilate these base supporters of British imperialism. Your sole hope of salvation lies in annihilating the Jews before they annihilate you.[39]

This was not the only effort to incite pogroms. After the landing, by 63,000 US and British soldiers in Algeria and Morocco in November 1942, the Nazis aimed to provoke clashes between Moroccans and Americans. A point of entry is "provided by the Jewish element," reads the introduction to a set of *Guidelines for Underground Propaganda in Morocco*, personally endorsed by the Foreign Minister, Joachim von Rippentrop: the indigenous inhabitants should be "encouraged to engage in acts of anti-Jewish violence; since the Americans will then be compelled to take action to protect the Jews, the desired American clash with the locals will be brought about." Recommended were the "fomenting of demonstrations, clashes and pogroms against Jews. Calls for the looting of Jewish businesses, refusal to pay taxes and loan repayments." This incitement should "be disseminated by the new secret radio station."[40] Did this calculation pay off?

Farhud – The Massacre of Iraqi Jews

On the whole, the radio propaganda had little immediate impact on Muslim behavior. The uprisings called for by the Mufti in the British and American-occupied territories failed to materialize. Most of the Arab leaders collaborated with Britain and desertions by Muslims fighting in the Allied ranks were rare.

No definitive answer can be given to the question of whether Muslims in, for example, Palestine would have participated in massacres of Jewish civilians as the Nazis hoped. The turning of the tide of war in 1942 ensured that the matter was never put to the test.

The same can be said for Western North Africa. Following the landing by German troops in Tunis, in November 1942, Jews were looted, terrorized and abused as forced laborers, but not murdered. In Tunisia, as in Morocco and Algeria, Germany had to pay heed to its French, Italian and Spanish allies, who placed obstacles in the way of the murder of Jews. In individual cases, Jews were also protected by Muslim leaders. Thus, the Moroccan Sultan Mohammad V was outraged by the racialist nature of the anti-Jewish laws issued by Vichy France. He was guided by Islamic law, which deemed a Jew who had converted to Islam equal in status.[41] Moreover, Allied forces had already landed in Morocco and Algeria, so that – unlike in Eastern Europe – any mass murder of Jews would have swiftly come to light. Nonetheless, one anti-Jewish pogrom by thousands of Muslims did take place.

The *Farhud*, as this massacre has since been known, occurred on 1 and 2 June 1941 in Baghdad and went on for 30 hours. Jews, members of a community that had lived in Iraq since time immemorial, were mutilated and murdered; children were killed and women raped in front of their husbands, synagogues set on fire and Torah scrolls destroyed. The corpses of 180 Jewish women and men could be identified, but according to BBC report a further 600 victims were alleged to have been buried in mass graves.[42]

Prior to this mass murder, Fritz Grobba, since 1932 the German envoy in Iraq, and Amin el-Husseini, active in Baghdad since October 1939, had been campaigning in support of the Nazis. Their efforts had culminated on 1 April 1941 in a coup by a pro-Axis Iraqi politician, Rashid Ali al-Gailani. For London a red line had been crossed. On 2 May, the Anglo-Iraqi War began. Hitler, preoccupied with the imminent invasion of the Soviet Union, gave the Iraqi putschists only half-hearted support. By 28 May, British forces were at the gates of Baghdad, and on 31 May, El-Husseini and the putschists fled to Iran. By then, the decision to perpetrate a massacre had probably already been taken; Jewish dwellings had been marked in advance.

A subsequent official inquiry by the Iraqi government identified two causes of the massacre: the Mufti's agitation and Nazi–German radio propaganda.[43] What was the content of this propaganda immediately before the massacre?

The Anglo-Iraqi conflict "opens … a fertile field for our Arabic broadcasting," asserted Joseph Goebbels on 3 May 1941. "We must try to use Arab instincts … solely for our aims."[44] In this period, the Mufti, now resident in Baghdad, was in constant contact with the Berlin-based Orient Zone team. On 5 May 1941, Radio Zeesen reported on an appeal by the Mufti, "for arms to be taken up against England." It featured Iraqi spiritual leaders according to whom "no Mohammedan will any longer fight on the side of Britain without thereby sinning against the interests of Islam."[45] On 11 May, the Nazi radio station once again quoted Amin el-Husseini: "The Iraqi struggle is a struggle for all Mohammedans and thus a holy war for Islam."[46]

The Mufti designated Baghdad's 80,000-strong Jewish community as the scapegoat for Al-Gailani's looming defeat. He accused the Jews of passing information to the British, thus paving the way for their victory. In the memoirs he wrote several decades later, he continued to attribute the coup's failure to the Jews. On 26 May, a few days before the massacre, Younis Bahri graced Radio Zeesen with one of his notorious tirades. Taking up El-Husseini's conspiracy theory, he linked it to Islam.

> The Arabs fought the Jews and expelled them from the Arabian peninsula 1,400 years ago. Muhammad was the first who expelled them. … The Arabs of Iraq bear witness now to the actions taken by the Jews … in accordance with British orders [so allegedly as traitors – M.K.] … The Jews everywhere are an abomination. Remember the words of the Koran: The greatest enemies of mankind are those who believe as the Jews.[47]

Despite the fact that not a word of it is true, the talk appears to have been emotionally effective. While this was not in itself enough to effect a massacre, in combination with the prior efforts of Grobba and the Mufti and the bitterness of the Iraqi defeat in this short war, it is likely to have contributed to the fact that deeds followed words and hundreds of Jews were murdered.

What Was the Impact of the Radio Propaganda?

Many contemporary sources emphasize the German broadcasts' attractiveness and popularity. This remained true in Iraq even after the defeat of the pro-Nazi coup and the *farhud*. In September 1941, a British informant reported that "Those living in towns turn their radios on to Germany and encourage others to listen in defiance of instructions to the contrary."[48]

The Arabs in Palestine too listened to the Nazi radio "most attentively, particularly in town and village coffee shops where large crowds gather for the purpose. Whilst the distorted information does not have any great effect on the intelligentsia, the uneducated classes are undoubtedly being influenced," reported Palestine's Criminal Investigation Department on 15 September 1939.[49] This finding is corroborated by an internal report of the Jewish Agency that cites an Arab informant, who on 7 October 1939 observed a crowd in an Arab coffee house in Jaffa.

> 10 days after the war broke out, the police in Nablus imposed a ban on listening to Arabic-language broadcasts from Berlin (the ban was conveyed verbally to those in the coffee houses). I was told that there is a similar ban in place in Jaffa, but in reality even in the coffee houses this station is turned on. One of the informants told me that on the eve of the Sabbath (7 October) he went into a café and heard a German broadcast. Arabs were standing around the café – even on the surrounding balconies – to listen to the program.[50]

The British took a whole range of measures to counter this propaganda, including using jamming equipment to hinder reception. In 1941, they launched an Arabic-language radio station *Sharq al-Adna* in Jaffa.[51] They tried to ban listening not only in public places but also in private dwellings. In December 1942, SS-*Standartenführer* Walter Schellenberg complained in a report on the situation in Palestine that "the radio equipment in the possession of Arabs has to a large extent been confiscated or rendered useless."[52] Last but not least, BBC in Arabic began to increase the number of citations from the Koran, celebrate Islamic festivals and present Britain as the real friend of Islam.

Just as the Berlin broadcasters had put up Amin el-Husseini as their front man, so the BBC now promoted such opponents of the Mufti as Emir Abdullah of Transjordan and the pro-British leader of the North African Sanussi Brotherhood. "In the recent period, the English radio propaganda … has become especially good and effective," commented Schellenberg in a message to the German Foreign Office of December 1942.[53]

To Radio Zeesen's most important speciality, its antisemitism, however, the Allies provided no counter. The antisemitic anti-Zionism disseminated day in, day out by the German radio was popular throughout the Arab world, far more indeed than was Nazi Germany itself. The Orient Zone skillfully exploited every opportunity to underline the alleged identity of interests of Zionists and Allies.

On this front, the BBC and the other Allied stations had nothing to say. None of them wanted to be seen as defenders or even "accomplices" of the Jews. They feared that if they drew attention to the topic of antisemitism, they would end up confirming the Nazi propaganda to the effect that the Allies were the instruments of the Jews. The more popular the Nazis became in the Middle East, the less ready were the Allies to oppose their use of antisemitism there.

Anne Fuller, an employee of the United States Office of War Information, addressed this dilemma in a report of September 1941: "The Zionist problem," she concluded, presented "the most difficulties in [Allied] broadcasting to the Arab world." The BBC meanwhile avoided the theme entirely. It thereby left "the Axis powers with an important weapon with which to stir up discontent within the Arab world." Fuller advised that the USA should follow the BBC's policy and "make no mention of the thorny subject. Admittedly this is far from satisfactory. But until the precarious future of the Near and Middle East is better defined there seems no other course."[54]

This position was the one implemented. Wary of the Arab mood, the Allies decided *de facto* to dissociate themselves from Zionism, while ignoring rather than opposing the German broadcasters' antisemitism.

If the Nazis' radio propaganda succeeded in doing anything, it was in disseminating and escalating Jew-hatred in this part of the world. The reverse conclusion is that in Muslim-populated centers that were beyond the reach of the Zeesen hate propaganda, there was less hatred of Jews. This was, for example, the case in Bosnia–Herzegovina, home to some 950,000 Muslims and 14,000 Jews. Here the Nazis only had written material at their disposal to stir up the Muslims against the Jews. This material included the widely distributed *Islam and Judaism*. There was, however, no radio propaganda in Serbo-Croat. In this region, antisemitism failed to gain a foothold, the Middle Eastern conflict attracted little attention and there were no attacks by Muslims on Jews in the postwar period.[55]

Even at the beginning of 1944, when it was very hard to believe that the Nazis could still win the war, Radio Zeesen continued to attract a large audience. This was in any case the view of two employees of the US Military Intelligence Division. Even though only a small percentage of Arabs owned a radio, yet from "reliable sources in both Syrian and Lebanese capitals," they had learned that "practically all Arabs who have radios and listen to any variety of programs, listen to Berlin."

The Arabs, they continued, did not "take German 'news' at all seriously," and the effect of German news reporting was "practically nil." Rather, Berlin radio broadcasts achieved their impact through "the clever and full exploitation of half-truths, and occasional events." Berlin broadcasts seized on "the curiosity, the credulity, the avarice, the aspirations, the religious instincts or the racial prejudice, etc., of the Arabs" to fan their antagonism to the Jews and the Allies.[56] Only by the end of 1944, when there had, for a long time, been no German military victories to report, did the numbers of listeners and the impact of the propaganda markedly decline.

As Seth Arsanian, a close observer of the radio scene during World War II, wrote correctly in 1948, the effect of the propaganda – the resulting changes in attitude – cannot really be measured. His prognosis seems, nonetheless, to have been confirmed:

It may be surmised that the campaign of hate, the name calling, the derision, and the accusations which the Axis propagandists directed against the Allied nations will continue to have their subtle effect for some time to come. This devaluation of the European nations in the minds of the Arab masses will not be limited to any specific nation but will extend to Western civilization in general, tending to strengthen traditionalist, conservative groups in the Middle East.[57]

An example is Iran. Here Germany's Farsi-language wartime broadcasts enjoyed great popularity. When the 36-year-old cleric Ruhollah Musavi, later to become famous under the name Ruhollah Khomeini, returned in winter 1938 from Iraq to Qum in Iran, writes his biographer Amir Taheri,

> He had brought with him a radio set made by the British company Pye which he had bought from an Indian Muslim pilgrim. The radio proved a good buy ... It also gave him a certain prestige. Many mullahs and talabehs would gather at his home, often on the terrace, in the evenings to listen to Radio Berlin and the BBC.[58]

Even though Khomeini remained opposed to Hitler and National Socialism, it is reasonable to assume that there is a link between the eruption of his Jew-hatred in 1963 and the invective from Berlin that he had imbibed over the radio 15 years previously.

Excursus: The Nazis and Iran

A photo taken in 1940 in Tehran shows a big crowd listening carefully to a large pipe radio placed in an elevated niche on a wall.

> In some newspapers and private notes of the time we find reports of how in the late 1930s ... during the broadcast of the Farsi-language news from Berlin people would gather together on the steps of the tea houses with a radio set in order to listen to the Germans' reports of their territorial gains on the various fronts,

writes Iranian writer Amir Hassan Sheheltan. "The reports inspired the fantasy of the crowd on the street that every victory corresponded to a defeat for the colonial powers, the Soviet Union and Britain, which they cheered and applauded."[59] Already in World War I, most Iranians had supported the Germans, who were fighting their common enemies, the British and the Russians. Moreover, the Germans also enjoyed great prestige as technicians and engineers. Since the mid-1920s, Germany had not only laid the foundations of an Iranian industrial infrastructure but also exported "made in Germany" technical education to Iran. Soon enough the "German work ethic" had become the stuff of legend. In addition, after 1933 the German–Iranian friendship had also taken on a racist dimension through a purported shared membership in the "Aryan" race. All this created a bond between Germans and Iranians of a quite different quality to their respective relationships with the Arab world.[60]

With the start of World War II, cooperation became especially close. In 1940, 47% of all Iranian exports went to Nazi Germany, while Germany's share of Iranian imports had reached 43%. In the same period, between 1939 and 1945, a special German export product – European antisemitism – was marketed in Iran albeit in an Islamic guise.[61]

A 14-page report by Alexander Winkler, the former Cultural Attaché at the German Embassy in Tehran, on "Lessons of German propaganda work in Iran between November 1939 and September 1941" dated 10 January 1942 is highly revealing.

One did not get far with conventional antisemitism in Iran. "The broad masses of Iranians lack a feeling for race theory." Instead, religion was the appropriate vehicle. "The propaganda that promises the greatest success," writes Winkler, "ties in with Iranian religious ideas and expectations." In this respect, Winkler mentions the belief in the Shiite Messiah, the Twelfth Imam, and the readiness of Iranians to view Hitler as this very Messiah. "In the inclination of the Iranians towards religious fanaticism powerful forces lie ready that we can exploit for our own ends." But how could Nazi Germany of all places conduct religious propaganda? Winkler had the answer: "The immediate point of connection with Shiite beliefs lies in the treatment of the Jewish question, which the Mohammedan perceives in religious terms, so bringing him close to National Socialism on a religious basis."[62] Hatred of Jews is to provide the way into the Shiite belief system, while at the same time that belief system is seen as the natural medium for the propagation of National Socialism.

The German Ambassador to Iran, Erwin Ettel, gave this idea concrete form when he connected the seventh with the twentieth century. "One way to promote this [anti-Jewish – M.K.] development would be to highlight Mohammed's struggle with the Jews in the olden days and that of the Führer in the present day," he recommended to the Foreign Office at the beginning of 1941. He also provided the relevant citations: on the one hand, verse 5/85 of the Koran which reads, "Truly you will find, that among all people the Jews ... are the most hateful towards the faithful," and, on the other, the final sentence of the second chapter of Hitler's *Mein Kampf*: "in resisting the Jews, I am doing the Lord's work." If we succeed, writes Ettel, "in bringing the country's spirituality to a large extent under the influence of German propaganda, the mass of the people in its full breadth can be captured."[63]

It was, however, not only the pseudo-religious approach of the propaganda that accounted for the Zeesen broadcasts' popularity but also the style of the programming. In 1940, Reader Bullard, the British Ambassador to Iran, complained that "Even if we [the British] do broadcast in Persian, we cannot hope to rival the Germans in interest, as their more violent, abusive style, with exaggerated claims ... appeals to the Persian public."[64]

In addition, Zeesen had in Bahram Shahrokh an outstanding speaker with a good voice and excellent diction. Shahrokh's antisemitic incitement had at times a direct impact on the situation of Iran's Jews. An Iranian Jewish woman, Parvin R., who was 17 years old at the time, remembers,

In particular a speech by Bahram Shahrokh on Radio Berlin on the occasion of the Jewish Purim festival. Shahrokh urged the audience ... to exact revenge for the alleged Massacre of Persians by Jews in the Purim story. Parvin: "The next day, some of my father's Muslim friends came to my father's pharmacy to demand an explanation. I was there that day and I heard them belittle and mock the Jews. When my father tried to explain the issue … they attacked him and grabbed his neck whereupon my father told me to run home. I never asked nor did I ever find out how he got rid of them."[65]

At the same time, Shahrokh presented himself as brave and cheeky. He repeatedly made barbed remarks about Reza Shah, the by now thoroughly detested ruler. Following angry protests from Reza Shah, who was a regular listener of the German radio station, at the end of 1940 the German Foreign Office had to take Shahrokh off air, but only temporarily. In August 1941, Britain and the Soviet Union occupied Iran, which sympathized with Germany, in order to create a land bridge for the delivery of arms to the Soviet Union – arms without which the battle of Stalingrad would not have been won.[66] The occupying powers ousted Reza Shah Pahlavi from his throne and installed his son, Mohammed Reza Shah, in his stead. Shortly thereafter, Shahrokh was back on air. However, even though the British–Soviet coup had put an end to the flirtation between Tehran and Berlin, the situation of the Iranian Jews remained insecure. Already under Reza Shah the effects of Nazi propaganda had impacted their daily life.

"Teachers were sacked along with holders of government offices or employees of state railways. Schoolchildren were expelled from the public schools and refused places in public universities."[67] Moreover, after the deposition of Reza Shah, the mass of the population fervently awaited the German invasion of Iran envisaged by Hitler, hoping that it would put an end to the hated British–Soviet occupation. Now the Nazis' radio propaganda was more than just commentary on the war: it was an instrument in the service of the "liberation" of Iran by German forces.

In those days swastikas were painted on the walls of many houses in Tehran. Bazaar traders sold pictures of Hitler. The new Shah recalled that "…the German … propaganda was very effective. … The propagandists always depicted Hitler as a Muslim and descendant of the Prophet. He was said to have been born with a green band around his body".[68]

As the US Ambassador in Iran, Louis Dreyfus reported in May 1942,

German propaganda … made a deep impression on the masses. The daily radio broadcasts from Berlin had been particularly effective and a film audience in the poor section of Tehran had cheered wildly for Hitler and at decidedly the wrong places when a British war film was shown. At one point, the British pressured the Iranian police to remove all radios from public places, but they were quickly restored, again at British request, when it was found, strangely, that one could not tune in the British broadcasts either, without a radio.[69]

Following the coup of August 1941, the radio provided the only way of getting news about the Axis.

> Although action is been taken to make effective the ban on public listening to Axis broadcasts, it seems that listening in private houses is still widely practiced. As a result it appears that many people are still convinced that the Axis powers will win the war; Hitler, moreover, is said to enjoy great personal popularity,

reported the BBC in June 1942.[70]

At the same time, after the fall of Reza Shah, who, despite his admiration for Hitler, did not share the latter's antisemitism, Jew-hatred began to play a greater role in the Zeesen broadcasts. This fell on the fertile soil of Iranian anti-Judaism.

Indeed under Shiite rule, the Jews had fared even worse than in the Sunni sphere. Only in post-sixteenth-century Iran had they been deemed *najes* ("unclean") so that they were forbidden to leave the house when it rained or snowed in order to prevent their "uncleanness" from polluting Muslims. Ayatollah Khomeini gave expression to this radical Shiite anti-Judaism in a widely disseminated basic guide for Muslims:

"There are eleven things which make unclean: 1. urine; 2. faeces; 3. sperm; 4. carrion; 5. blood; 6. dog; 7. pig; 8. unbeliever; 9. wine; 10. beer; 11. the sweat of a camel which eats unclean things." In a comment on point 8 he adds: "The entire body of the unbeliever is unclean; even his hair and nails and body moistures are unclean."[71]

While, in the above-cited passage, he places Christians and Jews on the same level as dogs and pigs and so disparages both to the maximum extent, on other occasions he would present the Jews alone as uniquely dangerous to the future of Islam.

"We see today that the Jews (may God curse them) have meddled with the text of the Koran," he wrote in his most important work, *The Islamic State*, published in 1971.

> [T]he Jews and their foreign backers are opposed to the very foundations of Islam and wish to establish Jewish domination throughout the world. Since they are a cunning and resourceful group of people, I fear that – God Forbid – they may one day achieve their goal.[72]

Such fantasies about Jewish world domination are not part of the Shiite tradition. Here Khomeini has adopted a key idea of European antisemitism and linked it to his religion-based anti-Judaism. Khomeini had been a regular listener to the Nazis' wartime Farsi-language broadcasts, and, although it cannot, in retrospect, be proven, it would seem obvious that his fantasy had been shaped by this six-year-long barrage of antisemitic propaganda.

Khomeini's great campaigns of the 1960s that made the later revolutionary leader famous throughout Iran were conducted under the sign of Islamic antisemitism.

"Israel does not wish the Koran to exist in this country," he roared out in June 1963 to tens of thousands of people who had streamed into Qum. "Israel does not wish the *'ulama* to exist in this country. Israel does not wish to see Islamic precepts in this country." At the climax of the speech, he also personally attacked the Shah, "What exactly is the relationship between the Shah and Israel ...? Can it be that the Shah is an Israeli? Does the secret service believe him to be Jewish?" He finally introduced the threat of excommunication: "Shall I declare you, Mr. Shah, to be a heathen so that you are chased out of this country?"[73]

The image of the Jew as the enemy permeates Khomeini's early writings. Thus the following extract from his foreword to *The Islamic State* could easily have been written by Amin el-Husseini or Sayyid Qutb.

> From the very beginning, the historical movement of Islam has had to contend with the Jews, for it was they who first established anti-Islamic propaganda and engaged in various stratagems, and as you can see, this activity continues down to the present.

Khomeini recalls that the Prophet Muhammad had hundreds of members of the Jewish Qurayza tribe beheaded and praises him for this.

> When he [the Prophet] gave orders for the conquest of a certain area, the burning of a certain place, or the destruction of a certain group whose existence was harmful for Islam, the Muslims and mankind in general, his orders were just. ... Since the Jews of Bani Qurayza were a troublesome group ... the Most Noble Messenger (peace and blessings be upon him) eliminated them.[74]

In a classic case of projection of his own megalomania, Khomeini was convinced that he was called upon to fight against the establishment of Jewish world domination: "Can you not see that the Israelis are attacking, killing and destroying and that the British and Americans are helping them? (...) Islam is being wiped out (...) Wake up!"[75]

Khomeini addressed these words to the Iranian clergy, whom he derided as "pseudo-saints." Hidden behind his attack on Israel lay a fundamental divide *within* Islam. On the one side were those clerics who advocated the abolition of sharia and the adaptation of Islam to modernity and so supported the Shah's modernizing reforms, including the introduction of votes for women. On the other side were those who, like Khomeini and his successors, sought to defend an interpretation of the religious law based on a literal reading of texts and the example of the time of Muhammad against the temptations of the social model of liberal democracy.

Khomeini railed against those who introduce "an evil innovation into Islam ... claiming to be acting in accordance with the requirements of Islamic justice." With such modernizers in mind, he called for a Holy War to begin among Muslims. Thus, his 1971 book calls for the religious teaching institutions to be reformed in order to remove "the traces left on their [the people's] minds and spirits by the insinuating propaganda of the foreigners."[76]

Such statements reveal the aim of Khomeini's return to Muhammad and struggle with the Jews: the wish to repudiate all aspects of modernity that undermine his conservative concept of Islam. This connection between antisemitism and anti-modernism also explains the popularity of the *Protocols of the Elders of Zion,* which is of Russian origin, in the Islamic world. This text was conceived as a rallying cry against liberalism: in order to drive forward the struggle against individual freedom, the latter is denounced as the main tool of a global Jewish conspiracy. Ideas originally disseminated a hundred years previously by Tsarist agents in order to save Tsarism are today being repeated by key leaders of Islam in order to promote the domination of a conservative Islam.

Between April 1939 and April 1945, the Nazi radio station in Berlin had promoted that very "return to the religious traditions of Islam" and the related "fierce opposition to Western liberalism" that Khomeini later espoused and warned against the establishment of a Jewish state in Palestine as the worst possible catastrophe. This propaganda was one of the reasons why it was not an Atatürk-style modernism that prevailed in the Arab part of the Islamic world but a conservative interpretation of the Koran and Islamic antisemitism.

The shortwave radio transmitter in Zeesen appears, in retrospect, as the interface across which the antisemitic worldview streamed into the consciousness of the Arab masses. Radio Zeesen fell silent in 1945, but its frequencies of hate continued to resound in the Arab world.

Notes

1 Hans Goldenbaum, "Nationalsozialismus als Antikolonialismus. Die deutsche Rundfunkpropaganda für die arabische Welt", *Vierteljahreszeitschrift für Zeitgeschichte,* Vol. 3, 2016, 449–489, here 479.
2 Jeffrey Herf, "Nazi Germany's Propaganda Aimed at Arabs and Muslims during World War II and the Holocaust: Old Themes, New Archival Findings", *Central European History,* Vol. 42, 2009, 709–736, here 715.
3 According to Goldenbaum, "Given the Fact That the Number of Recipients of the Radio Broadcasts in, for Example, Coffee Houses, Was Located in the High Double Or Triple Digits, the Total Should Probably Be Adjusted Upwards", Op.cit., 479.
4 Callum A. MacDonald, "Radio Bari: Italian Wireless Propaganda in the Middle East and British Countermeasures, 1934–1938", *Middle East Studies,* Vol. 13, No. 2, May 1977, 195. See also Heinz Pohle, *Der Rundfunk als Instrument der Politik,* Dissertation, Hamburg 1953, 442.
5 PAAA R 104 800, Dok. 188, Werner von Hentig, Schreiben, 9 March 1938.
6 Werner Schwipps, "Wortschlacht im Äther", Deutsche Welle (ed.), *Wortschlacht im Äther. Der deutsche Auslandsrundfunk im Zweiten Weltkrieg,* Berlin 1971, 13, 16, 58.
7 Klaus-Michael Mallmann and Martin Cüppers, *Halbmond und Hakenkreuz. Das Dritte Reich, die Araber und Palästina,* Darmstadt 2006, 100.
8 Pohle, *Rundfunk,* 439. I use the terms "Radio Zeesen" und "Radio Berlin" interchangeably.

9 Willi A. Boelcke, *Die Macht des Radios. Weltpolitik und Auslandsrundfunk 1924–1976*, Frankfurt/M. 1977, 406.

10 Kirk to Secretary of State, No. 502, Cairo (21 July 1942), Axis Broadcasts in Arabic … 3 to 9 July 1942, 3–6, National Archives, College Park (NACP), RG 84, Egypt: Cairo Embassy General Records 1936–1955.

11 Fritz Grobba, *Irak*, Berlin 1941, 82.

12 David Motadel, *Islam and Nazi Germany's War*, Cambridge, MA 2014, *Islam*, 93.

13 BA-MA, RW4/286, Anlage zu "Betr.: Berliner arabische Sendungen", 11.02.1942.

14 Nevill Barbour, "Broadcasting to the Arab World. Arabic Transmissions from the BBC and Other Non-Arab Stations", *Middle East Journal*, Vol. V, Winter 1951, 57–69, here 65.

15 "Die arabische Sendung aus Berlin" [hebr.], S[asson) an Sh[ertok], 22.6.1939, in Zionistisches Zentralarchiv Jerusalem, S25/10013-87, cited after Goldenbaum, op. cit., 470.

16 BNA, WO 208/1701, German Propaganda, 13 October 1939.

17 Henry Picker, *Hitlers Tischgespräche im Führerhauptquartier 1941–42*, Bonn 1951, 362ff. See also Stefan Ihrig, *Atatürk in the Nazi Imagination*, Cambridge, MA, 2014.

18 Höpp-Archiv, 01.04.021, ZMO, "Panislamismus", *Völkischer Beobachter*, 19 April 1936.

19 Höpp-Archiv, 01.04.021. ZMO, "Der islamische Nationalismus", *Rheinisch-Westfälische Zeitung*, 6 August 1937.

20 Giselher Wirsing, *Engländer Juden Araber in Palästina*, Leipzig 1942, 136ff.

21 Motadel, *Islam*, 103.

22 Bundesarchiv Berlin (BAB), R 78/1802: Sendungen für den Nahen und Mittleren Osten – Manuskripte in deutscher Sprache, 8. Januar 1940–31. Januar 1940.

23 Kirk to Secretary of State, No. 639, Cairo (3 October 1942), "Axis Broadcasts in Arabic for the Period September 18 to 24, 1942", NACP, RG 84, Egypt: Cairo Embassy General Records 1936–1955, 5.

24 BAB, R78/1802 bis R78/1826: Sendungen für den Nahen und Mittleren Osten – Manuskripte in deutscher Sprache. No scripts are available for 26 May–24 July 1941.

25 Jeffrey Herf, *Nazi Propaganda for the Arab World*, New Haven, CT 2009. I am grateful to Professor Herf for making copies of these scripts available to me.

26 Jeffrey Herf, *The Jewish Enemy. Nazi Propaganda during World War II and the Holocaust*, Cambridge MA, 2006, 209.

27 ADAP 1918–1945. Serie D: 1937–1941, Bd. XIII/2: Die Kriegsjahre, Sechster Band, Zweiter Halbband, 15. September bis 11. Dezember 1941, Nr. 515, Göttingen 1970, 720f. Aufzeichnung über die Unterredung zwischen dem Führer und dem Großmufti von Jerusalem […] in Berlin am 28. November 1941.

28 Cüppers and Mallmann were the first to identify the existence and function of this unit. Mallmann and Cüppers, *Halbmond*, 137–147.

29 Kirk to Secretary of State, No. 340, Cairo (18 April 1942), "General Summary of Tendencies in Axis Broadcasts in Arabic", NACP, RG 59, 4.

30 SFA, "Palestine between the Bolsheviks and the Jews" (3 November 1943), Kirk to Secretary of State, No. 1410, Cairo (19 November 1943), Axis Broadcasts in Arabic […] 3 to 9 November 1943, NACP RG 84, Egypt: Cairo Embassy General Records, 1936–1955, cited after Jeffrey Herf, *Nazi Propaganda for the Arab World*, New Haven, CT 2009, 184.

31 Kirk to Secretary of State, No. 574, Cairo (27 August 1942), Axis Broadcasts in Arabic for the Period 14 to 20 August 1942, "Berlin in Colloquial Arabic" (15 August 1942), NACP, RG 84, 10.

32 Herf, *Nazi Propaganda*, 197.

33 Motadel, *Islam*, 76, 97.

34 NACP, RG 84, The Arab Nation, 23 December 1942, Kirk to Secretary of State, No. 782 (8 January 1943). See also Herf, *Nazi Propaganda*, 153.

35 Jeffrey Herf, "Hitlers Dschihad. Nationalsozialistische Rundfunkpropaganda für Nordafrika und den Nahen Osten", *Vierteljahreszeitschrift für Zeitgeschichte*, Vol. 58, Nr. 2, April 2010, 259–286, here 280ff.
36 Herf, *Nazi Propaganda*, 255–59.
37 Mallmann and Cüppers, *Halbmond*, 134. – NACP, Kirk to Secretary of State, No. 640 Cairo (3 October 1942), "Comment on Axis Broadcasts in Arabic with Particular Reference to Items Concerning Egypt", Egypt: Cairo Embassy General Records 1936–1955, 2.
38 Kirk to Secretary of State, No. 479, Cairo (6 July 1942), "Subject: Arabic Broadcasts for the Period June 19–25, 1942", NACP, RG 84, 19.
39 Kirk to Secretary of State, No. 502, Cairo (21 July 1942), "Arabic Broadcasts for the Period July 3–9, 1942", NACP, RG 84, 13–14 and Herf, *Nazi Propaganda*, 126.
40 Höpp-Archiv, 01.10.012. ZMO, "Westfalen", 20. November 1942, Sprachregelung für Flüsterpropaganda nach Marokko.
41 Robert Satloff, *Among the Righteous. Lost Stories from the Holocaust's Long Reach into Arab Lands*, New York 2006, 109.
42 Sarah Ehrlich, "Farhud Memories: Baghdad's 1941 Slaughter of the Jews", *BBC*, 1 June 2011. https://www.bbc.com/news/world-middle-east-13610702.
43 Edy Cohen, "Remembering the Destruction of Iraqi Jewry", *The Tower*, No. 40, July 2016, 1.
44 Boelcke, "Macht", 407f.
45 BAB R 78/1823, 24.4.41–9.5.41: Program script for 5 May 1941.
46 BAB, R 78/1824, 10.5.41–26.5.41: Program script for 11 May 1941. In the script for Turkey, there is no mention of Holy War. The relevant text reads, "The Iraqi struggle [is] a struggle for all Muslims who today await the moment of liberation from the English yoke."
47 Cohen, "Remembering", 5. The radio quotation can be found in: Hagana-Archiv, Tel Aviv, Akte Nr. 105/394. I am grateful to Edy Cohen for this information.
48 Elie Kedourie, *Arabic Political Memoirs and Other Studies*, London 1974, 310.
49 Criminal Investigation Department, Headquarters, Palestine Police, Intelligence Summary No. 60/39, 15th September 1939. I am grateful to Edy Cohen for providing me with this document.
50 Central Zionist Archives (CZA), S25/2971 Bericht Kapeliuk vom 18.10.1939: "Al ha-Mazav ha-politi bein ha-Aravim" ["On the Political Situation among the Arabs"], cited after René Wildangel, *Zwischen Achse und Mandatsmacht. Palästina und der Nationalsozialismus*, Berlin 2007, 359.
51 Meir Zamir, *The Secret Anglo-French War in the Middle East. Intelligence and Decolonization, 1940–1948*, London and New York 2015, 24.
52 BAB NS 19/186, Blatt 37–48, 7: Walter Schellenberg, Lage in Palästina, 21. Dezember 1942. According to an American estimate, in 1941 there were 90,000 shortwave radios in the region, of which 55,000 were in Egypt and 24,000 in Palestine. See also Herf, "Dschihad", 263.
53 Wildangel, "Achse", 360.
54 Anne H. Fuller, "General Argument Used in German Propaganda to the Near East (September 29, 1941)", cited after Herf, *Nazi Propaganda*, 71.
55 Boris Havel, "Haj Amin al-Husseini: Herald of a Religious Anti-Judaism in the Contemporary Islamic World", *The Journal of the Middle East and Africa*, Vol. 5, No. 3, September–December 2014, 221–243, here 235 and 238–241.
56 Herf, *Nazi Propaganda*, 218.
57 Seth Arsenian, "Wartime Propaganda in the Middle East", *Middle East Journal*, October 1948, Vol. II, No. 4, 428.
58 Amir Taheri, *The Spirit of Allah*, Bethesda 1986, 99ff. On 30 April 2014, Taheri informed me of the source of this information. It is based on several interviews with people who had known Khomeini in Qum in the 1940s – among them Ayatollah Shubeir Zanjani, Hojat al-Islam Ali Davani and Seyyed Hussein Abdi.

59 Amir Cheheltan, "Von der Differenz zwischen Gott und Teufel", *FAZ*, 30 July 2010.
60 Matthias Küntzel, *Germany and Iran. From the Aryan Axis to the Nuclear Threshold*, Telos, NY 2014, 30–36.
61 Ibid., 27.
62 PAAA, R 60690, Winkler, Erfahrungen aus der deutschen Propagandaarbeit in Iran von November 1939 bis September 1941, Aufzeichnung vom 10. Januar 1942, 2f.
63 PAAA, R 60690, Deutsche Gesandtschaft Teheran an das AA Berlin: Teheran, den 2. Februar 1941: "Propagandistische Möglichkeiten unter der iranischen Bevölkerung im Hinblick auf die religiösen Erwartungen der Schiiten", 3.
64 Reader Bullard, *Letters from Tehran*, London 1991, 28.
65 Kathrin Haurand, "Vom Nazi-Kollaborateur zum Gastland – Iran während des Zweiten Weltkrieges", *Medaon*, Vol. 11, Nr. 20, 2017, 7.
66 Küntzel, *Germany and Iran*, 5–9.
67 Haurand, "Nazi-Kollaborateur", 7.
68 Cyrus L. Sulzberger, *Auf schmalen Straßen durch die dunkle Nacht*, 1971, 142, cited after Boelcke, *Macht*, 420.
69 Dreyfus to Hull, 13 May 1942, as cited in Barry Rubin, *The Great Powers in the Middle East 1941–1947. The Road to the Cold War*, London 1980, 81.
70 NACP, RG 84, Foreign Service Posts of the Department of State, Tehran Embassy General Records. 1942: 820.2–851, Box 53: William p. Farrell (Bagdad) to Louis G. Dreyfus Jr. (Tehran), 13 September 1942. Excerpts from the Arab World, Iran, Turkey, Bi-Monthly Service Report of the Near East Department of the British Broadcasting Corporation, 18 June 1942.
71 Risala-i Tawzih al Masa'il (Teheran 1962), as cited in Bernard Lewis, *The Jews of Islam*, Princeton, NJ 1984, 34.
72 Ruhollah Khomeini, "Programme for the Establishment of an Islamic Government", *Islam and Revolution: The Writings and Declarations of Imam Khomeini*, Translated and annotated by Hamid Algar, London 2002, 127.
73 The Institute for the Compilation and Publication of the Works of Imam Khomeini (ed.), *Kauthar – Volume One*, Tehran 1995, 122, 127 and Taheri, *Spirit*, 140.
74 Algar (ed.), *Islam and Revolution*, 89.
75 Algar (ed.), *Islam and Revolution*, 142.
76 Algar (ed.), *Islam and Revolution*, 114, 135–136.

4

1948

Arab–Israeli War

By the early summer of 1943, the mood in the Nazi camp was gloomy. The tide of war had turned. The Battle of Stalingrad was lost and Rommel's forces had been defeated in North Africa; the prospect of an Allied victory loomed. In a radio speech on 19 March 1943, El-Husseini depicted the horrors that awaited "if, may God preserve us, the Jew-controlled Allies are victorious in this war."[1] At the end of May 1943, one of Zeesen's secret stations, The Voice of the Free Arabs, echoed the sentiment:

> The British have not won the war yet; but we must confess that we have to prepare ourselves for the obscure future awaiting us should the British, the Jews and their Allies emerge from the war as victors. It is our duty to prepare for the future,

declared the speaker in Arabic.[2] Of special concern was the future of Palestine. If Nazi Germany were to fall, one should at least ensure that the Zionist project met the same fate. In his memoirs, the Mufti mentions some of the steps he took to ensure that his struggle against Zionism in Palestine could continue even after a defeat of the Third Reich.

"On November 2, 1944, … Germany agreed to supply us with arms *for the approaching tasks*," El-Husseini recounts,

> and to this end created a large store with light arms suitable for guerilla action. … In addition, the authorities put at our disposal four light four-engine airplanes for the transportation of war material to Palestine, to be stored in secret shelters, for the training of Palestinian fighters and *for their preparation for the battles to follow*.

DOI: 10.4324/9781003369110-5

Walter Schellenberg, one of Nazi Germany's most senior intelligence officials, had selected two Arab and three German Wehrmacht officers to undertake this operation. "It was decided that they must not enter into conflict with the British authorities during the war, but limit themselves to *preparations for the days after the end of World War II.*" The planned supplies included "tens of thousands of rifles, machine guns and light weapons and large quantities of equipment and ammunition."[3]

On 6 October 1944, the five parachutists did indeed fly out from Athens to land in the Jordan valley with the task of hiding the crates of weapons they had previously dropped from the plane.[4] Ten days later, they were captured by the British. The three German officers turned out to be Palestinian Germans. The two Arab officers were Abdul Latif, who had previously been involved in editing the Mufti's radio broadcasts in Berlin, and Hassan Salameh, who had led a gang in the Nablus area during the 1936–1939 Arab Revolt. While this may have been an isolated and ineffective action, it nonetheless provides a direct link between the Nazis' world war and the "battles to follow" in Palestine.

Moreover, Radio Zeesen too was preparing the Muslims of the Middle East for the "battles to follow." It relentlessly assailed its listeners with horror stories according to which the Jews were planning not only to destroy the Al-Aqsa Mosque but also, starting out from their base in Palestine, to embark on the total destruction of Islam and the Arabs. Here are some of the slogans disseminated by Radio Zeesen between May and November 1942:

The Jews are the deadly enemies of Islam.

(3 May 1942)

The aim of the Jews is to make the Arab countries a Jewish colony.

(2 June 1942)

The Jews are the enemies of all Arabs and Muslims.

(13 September 1942)

The Jews are the enemies of the Arabs and the Holy Koran.

(21 October 1942)

An Allied victory will mean a victory for the Jews and the destruction of the Muslims.

(23 October 1942)

If Britain wins this war, the Jews will rule our countries and will deprive the Arabs of their freedom and independence.

(14 November 1942)[5]

After mid-1943, as it became ever clearer that Germany was heading for defeat, the warnings about what "World Jewry" would do when it got the chance became ever shriller. In his diary entry for 10 May 1943, Goebbels reported on a "sharpening of our antisemitic propaganda in the press and on the radio ... At times, it forms 70% to 80% of our entire foreign broadcasting."[6] In his famous *Wollt-ihr-den-totalen-Krieg* ("Do you want total war?") speech on 18 February 1943, Nazi Propaganda Minister Josef Goebbels had conjured up before the German people the dreadful prospect of their destruction in the event of defeat. The Nazis' Arabic-language propaganda now began to scaremonger in the same terms about the consequences of an Allied victory for the Arabs.

Finally, money the Mufti had received from the Nazis in the later stages of the war was redirected towards the new "battles" of the postwar period. Before 1945, according to his biographer, Joseph Schechtman, "With astute foresight, the Mufti managed to get a large proportion of the Nazis' subsidies out of Germany even while the war was still in progress," transferring it to Switzerland and Iraq.[7] Walter Schellenberg admitted during the Nuremberg war crimes trials that he alone had given the Mufti "half a metric hundredweight of gold and 50,000 dollars." "The Mufti took it all with him," added Schellenberg, who also referred to the Mufti's "excellent" contacts in Switzerland.[8] The Nazi Foreign Office too had invested in the post-1945 period. First, as late as April 1945, they gave the Mufti 50,000 Reichsmarks – money which the Mufti put to effective use in his anti-Jewish campaigning between 1946 and 1948.[9] Second, it stated in writing its readiness to pay the Mufti 12,000 Marks a month even after 1 April 1945, an arrangement that shows that "Nazi officials ... hoped to continue their joint or complementary political-ideological campaigns in the postwar period."[10] But was El-Husseini in a position to pursue his anti-Zionist activities? What became of this man, who had done more than anyone to infect the mass of Muslims with the virus of antisemitism before and during the war, after the unconditional surrender of the Third Reich?

On 7 May 1945, the Mufti fled to Bern on the advice of the German Foreign Office. Upon arrival in Switzerland, the authorities immediately handed him over to France. There he was placed in a villa near Paris from which he was able to make an easy escape and fly to Cairo at the end of May 1946.[11] Here he had to remain in hiding for some weeks since, at least on paper, he was being sought as a war criminal by Britain, Yugoslavia and the USA. He was, moreover, the target of major anti-Nazi campaigns. Thus, a memorandum from the American Zionist Emergency Council dated 12 December 1945 states that:

> In the case of practically all of the Axis criminals an end has, as far as we know, been put on their ability to cause additional damage. ... But the ex-Mufti, should he escape punishment ... will undoubtedly be in a position to stir up further trouble and to cause more massacres of Jews. It is earnestly hoped that our Government will realize the serious moral responsibility, which ... it would share for the loss of human lives and for the other grave consequences which would

result from a policy of allowing the Mufti to go unpunished for his past crimes and free to commit new ones.[12]

There was no lack of grounds for putting him on trial. As an active supporter of the "Final Solution," the Mufti had repeatedly intervened to block Jews from escaping the Holocaust. Thus, he had actively opposed plans for Jewish children from Slovakia, Poland, Hungary and Bulgaria to be allowed to travel to Palestine. Instead, he recommended that they be sent to the gas chambers or, in his own words, to "where they are subject to strong control, e.g. Poland." At the end of 1942, when Romania wanted to allow 80,000 Jews to emigrate to Palestine in return for a per capita payment, the Mufti stepped in again to derail the scheme.[13] Moreover, he had recruited the Bosnian-Muslim Handschar SS division that had fought the Yugoslav Partisans with extreme cruelty, hunted Jews in Croatia and murdered Bosnian civilians.[14]

Despite these crimes and despite the anti-Mufti campaigns, the Allied victors refused to indict him as a war criminal and so risk conflict with the Arab world. Just as during the war they had shied away from combating Radio Zeesen's anti-semitism out of opportunism, so now they once again failed to make an issue out of the Mufti's Jew-hatred. This omission would have serious consequences. To quote Jeffrey Herf:

> The absence of a trial and punishment enabled the leading voice of Arab extremism and radical antisemitism to be welcomed home to the Middle East as a hero of an anti-imperialist struggle rather than as a disgraced collaborator with Nazism and its crimes against the Jews.[15]

The Muslim Brotherhood and the Mufti

As we saw in Chapter 2, in summer 1937, shortly after the attempt to arrest the Mufti, London had dissolved the Arab Higher Committee that he had headed, leaving the Arabs in Palestine leaderless. The Arab League, founded in 1944 by Egypt, Iraq, Saudi Arabia, Yemen, Syria, Transjordan and Lebanon, nonetheless considered it important that Palestine be represented. In November 1945, they therefore established a new Palestinian Arab Higher Committee with a balanced composition: five supporters and five opponents of El-Husseini plus two neutrals.[16]

At the end of May 1946, El-Husseini himself arrived in Cairo. His return was greeted not only by the Muslim Brotherhood but also by secular forces.[17] The preparations for his return had begun several weeks previously, and it was likely no accident that a meeting of the Arab League in the Syrian resort of Bloudan coincided with the event.[18] That conference reached a surprising decision: following an Egyptian proposal an entirely new Palestinian body, the so-called "Arab Higher Executive Committee of Palestine," was established, but this time under the leadership of Amin el-Husseini and his cousin Jamal el-Husseini.[19] The Mufti's opponents were excluded.

We do not yet know how this decision came about or what positions the various actors took towards it behind closed doors. What is certain is that "The Bloudan decision resembled a seizure of power, a coup, except that here it involved not a state, but the leadership of a national movement," writes David Schiller, while the Mufti's biographer, Joseph Schechtman, talks of a "Bludan 'Diktat'" that "was a complete victory for the Mufti."[20]

Although at British request Amin El-Husseini was not allowed to set foot in the Palestinian Mandate Territory, the Arab League decision had now enthroned him as the new leader of the Palestinian Arabs, with access to an annual budget of 10,000 British pounds.[21] For the Jews in Palestine, this decision was a blatant provocation, while the Palestinian Arabs saw their last chance of a policy not dictated by the Mufti slip away.

As a result, between 1946 and 1948, the terrorism that had crushed the supporters of the first partition plan resumed.

> The Mufti and his associates tolerated neither criticism nor opposition – even in non-political contexts – and did not hesitate to use pressure, violence and even murder to crush any reserve or disapproval. Anyone who broke the consensus of non-recognition of Jewish rights (or was even suspected of doing so) exposed himself to threats.[22]

One victim was Fawzi Darwish el-Husseini, a respected personage and cousin of the Mufti. He sought agreement with representatives of the Jewish Agency on a binational state in which neither nation would dominate. On 11 November 1946, five members of Fawzi group's signed an accord on common activities with Jews. Twelve days later, Fawzi was murdered by the Mufti's henchmen and his group disintegrated. "My cousin strayed and received his just punishment," commented Jamal el-Husseini.[23] Another was Sami Taha, a prominent trade union leader from Haifa, who had advocated giving the Jews certain rights and for this very reason was murdered in September 1947.[24] In the same year, when UNSCOP (United Nations Special Committee on Palestine) tried to obtain information about the situation in Palestine, the Arab Higher Executive Committee threatened to kill anyone who spoke with the UN representatives.[25]

However, the Mufti was unpopular not only with many of Palestine's Arabs but also with most Arab rulers. His extremism was "at least, if not more, harmful to the Arabs than to the Jews," commented the Arab League's Secretary-General, Abd al-Rahman Azzam.[26] Egypt's Prime Minister, Isma'il Sidqi, described him as "a schemer seeking his own personal interest [who] couldn't care less if the entire Arab world were destroyed so long as he achieved his own goals."[27] Abdullah of Transjordan held him responsible for the "misery" in Palestine, while the Saudi King Ibn Saud banned the Mufti from his country.[28] It is all the more surprising therefore that the Arab League should decide to appoint El-Husseini leader of the Arabs in Palestine. Why did it do so?

Despite his unpopularity among sections of the Arab elite, in 1946 Amin el-Husseini's fame was at its height. His speeches on Radio Zeesen and a photo of him talking with Adolf Hitler that had been massively disseminated by the Nazis had given him unrivalled celebrity throughout the Arab world. Very many Arabs beyond the ranks of the Muslim Brotherhood hailed him as a charismatic hero who had defied not only the British arrest warrant of 1937 but also the extradition requests of London, Belgrade and Washington in 1945.

"The impunity of his deeds has lifted his prestige amongst the Arabs," Simon Wiesenthal reported in 1947. "A man ... who is the enemy no. 1 of a powerful empire – and this empire cannot keep him away – seems to them to be exactly the right kind of 'leader'."[29]

The Muslim Brotherhood built on and further fueled this mood. Since the Mufti's detention in May 1945, it had tirelessly defended and extolled him and threatened anyone who dared to stand up to him. Thus, in response to a rumor that the Zionists had sentenced the Mufti to death, the Brotherhood declared that "One hair of the Mufti's is worth more than the Jews of the whole world. ... Should one hair of the Mufti's be touched, every Jew in the world would be killed without mercy."[30] This terrible threat was made at a time when the revelations about the Shoah had already made the headlines throughout the world, including in Egypt.

The Muslim Brotherhood had already in the 1930s grown into a mass movement on the back of its antisemitic Palestine campaigns. It had been materially and ideologically supported by the Nazis in this process.[31] By the end of 1945, it had 1,500 branches and 500,000 members in Egypt alone, making it the world's largest antisemitic movement. By 1948, membership had risen to over a million.[32] It had offshoots in Syria, Jordan, Palestine and Lebanon and inspired fear. An American secret service report from September 1947 describes the Brotherhood as a society of "anti-Occidental religious fanatics, thus powerful enough to arouse 70,000,000 devout Moslems in this part of the world."[33]

Their ideology was then as now marked by Islamic antisemitism. "The hostility of the Society to the Jews had its origins in a particular reading of the Qur'an [and] the Prophetic Tradition." For them, the conflict in Palestine was not territorial, but "one between Islam and Judaism." "They emphasized that jihad in the way of God, and the defense of the Holy Land, was an inescapable religious duty."[34]

While not a member of the Brotherhood, Amin el-Husseini had been on friendly terms with its leader, Hassan al-Banna, since 1927. His daughter was married to one of the Muslim Brotherhood's leaders.[35] He voiced his gratitude for the Brotherhood's support with these words of praise: "I believe in the Muslim Brothers as they are the troops of God who shall defeat the troops of Satan."[36] Indeed the Mufti's very return to Egypt was a result of Brotherhood campaigning, a success which the Muslim Brotherhood celebrated exuberantly, comparing El-Husseini to the Prophet Muhammad:

Oh Amin! What a great, stubborn, terrific, wonderful man you are! ... What a hero, what a miracle of a man. ... He is but one man, but Mohammed was also one man, and so was Christ, and they achieved great results. ... There must be a divine purpose behind the preservation of the life of this man. ... Amin! March on! God is with you! We are behind you! We are willing to sacrifice our necks for the cause. To death! Forward March.[37]

Then, upon hearing in June 1946 of the Mufti's return to Egypt, the Brotherhood began to bombard the delegates to the Arab League meeting in Bloudan with pro-Mufti telegrams.[38]

Combined with the power-political calculations of certain Arab leaders,[39] these pro-Mufti campaigns and the Brotherhood's potential for making trouble made a major contribution to the fact that the Arab League chose the Mufti – and he alone – to lead the Palestinian Arabs.

This decision was, however, not only challenged by Palestinian Arabs but also from within the United Nations, which in May 1947 had to decide whom to authorize to represent Palestine's Arabs alongside the Jewish Agency. In regard to this matter, Poland's ambassador to the United Nations, Alfred Fiderkiewicz, himself a survivor of Auschwitz, on 12 May called on the United Nations "to examine the political role and influence of former Nazi collaborators whose very political records make Arab-Jewish co-operation impossible, and whose political records forbid any real co-operation with them by the United Nations."[40] In the same vein, Moshe Shertok, the representative of the Jewish Agency, pointed out that Amin el-Husseini "was directly involved during the war in the Nazi policy of the extermination of the Jews of Europe."[41] A few hours later, however, Emile Ghoury, representing the Arab Higher Executive Committee, turned the tables: according to him, the Zionists had persecuted the Mufti so relentlessly that he had been compelled to turn to Germany "in self-defense." "That was the only alternative to arrest and exile which were being urged on Great Britain by the Zionists. His sole crime was that he had stood in the way of Zionist aims."[42]

It is striking that Ghoury, precisely in the framework of the United Nations and only two years after the Holocaust, felt able to present the "Zionists" as the perpetrators and the Mufti as their victim. Regardless, the United Nations recognized the Mufti and his accomplices as the representatives of the Palestinian Arabs.

The First Middle East War

On 29 November 1947, over two-thirds of the UN member states voted in favor of a two-state solution for Palestine. Fifty-six percent of the Mandate territory was to become a Jewish state containing 500,000 Jews and 500,000 Arabs. Forty-three percent would form an Arab state comprising 750,000 Arabs and 10,000 Jews. Jerusalem was to be placed under international control.[43] Jews danced the night away in the streets for joy. The next day, six were murdered. The Arab war to prevent the implementation of the decision had begun.[44]

The fighting lasted for well over a year. Initially it was a civil war conducted on the Arab side by two irregular guerilla bands. The second and decisive interstate phase began in May 1948. On 14 May 1948, Ben Gurion proclaimed the establishment of the State of Israel. A few hours later, Arab armies invaded the infant country: from the north came 6,000 Syrian, 2,000 Lebanese and 4,500 Iraqi troops; from the east 6,500 Jordanian forces and from the south 5,500 Egyptian soldiers.[45] Since the British Mandate had ended on 15 May, there was no one to stop the Arab armies entering the country.

In October 1947, a few weeks before the UN partition resolution, the General-Secretary of the Arab League, Abd al-Rahman Azzam, had warned of a "war of annihilation" that would follow a decision for partition:

> I personally wish that the Jews do not drive us to this war, as this will be a war of extermination and momentous massacre which will be spoken of like the Tartar massacre or the Crusader wars. ... This war will be distinguished by three serious matters. First – faith: as each fighter deems his death on behalf of Palestine as the shortest road to paradise; second [the war] will be an opportunity for vast plunder. Third, it will be impossible to contain the zealous volunteers arriving from all corners of the world to avenge the martyrdom of the Palestine Arabs.[46]

Judging from later remarks by Azzam, his martial words were intended, on the one hand, to impress the "Arab Street" and, on the other, to forestall a military clash. Nevertheless, his threat of annihilation echoes the scenario that the Nazis had foreseen in summer 1942 after Rommel's military victories. At that time the tone was set by the Wehrmacht and SS. Six years later others were making the decisions, but former Wehrmacht and SS officers were still involved.

Already before the war, the Arab Higher Executive Committee had contemplated employing European mercenaries.

> Potential recruits included German POWs who had escaped and found shelter in the Middle East; Polish veterans of General Anders' army who had refused to return to communist Poland; Bosnians who had served in the Nazi Muslim legion; Croat *Ustasha* and Serb *Chetniks* who had fled from Yugoslavia to Italy; and British defectors from the Army and the Palestine police. In November 1947, the first mercenaries arrived in Syria.[47]

Thus, Bosnian mercenaries joined up with Hassan Salameh, who had parachuted into the Jordan valley in October 1944 as a major in the Wehrmacht and was now one of the leaders of a guerilla force set up by the Mufti known as the Jihad Army (*Al-Jihad al-Muqaddas*). At his side was a former German Wehrmacht officer.[48]

The best-known Commander of the Jihad Army, Abd al-Qadir el-Husseini, in charge of Jerusalem, had also been a Nazi collaborator and had taken part in the defense of the pro-Nazi regime in Baghdad. At his headquarters in Bir Zeit, he hosted 36 Germans and 10 Britons.[49] His closest associate, Fawzi el-Kutub, had undertaken a training course in bomb making in Nazi Germany.[50]

The second guerilla group – the Arab Liberation Army, established by the Arab League – was also led by a former Wehrmacht officer, Fawzi el-Qawuqji. According to *Spiegel* in 1948, "Important posts in Fawzi's headquarters are occupied by members of the former German Wehrmacht who otherwise form a large volunteer contingent of the Arab invasion army for Palestine. They are mainly former soldiers in Rommel's Africa Korp" and "escaped prisoners from Egyptian POW [Prisoners of War] Camps." No one appeared troubled by the fact that "the German volunteers have adopted 'Die Fahne hoch'[51] as their theme song from the old days."[52]

In addition, many former members of the Muslim SS Divisions who took part in the war against Israel had previously killed civilians in Bosnia and hunted Jews in Croatia. At the end of World War II, facing prosecution if they returned to Tito's Yugoslavia, they had remained as stateless exiles in Italy from where some hundred had moved to Beirut in 1947 and 1948. "By the end of April almost 1,000 Bosnian, Croatian, and Albanian volunteers may have been in Palestine as members of three different units" along with "53 Germans and Britons" who also fought in the Arab ranks.[53]

Militarily, these former Wehrmacht and SS soldiers played a secondary role. Politically, however, they were significant in that they embodied the continuity of the anti-Jewish war of extermination that had begun under Hitler. *Aufbau*, a Jewish weekly published in New York, at that time denounced the "absolute belief of these murderers in uniform that they did not even lose the war. The world is allowing them, indeed, to complete Hitler's fanatical campaign to destroy the Jewish people."[54]

This first Middle Eastern war claimed the lives of 6,000 Jews (1% of the Jewish population of Palestine at that time) and probably an even higher number of Arabs before the signing of the first armistice agreements at the beginning of 1949.[55] This fateful Arab invasion shaped the Middle East conflict as we know it today. It resulted in the flight and expulsion of hundreds of thousands of Arabs from Palestine. It ended in the destruction not of the Jewish state as originally predicted but of the prospect of an Arab Palestinian state, a prospect which remained extinct for decades to come.

Qualms of the Arab League

In most textbooks on the history of the Middle East, the onslaught of the Arab armies on the newly founded Israel is viewed as an inevitability. In the view of Israeli historian Benny Morris, "the War of 1948 was the almost *inevitable* result of … Arab-Jewish friction and conflict that began with … the first Jewish immigrants from Eastern Europe in the early 1880s."[56] Admittedly, the Arab world was – at least in public – unanimous in its rejection of the UN partition plan. According to the *Middle East Journal*, early in 1948, "even those Arabs who sincerely hoped for an eventual understanding with the Jews of Palestine could see no reasonable basis for acquiescence in the partition scheme."[57]

After World War I, many Arabs considered that they had been betrayed by the secret Sykes–Picot Agreement of 1916 in which Britain and France had delimited their respective spheres of influence, disregarding the prospect of independence that London had been holding out to the Arabs. Following World War II, according to the *Middle East Journal*, "Palestine had become the test of the Arabs' independence; to surrender would mean a repetition of the defeat which had come upon them after World War I."[58]

The Arab camp, however, was divided "over the extent of the means to be invested in the effort to prevent the establishment of the Jewish State."[59] An especially controversial question was whether regular Arab armies should be used to thwart a two-state solution. Indeed, in the event the Arab states and notably Egypt delayed deploying their armies until the last minute.

In March 1948, they declared themselves ready to set up training camps for guerilla fighters and provide them with arms for a civil war in Palestine. At the same time, however,

> the Arab League, in decisions made at conferences in Inhas and Bloudan in 1946, and Alay and Cairo in 1947, stated that Arab armies would not invade Palestine. ... Instead, they would supply the Palestinians with arms, money, and volunteers.[60]

Three months prior to the Arab armies' invasion, the League's General-Secretary, Abd al-Rahman Azzam, had stated that the League's member states "viewed the struggles in Palestine as a civil war in which they would only intervene with regular forces if foreign armies attack the country and attempt to push through the partition by force."[61] He was backed up by General Muhammad Haidar, Egypt's Defense Minister, "We shall never even contemplate entering an official war," he declared at the beginning of May 1948. "We are not mad. We shall allow our men and officers to volunteer for service in Palestine, and we shall give them weapons, but no more."[62]

It was only at the very last minute, on 12 May 1948, that the Egyptian Parliament agreed to send regular Egyptian troops to Palestine.[63] Even then, on 14 May, the very eve of the invasion, Azzam made "no secret of his fears," caused by "the strength of the opponent" and "their support in the UN and from the great powers in East and West."[64] What lay behind the Arab leaders' months of reluctance, so starkly at odds with their grandiose proclamations of a "war of annihilation"?

In 1948, there were at least five good reasons for these leaders to recoil from a full-scale war in Palestine.

Firstly, it would be an affront to the United Nations. The partition resolution of November 1947 had been prepared with unusual care. In April 1947 several weeks of debate on the Palestine question began in the General Assembly.

On 15 May the UN decided to establish an 11-member Special Committee on Palestine (UNSCOP) to investigate and report on the situation in the territory. The membership of this committee was drawn not from the Security Council veto-wielding powers, but middle-ranking and neutral countries: Australia, Guatemala, India, Iran, Yugoslavia, Canada, the Netherlands, Peru, Sweden, Czechoslovakia and Uruguay. On 1 September 1947 the Committee issued its eagerly awaited report. Eight countries supported the partition of Palestine into a Jewish state and an Arab state, whilst three – India, Yugoslavia and Iran – voted for a single federal state. In the light of these preparations, on 29 November 1947 over two-thirds of the UN member states voted in favor of partition.

Starting a war in the face of such a clear decision was reckless, especially given that since 1945 Egypt, Iraq, Saudi Arabia, Syria and Lebanon had been UN members. According to Dean Rusk, then director of the State Departments's Office of United Nations Affairs, "armed interference in Palestine by the Arab States to prevent the implementation of the Asssembly's resolution would clearly be aggression contrary to the obligations of those states under the [UN] Charter."[65] And the newly founded UN Ad Hoc Commission on the Palestinian Question stated in its report to the Security Council that "It would be a dangerous and tragic precedent if a decision of the UN General Assembly should be thwarted by force". This report also suggested that the partition decision should be implemented by force.[66]

Second, it was a slap in the face of the superpowers, the USA and USSR. Both had backed partition, and both were opposed to the Arab war against it. No one believed "that the Arabs would be so foolhardy as to challenge the combined authority of the United Nations, the United States and the Soviet Union," wrote Israeli diplomat David Kimche.[67] On 25 February 1948, Warren Austin, the US representative at the United Nations, presented the Security Council with a draft resolution stating that the Council "has to implement the partition decision" and that "any attempt to change the decision of the General Assembly by force may be viewed as an act of aggression." The Security Council had the task of "maintaining international peace and implementing the partition decision."[68]

Moscow too was outraged by the invasion. "It is now an obvious and undeniable fact," the Soviet UN representative, Yakov Malik, stated in August 1948,

> that ... the development of the new problem of Arab refugees in the Near East, results from the sabotage of the General Assembly resolution on Palestine. Those who have contributed to that sabotage are directly responsible for the sufferings of these people.[69]

In November 1948, the Soviet representative to the United Nations, Semjon Zarapkin, spoke in the same vein:

> The presence of Arab forces in Palestine was a direct violation of the appeal which the Assembly had issued ... calling upon all States and individuals to refrain

from any acts likely to … hinder the implementation of the recommendation of the General Assembly.

He went on to praise, "…the quick action of the Jewish people in defending the area assigned to them…" and criticized the statement by the Egyptian UN representative, who had claimed that his country's armed forces were a stabilizing force in Palestine.

> It would have been more true if he had said that those who had directed the invasion of Palestine had done so in order to wreck the November resolution and their action had only served to increase the enmity between Jews and Arabs.[70]

Today this Soviet support for Israel seems surreal. This is due, first, to the still dominant narrative of the Palestine Liberation Organization (PLO) which has, for 50 years, defined the UN partition plan rather than the Arab invasion as the real crime and, second, to the reversal in the attitude of the Soviet Union, which by 1967 had begun to equate Zionism with Nazism. Back in 1948, however, Moscow even wanted the partition decision to be imposed by an international force, an idea rejected by the USA which wanted to prevent Soviet troops from entering the Middle East.[71]

Third, many Arab leaders were not nearly as hostile to the partition plan as might appear from the outside. Thus, Emir Abdullah's real view was "that partition was the only solution." The ruler of Transjordan "hoped that every effort would be made to ensure that it was adopted."[72] In private discussions, the Egyptian Prime Minister, Isma'il Sidqi, also expressed a wish to accept the partition plan. According to Eliyahu Sasson, Sidqi, "repeatedly stressed that he is a businessman. He is neither pro-Jewish nor pro-Arab. He looks out for the welfare of Egypt. If that dictates Jewish-Arab understanding, so be it."[73] Muzahim al-Pachachi, Prime Minister of Iraq, echoed the sentiment, agreeing, according to a British source, that "eventually there would have to be an acceptance of the Jewish state's existence, but for now it was politically impossible to acknowledge this publicly."[74] Moreover, this was also the original position of the Arab League Secretary-General, Abd al-Rahman Azzam.

According to a report by the Jewish Agency of August 1946,

> There was only one solution, in his view, and that was: partition. But … as Secretary of the Arab League he could not appear before the Arabs as the initiator of such a proposal. … He would be prepared to support partition on [one of] two conditions: if one of the Arab states took into its hands the initiative and found the strength and courage to propose the thing in the League Council, or if the British requested him to work along these lines. … He respected very much the Jewish achievements and strength in Palestine, and believed that if the Arab East came to an understanding with them, it would be able to reap great benefits.[75]

Fourth, with the exception of the Arab Legion of Transjordan, the Arab armies were "young, untrained, inexperienced and poorly equipped with pre- or early Second World War types of armaments. ... None of the Arab armies had any battle experience beyond repressing tribal insurrections, and all were by no means fit for combat."[76] Their main task up until that point was defending their respective regimes against domestic subversion, since all the regimes, none of them elected, "suffered from a sense of illegitimacy and, hence, vulnerability."[77] No wonder that the generals were even less eager to fight in Palestine than the political leaders who were amateur in military matters.

Fifth, the Arab inhabitants of Palestine had not been consulted. "Most of the Palestinian Arabs have refused, and still refuse, to be drawn into the fighting," noted Ben Gurion in February 1948.[78] One reason for this was that tens of thousands of them had found jobs and livelihoods in Jewish-controlled economic spheres such as citrus fruit farming that they did not wish to jeopardize. Another was that they were better informed about the military capabilities of the Zionists than the exile Palestinians operating out of Cairo. And, finally, the Mufti was far less popular among the Palestinian Arabs, whom they well remembered for his terrorism of the 1930s, than in other parts of the Arab world, and some indeed actively loathed him. A state run by Amin el-Husseini was the last thing they wanted to help bring about. In his study *Army of Shadows*, Hillel Cohen provides examples of the determination with which Palestinian Arabs resisted their leaders' calls to arms, made nonaggression pacts with local Jews and even supported the Jewish fighting forces. Here is a brief extract from Cohen's comprehensive survey:

In December 1947 the inhabitants of Tulkarem refused to attack Jewish towns to their west, to the chagrin of the local Holy Jihad commander, Hasan Salameh. Sources in Ramallah reported at the same time that many were refusing to enlist. ...

The villagers of the Bani-Hasan *nahiya* southwest of Jerusalem decided not to carry out military actions within their territory, and the people of al-Maliha refused a request from 'Abd al-Qader al-Husseini to attack the Jewish neighborhoods. ...

This unwillingness to fight was frequently buttressed by agreements with Jews in nearby settlements. Sources in many parts of the country reported that local Arab representatives had approached their Jewish neighbors with requests to conclude nonaggression pacts. ...

Arabs who made agreements with Jews, and many others as well, often refused to provide assistance to Arab military forces and even tried to prevent them from operating in their vicinity. In several cases Arab detachments could not find a village that would quarter them or allow them to deploy. ...

Many Palestinian Arabs thus not only refrained from fighting themselves but also did their best to prevent foreigners and locals from carrying out military actions.[79]

These Palestinian Arabs clearly saw advantages in allying with rather than fighting the Jews. Rather than a people united against injustice, the Palestinian

Arabs were a deeply divided community that above all wished to be left in peace and greatly distrusted the Mufti. Only a tiny minority of the 1.3 million Arab Palestinians enlisted in the war against Israel. Nimr al-Hawari, a contemporary Palestinian Arab activist, "estimated the number of conscripts at no more than a few hundred. ... To serve in a Palestinian army did not rank high in the population's ambitions."[80]

So, despite all the criticism of the partition plan, there was also much to be said from the Arab point of view against an invasion by regular Arab forces in May 1948. So why did it nonetheless take place? This brings us back to the topic of Islamic antisemitism.

Antisemitic Mobilization

Preventing the emergence of a Jewish state and wiping out the Jews living in Palestine had been constant themes of the Nazis' radio propaganda between April 1939 and April 1945. "The Prophet Muhammad fought the Jews and called upon Muslims to continue the struggle. Muhammad has chased the Jews from the Arab land and ordered Muslims to fight until they are extinct," Radio Zeesen had proclaimed to the Arab world on 15 March 1943.

Their propaganda campaigns changed the image of the Jews in the Arab world. They promoted an exclusively anti-Jewish reading of the Koran, popularized the European world conspiracy mythology, demonized Zionism and instilled genocidal rhetoric against Israel. In 1946, a British Foreign Office cable "spoke of Arab hatred of the Jews as being greater than that of the Nazis."[81] This was certainly exaggerated, but it nonetheless contained a kernel of truth.

One of the most important themes of the Nazi propaganda was the claim that Zionism was intrinsically expansionist and directed against Islam. The Jews, asserted Radio Zeesen on 8 September 1943, would not stop until they had made "every territory between the Tigris and the Nile Jewish." If they succeeded, "there will remain not a single Arab Muslim or Christian in the Arab world. Arabs! Imagine Egypt, Iraq and all the Arab countries becoming Jewish with no Christianity or Islam there."[82] The clearer it became that Nazi Germany was going to lose the war, the more insistent such warnings became. This demonization of Zionism and the Jews took firm root in the minds of many Arab leaders.

Of course, already in 1937, the Arab world had opposed the creation of a Jewish state in Palestine as envisaged by the Peel Commission. At that time, however, the Mufti and the Muslim Brotherhood were almost alone in their use of antisemitism. By 1947, however, antisemitism was part of the public discourse, even among those who previously had been regarded as moderates.

Thus, less than two years after the liberation of Auschwitz, Ibn Saud publicly characterized the Jews as "an aggressive people that uses force in the name of humanity in order to achieve its goals" and whose ambitions extended to "all Arab states in which holy places are to be found."[83] He was not alone in his opinions. On behalf of Syria, Iraq, Saudi Arabia, Yemen, Egypt and Lebanon, the Lebanese Foreign Minister, Hamid Frangie, spoke of the "expansionist efforts" of Zionism which presented "a serious threat to peace in the Middle East."[84]

For the Iraqi Crown Prince Abd al-Ilah, Zionism was even "the greatest tragedy of the twentieth century,"[85] while a member of the Egyptian parliament described it as "a cancer on the Arab body."[86] The Jordanian Prime Minister Samir Rifa'i went so far as to hold the Jews responsible for both world wars.[87]

Even during the United Nation's special session on Palestine, echos of Radio Zeesen could be heard in the speeches of the Arab delegates. Thus, during the special session in 1947, the Syrian representative, Faris al-Khouri, accused the Jews of conducting an extermination policy:

> They started to invade Palestine and occupy certain portions of it with the policy of exterminating everyone here – men, women, children, old and young, even animals – in order not to leave a trace of the living population of that country; and the places which they succeeded in conquering were subjected to utter destruction and extermination.

The USA too is controlled by Jews: "They have extended their influence into all circles," so al-Khouri. "They are influencing and dominating people here even though they are only one to thirty in this country."[88] It was grotesque, observes John Strawson, "that this image of the powerful Jew was deployed so soon after the evident weakness of the Jews to prevent their own destruction in Europe." This antisemitic discourse, however, "was never challenged by other [UN] participants."[89]

So we are forced to conclude that with the help of the Zeesen transmitter, Arab leaders had "traveled all or most of the way from the traditional contempt for the Jew as upstart to the modernized, Westernized nightmare of the Jew as the embodiment of evil."[90] It is therefore no surprise to find the Arab League rhetorically banging the same drum.

> We have decided that Zionism poses a danger not only to Palestine but also to all other Arab countries and to all nations of Islam. Therefore it is the duty of all Arab countries and Islamic countries to resist the danger of Zionism.[91]

How can a few thousand Zionists in Britain and the USA plus the small Jewish community in Palestine become a dangerous global power that threatens the whole Islamic nation? This paranoid delusion had nothing to do with reality, but much to do with the years of relentless Nazi propaganda. As Egyptian Prime Minister, Ali Mahir, commented in 1946, "Arab opposition to Zionism was the product of both Nazi propaganda in the Arab East and Britain's confusing politics."[92]

The Arab League, however, still shrank back from deploying regular troops in the conflict. The Muslim Brotherhood's hour had come. By this time, the Brotherhood had fully adopted the Nazis' Jew-hatred. In 1944, one of its leaders had abused the Jews as the "parasites of the universe" and "an impudent people who used Muslim and Christian blood for their holy services in Passover." He called on his audience to hate the Jews and unite in jihad against them, in order to "destroy them like sick dogs."[93] This hatred was not restricted to words.

On 2 November 1945 – six months after the end of the war – Hassan al-Banna led a 100,000-strong demonstration in Cairo which ended in the first pogrom of Egypt's modern history. A mob broke into Cairo's Jewish quarter, attacked Jewish shops and desecrated synagogues. "The riots which also spread to Alexandria and to the European quarter there, lasted two days. When they ended, police and press reports counted six dead, five of whom were Jews, and 670 injured."[94]

When in May 1946 a Commission formed by Britain and the USA recommended the entry of 100,000 Holocaust survivors to Palestine, the Muslim Brothers announced a bloodbath: "Seventy million Arabs and 400 million Muslims behind them, with the Muslim Brothers at their forefront, would make the implementation of the Report impossible. Blood would flow like rivers in Palestine."[95]

In 1947/1948, the money that the Nazis had invested ten years earlier in the Muslim Brotherhood paid off. Already its rejection of the United Nations reflected Nazi propaganda, which had constantly ridiculed what it described as the "United Jewish Nations." Even before the partition resolution, Al-Banna had called on the Arab states to leave the United Nations. In his view, its action in relation to Palestine was nothing more than an "international plot, carried out by the Americans, the Russians and the British, under the influence of Zionism."[96]

Then, in response to the UN partition resolution, the Brotherhood initiated violent demonstrations in every major Egyptian city in which people "were summoned to bring down the British, the Zionists and the Jews, while European, Coptic, Greek and Jewish institutions were attacked and partially destroyed."[97]

It was the Brotherhood too that drove Egypt's hesitant elite to attack the newly established Jewish state with regular troops. On the one hand, it established its own branches in Palestine which, by the close of 1947, numbered over 25 units and 20,000 personnel. On the other, it put pressure on the Arab League by providing 10,000 fighters for Palestine.[98] Above all, however, it brought hatred of Zionism onto the streets. Under its influence, a nationalist mass movement was created that longed for the catharsis of a military confrontation, and a tidal wave of public anger whipped up that no one could withstand. Barry Rubin describes the mood:

> In Egypt ... a proliferation of organizations ... proclaimed their devotion to an exclusively Arab Palestine. The Muslim Brotherhood, the Nile Valley Committee for the Defense of Palestine, the Al-Azhar religious notables, the Mufti, Young Egypt, the Young Men's Muslim Association, the Arab Land Committee, and the Arab Union, poured out exhortations and denunciations. ... In every country, April [1948] saw the pressures for war intensified. A student hunger strike in Baghdad urged the army's dispatch to Palestine. ... A citywide general

strike rocked Beirut on April 16, calling for an end to the official nonintervention policy. ... A Damascus general strike demanded Syrian intervention. ... The newspapers, political parties, mass organizations, religious officials, and university students all echoed the cry to arms over Palestine.[99]

Rubin provides an interesting detail regarding the fanatical religious agitation conducted by the Muslim Brotherhood: "God has allowed this decision to be taken by the UN," Al-Banna declared in relation to the partition plan,

> to give you a chance to enter Paradise as well as enrich yourselves in this world. You have always yearned for this change and now you have it, so do not hesitate. A wind is blowing from Paradise, sweet with the smell of martyrdom![100]

Mullahs from Al-Azhar University further whipped up the hysteria. On 29 April 1948, they

> called on all Muslim countries for immediate military and economic action to save Palestine. Seventy thousand copies of the resolution were circulated to the press, Muslim representatives, the palace, and the cabinet. This resolution declared as well that "saving Palestine" was a "religious duty of all Muslims everywhere," and resorted to the Koran's statement: "He who dies fighting for Allah will be greatly recompensed in life to come."[101]

No one could hope successfully to resist this mood. The Egyptian Prime Minister Mahmoud al-Nuqrashi was among those who had initially opposed a military intervention. Then, however, as he admitted, he had been swayed by a public opinion that "was all in favor of the war, and considered anyone who refused to fight as a traitor."[102] No Arab leader, asserted Abd al-Rahman Azzam, could make a compromise with the Zionists and hope to stay alive, let along in power.[103]

When the Arab League met in December 1947, Transjordan's Prime Minister, Samir Rifa'i, as well as Ibn Saud's foreign policy advisor, Yusuf Yasin, explained that "if their governments attempted to take a moderate stand, their lives and the lives of their respective kings would be in danger."[104] With the Conference in session, the Muslim Brotherhood brought 100,000 people out onto the streets under the slogan "we want weapons!" On the terrace of the elegant Savoy Hotel where the League was meeting, "the leaders of the Arab states stood with dignified, solemn faces ... to greet, fez in hand, the march past of the believers," reads a contemporary account.[105] The Arab leaders clearly got caught up in the atmosphere. "Ibn Saud who, despite gout and rheumatism, had hastened to Cairo, spoke the decisive word, 'my final wish is to die at the head of my troops entering Palestine,'" recounted *Der Spiegel* in 1947, while Syria's Defense Minister, Ahmed al-Sharabati promised that "the Arabs would wade in blood to purify themselves."[106]

At this meeting, the Arab League pledged to do no more than train volunteers for the jihad. The training was conducted partly by Egyptian officers and partly by Muslim Brotherhood cadre.[107] However, here for the first time, a previously reluctant Egypt had accepted responsibility for the struggles in Palestine.

Then rumors spread of a brutal massacre of Arab Palestinians that was alleged to have happened on 9 April 1948 in the village of Deir Yassin,[108] rumors that seemed to confirm all the horror stories about the cruel and bloodthirsty Zionists that had been part of the years of Nazi propaganda. Half of the hundred or so people who lost their lives in the assault on this village were women and children. The official Jewish bodies such as the Haganah and the Chief Rabbinate disassociated themselves from the ten-hour battle, which raged while civilians remained *in situ*. For propagandist reasons, the radical Jewish Irgun group gave a far higher death toll, while Husayn Fakhri al-Khalidi, then Secretary-General of the Arab Higher Executive Committee, spread the massacre narrative in order to pressure the surrounding Arab countries to invade. This propaganda was, on the one hand, effective: The war fury did indeed now reach new heights: "The Arabic press and public became hysterical in their call for intervention."[109] On the other hand, it boomeranged because tens of thousands of Arab Palestinians "believed the massacre narrative, and they started to run away."[110]

It was, in particular, the Muslim Brotherhood's propaganda, writes Thomas Mayer, that

> created an atmosphere in which war seemed the only logical and natural process. ... The Government's failure to suppress this propaganda encouraged the military intervention. ... The Society succeeded in drawing Egypt into a full scale military initiative in Palestine.[111]

Of course, other factors, such as the "confusing policy of the British" referred to by Ali Mahir, also played a role as did power-political rivalries. If London had exerted its influence to promote the two-state solution, a regular war might not have happened. In the event, however, the British government, while outwardly pretending to be neutral, leaned to the Arab side and sought to torpedo the partition plan by, for example, boycotting cooperation with the Ad Hoc Commission on the Palestinian Question set up by the UN General Assembly to secure the plan's implementation.[112]

Intra-Arab power struggles also played a role. Emir Abdullah of Transjordan hoped to annex both the envisaged Arab-Palestinian state and Jerusalem, while Egypt and Saudi Arabia wished to prevent such a growth of Abdullah's power. For the "Arab Street," however, such tactical calculations were irrelevant.

The reckless mobilization of the Arab armies presupposed and therefore gave credibility to the paranoid belief that Zionism represented an existential threat to the Arabs and Islam. The Arab leaders thereby further fueled the hysteria on which the Muslim Brotherhood, following in the footsteps of and giving new life to the wartime Nazi propaganda, fed.

In hindsight, even the Egyptian government would attribute responsibility for the fiasco of the Palestine war to the irresistible pressure that "the Muslim Brotherhood's unbridled propaganda" had exerted on Egyptian foreign policy.[113]

Aftershock of National Socialism

This war was not inevitable. It took place despite all the countervailing considerations because the Nazis' antisemitic Arabic-language propaganda had shaped the postwar political climate. In this feverish atmosphere, no one was in a position to resist the policy of the Mufti and Muslim Brotherhood. There are, therefore, good grounds for interpreting the Arab war against Israel as a kind of aftershock of the previous Nazi war against the Jews. The continuity of the two events was embodied by Amin el-Husseini, Mufti of Jerusalem. His religiously packaged antisemitism that had cost thousands of Jews their lives in 1944 was four years later directed against Israel. "Our battle with World Jewry ... is a question of life and death, a battle between two conflicting faiths, each of which can exist only on the ruins of the other," he had written after his return to Cairo.[114]

El-Husseini had played a key role in the decisive months preceding the outbreak of the war. According to Israeli Arabist Hillel Cohen, "there can be little doubt that the Mufti's inflexible position and refusal to accept any partition proposal were the major reasons for the outbreak of war in 1948."[115]

His militant antisemitism was backed by the Muslim Brotherhood, who hailed the Mufti as the man who would realize Hitler's dream. "This hero," they rejoiced after his return from Paris in 1946, "fought Zionism with the help of Hitler and Germany. Germany and Hitler are gone, but Amin el-Husseini will continue the struggle."[116]

In 1945, the Egyptian media had reported in detail on the Holocaust and the Nuremberg war crimes trials that had begun in the same year.[117] Moreover, prominent intellectuals in Egypt such as the author Tawfiq al-Hakim had called for a full-scale denazification program for the postwar period.[118]

Notwithstanding, the authorities were unable to counter the Islamists' pro-Mufti campaign. A final attempt to do so was undertaken by the head of the Egyptian government, Isma'il Sidqi, in June 1946. He criticized King Farouk's decision to grant asylum to the Mufti without consulting the government and referred to the Mufti's "political errors" during his exile in Germany.

The Brotherhood responded with a series of angry statements and declared that El-Husseini, rather than committing any errors, had used his time in Germany to "perform jihad."[119] By going on the offensive, the antisemitic current in the Arab world was able to seize the initiative between 1945 and 1948 and set the agenda. As a result,

> blinded by their belief in the inevitability of Arab victory, by their own propaganda about the unlikelihood of effective Jewish resistance, and unable to admit any hesitancy or weakness (for political as much as psychological reasons), Arab leaders marched their countries straight into a costly and humiliating disaster.[120]

After the first Middle East war had ended in an Arab defeat, El-Husseini's Arab Higher Executive Committee existed only on paper. Now the Egyptian government decided to dissolve the Muslim Brotherhood units in Palestine and ban the movement in Egypt. Had the Egyptian authorities summoned up the will to act so decisively after the Brotherhood's first pogrom in Egypt in November 1945 – three years previously – the history of the Middle East might have been very different. Instead, the echoes of National Socialism had been allowed to resonate unhindered.

Rather than distancing himself from the Nazis, the Mufti still in 1954 continued to emphasize his pride in Hitler's great admiration for the Palestinian Arabs' struggle.[121] The Muslim Brotherhood too never repudiated the Mufti's alliance with Hitler, while the intimidated Egyptian authorities kept quiet about this aspect of the Brotherhood's policies.

Within the contemporary global picture, the total amnesty that the Brotherhood won for the Mufti looks totally out of place. "The Arabs proved to be the only people in the whole world for whom close cooperation with Hitler and Mussolini was not a crime, not even a blemish on the record of a national leader."[122]

At the same time, this general amnesty continued a bad tradition. Even during World War II, the Allies had refrained from countering the Nazis' antisemitic propaganda so as not to be known as "Zionist-lovers." Once the war was over, the Allies missed the opportunity to put the Mufti on trial for his war crimes and his antisemitism in order not to complicate relations with the Arabs. When the Mufti – that "ton of dynamite on two legs," as Churchill described him – began to engage in political activity in Cairo, the Egyptian government shrunk away from confronting him so as not to arouse the fury of the Muslim Brotherhood. Even when Arab delegates to the United Nations engaged in antisemitic speech, no one opposed them. "It was allowed to stand as if it were just another legitimate opinion."[123] Finally, when the Islamists raised a war cry against the partition plan, the Arab League was afraid to stand up to them so as not to appear "Jew-friendly." All the actors followed the same logic of appeasement, a logic which repeatedly opened up new space for antisemitism and paved the way for war.

Israel's Guilt?

Despite all of the above, there is a widespread tendency today to pin the responsibility for the 1948 war not on the by-then-endemic antisemitism but on Israel and Zionism. Thus, in a booklet entitled *Antisemitismus im Islamismus* ("Antisemitism in Islamism") published by the German Federal Office for the Protection of the Constitution in 2019, we read the following:

In 1948 the establishment of the State of Israel and its victory over the allied Arab States, Egypt, Syria, Lebanon, Jordan and Iraq, in the war of independence was the climax of the escalation. During the war there occurred the flight and expulsion of hundreds of thousands of Muslim Palestinians, a fact that weighs heavily to this day on Israeli-Palestinian relations.[124]

There was no mention of either the UN decision of 1947 or the invasion by Arab armies in 1948. Instead Israel, although it had accepted the UN decision, is held responsible for the "climax of the escalation," creating the impression that it had attacked the Arab world.

Even more striking is the way in which these events are presented in the *Handbuch des Antisemitismus – Länder und Regionen* ("Handbook of Antisemitism – States and Regions") issued by the Berlin Center for Research on Antisemitism (ZfA) in 2008. This bulky reference work describes the process of the foundation of Israel in these terms:

> The foundation of the state of Israel in May 1948 is described as the *nakba* ("catastrophe") in Arab political discourse. The flight and expulsion of 700,000 Palestinian Arabs who left the country as a result of the fighting and the territorial loss of a large proportion of the former Mandate territory exemplify in Arab eyes the ongoing intrigues of the European powers. In the 1950s and 60s the Palestine question moved to the center of Pan-Arab ideology and politics as the symbol of imperialist threats.

Once again the impression is created that the real "catastrophe" was the creation of the state of Israel, rather than the invasion of the Arab armies that followed a few hours later. The Handbook deals with this key event in the Middle Eastern conflict exclusively from "the Arab viewpoint," omitting to mention contrary views or such relevant factors as the invasion of Palestine by the Arab states in 1948. Once the Arab aggression has been omitted, however, there is then no further reason to consider its motives and attendant circumstances, such as the Nazi's Arabic-language propaganda.

In contrast to the one-sided pro-Arab partisanship of the prestigious ZfA, let me quote from a document that expresses what a significant portion of US society, represented by both Democrat and Republican senators, thought at the time about the Arab guerilla war against the UN partition plan. "Openly defying the United Nations, the governments of the Arab States … are deliberately encouraging aggression against the Jews of Palestine," states the one-page statement by the American Christian Palestine Commitee, published in the newspaper PM on 19 January 1948.

> This campaign of violence has no moral justification. It is directed against a decision of the United Nations made after nearly twenty committees of inquiry had investigated the problem of Palestine over a period of more than twenty-five years. The decision of the United Nations was moreover a compromise which granted national states in Palestine to both Jews and Arabs.
>
> The campaign of violence we now witness is not a spontaneous uprising by the majority of Palestine's Arabs. On the contrary, they wish to live in peace with their Jewish neighbours. But they are terrorized by the ex-Mufti's bands assisted

by confederates in Cairo, Baghdad, Beirut and Damascus. ... The campaign of Arab aggression, led by a group of former Nazi allies and their accomplices across the frontiers, is therefore directed not only against the Jews, not only against the peaceful majority of Palestine's Arabs, but against the authority of the United Nations itself. This is a bold attempt to blackmail the United Nations into submission. ... If the United Nations cannot make its Palestine decision stick, if a handful of willful men can prevent a UN decision from being carried out because they do not like that decision, then no future action of the UN will have more worth than the paper upon which it is written.[125]

While Amin el-Husseini and the Muslim Brothers represented the continuation of Nazi antisemitism, the signatories of this statement stood in another tradition: their support for the Zionist project was a logical continuation of the anti-Nazi and anti-fascist passions of World War II.

But why then is the role of Nazi propaganda still today largely ignored in debates on the roots of antisemitism in the Middle East? Instead this antisemitism is either considered as something, "brought into the Arab world by missionaries and colonial powers", as ZfA researcher Juliane Wetzel wrote in 2009, omitting to mention the German policies of the 1930s and 1940s,[126] or attributed to the period after 1948, that is, after the founding of Israel. Islam expert, Michael Kiefer, for example, presents "antisemitism in the Arab-Islamic world as an import from Europe. The first phase of its mass dissemination began in the 1950s."[127] Again, there was no mention of the period between 1937 and 1945.

Professor Peter Wien, a historian of the Middle East who teaches at the University of Maryland, does not ignore the Nazi period. Nonetheless, he asserts that

There is ... no Islamic tradition of anti-Semitic readings of the Qur'an that predates World War II. It is therefore incorrect to speak of a specific autochthonous Islamic anti-Semitism, which in itself would motivate Muslims to oppose the State of Israel.

In his view, the Islamization of antisemitism began after the 6-Day War. "After 1967, ... references to selective and de-contextualized readings of anti-Jewish passages of the Qur'an and the broader Islamic textual tradition were a novelty."[128]

Arabist Esther Webman also believes that the Islamic variant of antisemitism emerged only in the post-1967 period. "The swift Israeli victory over the Arab armies in June 1967 ... brought to the fore a new type of antisemitism that perceived the Arab–Israeli conflict as a religious conflict between Islam and Judaism."[129] Only then did "antisemitism referring to the Koran and the Islamic tradition [undergo] a process of Islamization." In fact, however, religiously inspired texts such as *Islam and Judaism* (1937) or Qutb's *Our Struggle with the Jews* (c. 1950) had been widely disseminated long before 1967.

Michael Kiefer even dates the emergence of an "Islamistically-clad antisemitism" to the period after 1979, following Khomeini's Islamic revolution in Iran.

> *New*, on the other hand was the systematic referencing by the anti-Semites of an image of the Jew derived from the Koran and the hadiths. In the *new way of looking at things* the Jews now appeared as a group that had always threatened Islam.[130]

In fact, however, this "way of looking at things" was by no means new: it was already a potent force in the run-up to the 1948 war.

The dates selected by Webman and Kiefer are nonetheless significant. They relate to events that further radicalized a Jew-hatred already present in the Middle East beforehand.

1950: The foundation of the State of Israel and the allegedly impossible defeat of the Arab armies further fueled the antisemitism. Gamal Abdul Nasser, whose putsch in 1952 was one of the consequences of the defeat, disseminated the *Protocols of the Elders of Zion* in the Arab world and employed many of the Nazi war criminals who had evaded judgment by fleeing to Egypt in their field of special expertise – anti-Jewish propaganda.

1967: After Nasser's anti-Israel campaign had come to grief in the 6-Day War, the Islamic form of antisemitism came back into fashion. In particular, the religious establishment missed no opportunity to explain the military defeat as the result of a lack of faith. A religiously conservative Saudi Arabia now set about distributing millions of copies of Sayyid Qutb's pamphlet *Our Struggle with the Jews*, which he had previously published at the start of the 1950s. Palestine was once more declared to be holy Muslim soil and the destruction of Israel a religious duty. The degree to which Islamic antisemitism found its way even into school textbooks was exposed by a 1969 UNESCO report. Their investigation into the teaching materials used in Palestinian refugee camps revealed that in religious studies and history books,

> an excessive importance is given to the problem of relations between the Prophet Muhammad and the Jews of Arabia, in terms tending to convince young people that the Jewish community as a whole has always been and will always be the irreconcilable enemy of the Muslim community.[131]

1979: A further intensification of this enmity ensued after the Islamic Revolution in Iran. In its wake, in 1982 the Lebanese Shiite Hezbollah movement began to carry out religiously motivated suicide murders of Jews. Then in 1988 came the religiously argued Hamas Charter.

All these successive radicalizations built on the basic pattern of the Nazi antisemitism that had demonized Zionism and paved the way for the war of 1948.

In Germany, the "reappraisal of the Nazi past" is a matter of special importance. It is therefore all the more surprising that this aspect of our history – the dissemination of an Islamically garbed Nazi antisemitism in the Arab world – attracts so little attention.

The subject of post-colonialism – the connection between former colonial policies and the present-day – is currently attracting lively interest. There is, however, no such interest in the subject of post-Nazism – the links between Nazi foreign policy and current events.

Moreover, even when the Nazis' Middle Eastern policy is topical, its ideological dimension is as a rule ignored. Helmut Mejcher is undoubtedly one of the most prominent German historians of the Middle East. In the volume *Die Palästina-Frage 1917–1948* that he edited, the Italian and British radio stations are briefly mentioned. There is, however, no mention of Radio Zeesen or all the other Nazis efforts to embed antisemitism in the Middle East in either this work or the later (2017), *Der Nahe Osten im Zweiten Weltkrieg*.[132]

A plausible hypothesis is that this pattern of omission reflects a desire to protect a proposition that is accepted as dogma in many academic circles: the idea that Israel, that is, Jews, bears sole responsibility not only for the war in 1948 but also the antisemitism in the region. What follows is only a small sample of the available evidence:

Michael Kiefer: "The spread of antisemitism in the Arab-Islamic world is an immediate consequence of the Palestine conflict." Alexander Flores: "I suggest, that these [anti-Semitic] attitudes [among Palestinian Arabs] be seen not as a *cause* but as an *outgrowth* of the conflict." Gilbert Achcar: "The anti-Semitic statements now heard in Arab countries are fantasy-laden expressions, … for which 'the Jews' of Palestine in their majority, as well as Israel, the 'Jewish state' they founded, must, in fact, be held responsible." Stefan Wild: "Middle Eastern antisemitism is the consequence, not the cause of the Middle East conflict."[133]

Of course, the establishment of Islamic antisemitism did have *something* to do with the Zionist movement and the building of the Jewish state. However, there was more than one way to respond to these phenomena. There were, for example, Egyptians who welcomed the "victory of the Zionist idea [as] the turning point for … the revival of the Orient."[134] Others, such as the ruler of Transjordan, Emir Abdullah, sought sometimes more, sometimes less cooperation with the Zionists. A third group may have opposed Zionism, but not Judaism, while initially it was only the Mufti's supporters who adopted the antisemitic approach.

The Nazis exclusively backed the last group. They saw the clashes in Palestine as an opportunity to promote their form of Jew-hatred. "The understanding of the dangers of the Jews has not yet been awakened here," complained the Cairo Nazi local group in October 1933 in a letter to Berlin. To create an anti-Jewish mood, it was necessary to focus on the point "where real conflicts of interest exist between Arabs and Jews: Palestine. The opposition between Arabs and Jews there must be transplanted to Egypt."[135] We see here that, *originally*, antisemitism had very little to do with the actions of the Jews in Palestine. Instead, a specific anti-Jewish interpretation was imposed on the local conflict. Thereafter, to paraphrase

Jean-Paul Sartre's *Reflections on the Jewish Question*, it was no longer "experience that shaped the idea of the Jew." Instead, "prejudice distorted the experience."[136]

Moreover, the question about the causes and consequences of the Middle Eastern conflict does not permit an "either-or" answer. Even if one interprets the Muslim Brotherhood's Jew-hatred as a result of Zionist policies, it is still the case that their antisemitism contributed to the exacerbation and perpetuation of the conflict. Statements such as "Middle Eastern antisemitism is the consequence, not the cause of the Middle East conflict" do not capture the complexity. Finally, the systematic avoidance, the active ignorance, that seems to operate in relation to the Nazi role in fueling the Middle East conflict confirms the suspicion that historical truth is here being sacrificed to an ideological goal – that of placing Israel in the dock and making Jews responsible for antisemitism.

In reality, Nazi Germany influenced the situation in the Middle East in many ways. First, the Third Reich's policies, including the Transfer (Haavara) Agreement, forced many Jews to emigrate to Palestine, thus fueling the Jewish–Arab antagonism there.[137] Second, it was the German preparations for World War II that led London to consider it necessary to placate the Arab world by restricting Jewish emigration to Palestine. Third, Berlin acted to reinforce the most radical Jew-haters in the Palestinian–Arab camp, such as the Egyptian Muslim Brotherhood and the Mufti, not only ideologically but also through subsidies and supplies of arms. Fourth, the Nazi propagandists used every trick in the book to whip up and mobilize antisemitism on the "Arab Street" by radio and in print. Fifth, Berlin's campaigns fostered a one-sided image of the Jew in Islam, "German propaganda combined Islam with anti-Jewish agitation to an extent that had not hitherto been known in the modern Muslim world."[138] Sixth, the Nazis made arrangements to continue the war against Israel even after their own defeat.

All the above had a huge impact on the Middle Eastern conflict and so on the Arab world as we have known it since 1948. And we can go further: the legacy of the Nazis' influence continues to affect us to this day.

Notes

1 Gerhard Höpp (ed.), *Mufti-Papiere. Briefe, Memoranden, Reden und Aufrufe Amin al-Husainis aus dem Exil, 1940–1945*, Berlin 2001, 155.
2 NACP RG 84, Egypt: Cairo Embassy General Records 1936–1955, 820.00–822.00, entry 2410, box 93: VFA, 21 May 1943, "British Control", Kirk to Secretary of State, No. 1071, Cairo (1 June 1943), Axis Broadcasts in Arabic … 21 to 27 May 1943, 3–4, cited after Jeffrey Herf, *Nazi Propaganda for the Arab World*, New Haven, CT 2009, 172.
3 Hagana Archive, *The Mufti's Memoirs, Part II*, cited after Jennie Lebel, *The Mufti of Jerusalem Haj-Amin el-Husseini and National-Socialism*, Belgrade 2007, 149. Emphases – M.K.
4 Heidemarie Wawrzyn, *Nazis in the Holy Land 1933–1948*, Berlin 2013, 122.
5 All the information is derived from the program scripts translated at the time on the initiative of the US Ambassador in Cairo, Alexander Kirk.

6 Elke Fröhlich (ed.), *Die Tagebücher von Joseph Goebbels, Teil II, Band 8*, Munich 1993, 261.
7 Joseph B. Schechtman, *The Mufti and the Fuehrer: The Rise and Fall of Haj Amin el-Husseini*, New York 1965, 221.
8 Robert Kempner, *SS im Kreuzverhör*, Hamburg 1987, 300.
9 Klaus Gensicke, *Der Mufti von Jerusalem und die Nationalsozialisten. Eine politische Biographie Amin el-Husseinis*, Darmstadt 2007, 148.
10 Richard Breitman and Norman J. W. Goda, *Hitler's Shadow: Nazi War Criminals, US Intelligence, and the Cold War*, Washington D.C. 2010, 21.
11 The Mufti's "house arrest" in France was "so lax that he was able to escape with relative ease and return to the Middle East" see: Jeffrey Herf, *Israel's Moment. International Support for an Opposition to Establishing the Jewish State, 1945–1949*, Cambridge 2022, 106–130.
12 American Zionist Emergency Council, "Memorandum Submitted to the Secretary of State", cited after Herf, *Israel*, 46.
13 Klaus-Michael Mallmann and Martin Cüppers, *Halbmond und Hakenkreuz. Das Dritte Reich, die Araber und Palästina*, Darmstadt 2006, 117ff.
14 Israel Gutman (ed.), *Enzyklopädie des Holocaust Band II*, Munich 1995, 631.
15 Herf, *Israel*, 61.
16 Schechtman, *Mufti*, 202; Thomas Mayer, "Arab Unity of Action and the Palestine Question, 1945–48", *Middle East Studies*, Vol. 22, No. 3, July 1986, 331–349, here 334. The following excerpt follows Mayer.
17 Herf, *Nazi Propaganda*, 242.
18 Barry Rubin and Wolfgang G. Schwanitz, *Nazis, Islamists, and the Making of the Modern Middle East*, New Haven, CT and London 2014, 197.
19 Mohammad Khalil, *The Arab States and the Arab League, Vol. II, International Affairs*, Beirut 1962, "Res. June 12, 1946", 162.
20 David Th. Schiller, *Palästinenser zwischen Terrorismus und Diplomatie*, München 1982, 18; Schechtman, *Mufti*, 203.
21 Joseph Nevo, "The Arabs of Palestine 1947–48: Military and Political Activity", *Middle Eastern Studies*, Vol. 23, No. 1, January 1987, 5.
22 Ibid., 6.
23 Walter Laqueur, *A History of Zionism*, New York 1972, 267.
24 Ibid.
25 Benny Morris, *1948. The First Arab-Israeli War*, New Haven, CT 2008, 42.
26 Efraim Karsh, *Palestine Betrayed*, New Haven, CT 2010, 191.
27 Ibid., 81.
28 Ibid., 206, 81.
29 Simon Wiesenthal, *Großmufti: Großagent der Achse*, Salzburg 1947, 2.
30 Herf, *Nazi Propaganda*, 242ff.
31 See Chapter 2 in this book.
32 Abd al-Fattah M. El-Awaisi, *The Muslim Brothers and the Palestine Question, 1928–1947*, London 1996, 135.
33 Cited after Herf, *Nazi Propaganda*, 248.
34 El-Awaisi, Ibid., 203.
35 Ibid., 28, 163.
36 Ibid., 191.
37 Jeffrey Herf, "Hitlers Dschihad. Nationalsozialistische Rundfunkpropaganda für Nordafrika und den Nahen Osten", *Vierteljahreszeitschrift für Zeitgeschichte*, Vol. 58, Nr. 2, April 2010, 259–286, here 285.
38 El-Awaisi, *Muslim Brothers*, 188.
39 By protecting the Mufti, Egypt and Saudi Arabia wished to counter the ambitions of their common rival, Emir Abdullah of Jordan, an opponent of the Mufti.

40 Cited after Herf, *Israel*, 140.
41 Cited after Herf, *Israel*, 141.
42 Cited after Herf, *Israel*, 143.
43 Resolution 181 (II) Future Government of Palestine, A/RES/ 181 (II), 29 November 1947, accessed 3 October 2017, https://unispal.un.org/DPA/DPR/unispal.nsf/5ba47a5c 6cef541b802563e000493b8c/7f0af2bd897689b785256c330061d253?OpenDocument.
44 Yaacov Lozowick, *Israels Existenzkampf*, Hamburg 2006, 118.
45 *Keesing's Archiv der Gegenwart (AdG)*, 14 May 1948, 1498; figures according to David Tal, *War in Palestine 1948. Strategy and Diplomacy*, London 2004, 163.
46 According to Azzam on 11 October 1947 in the Egyptian daily newspaper *Akhbar al-Yom*, as cited by David Barnett and Efraim Karsh, "Azzam's Genocidal Threat", *Middle East Quarterly*, Vol. 18, Nr. 4, Fall 2011, 85–88.
47 Yoav Gelber, *Palestine 1948. War, Escape and the Emergence of the Palestinian Refugee Problem*, Brighton and Portland, OR 2006, 43.
48 Nevo, "The Arabs", 35; Morris, *1948*, 121. Salameh's son, Ali Hassan Salameh was one of the organizers of the massacre at the 1972 Munich Olympics.
49 Gelber, *Palestine*, 43.
50 Monty Noam Penkower, *Palestine to Israel. Mandate to State, 1945–1948, Vol. II: Into the International Arena*, New York 2019, 574.
51 Also known as the "Horst-Wessel-Lied".
52 "Empfehlende Belastung. Braune Kolonnen in Palästina", *DER SPIEGEL*, 13 March 1948, 11.
53 Seth J. Frantzman and Jovan Culibrk, "Strange Bedfellows: The Bosnians and Yugoslav Volunteers in the 1948 War in Israel/Palestine", *Istorija*, Vol. 20, No. 1, 2009, 189–200, here 196, 200. See also Tal, *War*, 20 , 72.
54 "Empfehlende Belastung. Braune Kolonnen in Palästina", *DER SPIEGEL*, 13 March 1948, 11.
55 On the stages in this war, see Morris, *1948*; Tal, *War*, and Gelber, *Palestine*. There is no record of the Palestinian Arab fatalities; Egyptian losses amounted to some 1,400 dead; the Jordanian, Iraqi and Syrian armies each suffered several hundred dead. See Morris, *1948*, 406–407 and Gelber, *Palestine*, 148.
56 Morris, *1948*, 1. Emphasis – M.K.
57 Developments of the Quarter: Comment and Chronology September 1–November 30, 1947, *The Middle East Journal*, Vol. 2, No. 1, January 1948, 60–75, here 61.
58 Ibid.
59 Tal, *War*, 469.
60 Philip Mattar, *The Mufti of Jerusalem. Al-Hajj Amin al-Husayni and the Palestinian National Movement*, New York 1988, 110.
61 *AdG*, 16 February 1948, 1385.
62 Cited in Jon and David Kimche, *Both Sides of the Hill. Britain and the Palestine War*, London 1960, 153–4.
63 Barry Rubin, *The Great Powers in the Middle East 1941–1947. The Road to the Cold War*, London 1980, 201; Gelber, *Palestine*, 11, Tal, *War*, 169.
64 Chairiyya Qasimiyya, "Palästina in der Politik der arabischen Staaten 1918–1948", Helmut Mejcher (ed.), *Die Palästina-Frage 1917–1948. Historische Ursprünge und internationale Dimension eines Nationenkonflikts*, Paderborn 1993, 123–188, here 184.
65 Memorandum by Mr. Dean Rusk of 26 January 1948, cited after Herf, *Israel*, 274.
66 UN-Bulletin, Report to the Security Council, cited in *AdG*, 16 February 1948, 1385.
67 Kimche, *Both Sides*, 64.
68 *AdG*, 25 February 1948, 1408. A month later, Austin temporarily backed away from supporting the partition plan. For more on the turbulent debates between US President Harry S. Truman and the opponents of the plan in the Pentagon and State Department, see Herf, *Israel*, 263–348.

69 Yaacov Ro'i, *From Encroachment to Involvement. A Documentary Study of Soviet Policy in the Middle East*, 1945–1973, New York 1974, 60.
70 Ibid., 62f.
71 Matthias Küntzel, "Als die Sowjetunion für den Zionismus Partei ergriff. Anmerkungen zum 70. Jahrestag der Rede Andrei Gromykos vor den Vereinten Nationen", *menawatch.com*, 9 May 2017.
72 Avi Shlaim, *The Politics of Partition. King Abdullah, the Zionists and Palestine 1921–1951*, Oxford 1998, 83; Mayer, "Arab Unity", 344.
73 Michael Doran, *Pan-Arabism before Nasser*, New York 1999, 100.
74 Bruse Maddy-Weitzman, *The Crystallization of the Arab State System 1945–1954*, New York 1993, 80.
75 Neil Caplan, *Futile Diplomacy Vol. II, Arab-Zionist Negotiations and the End of the Mandate*, London 1986, 264ff.
76 Gelber, *Palestine*, 11 and 118.
77 Morris, *1948*, 66; see also Barry Rubin, *The Arab States and the Palestinian Conflict*, Syracuse, NY 1981, 166 and 175.
78 Karsh, *Palestine*, 115.
79 Hillel Cohen, *Army of Shadows. Palestinian Collaboration with Zionism, 1917–1948*, Berkeley, CA 2008, 232ff. See also Tal, *War*, 45.
80 Ilan Pappé, *The Making of the Arab-Israeli Conflict 1947–1951*, London 2015, 65.
81 Morris, *1948*, 34.
82 *Berlin in Arabic*, 8 September 1943, "Talk: The Ambitions of the Jews," Kirk to Secretary of State, No. 1313, Cairo, 23 September 1943, cited after Herf, *Nazi Propaganda*, 181.
83 *AdG*, 18 October 1946, 901. "Ibn Saud in a Telegram to US President Truman."
84 *AdG*, 22 July 1947, 1151. "Erklärung im Namen der arabischen Staaten."
85 Meir Litvak and Esther Webman, *From Empathy to Denial. Arab Responses to the Holocaust*, London 2009, 39.
86 According to Abd al-Majid Ibrahim Salih in *Al-Ahram*, 7 March 1946. Cited after Litvak and Webman, *Empathy*, 41.
87 Ibid., 394.
88 Cited after John Strawson, *Partitioning Palestine. Legal Fundamentalism in the Palestinian-Israeli Conflict*, London 2010, 79 and 116.
89 Strawson, *Partitioning*, 117.
90 Bernard Lewis, *The Jews of Islam*, Princeton, NJ 1984, 188. Emir Abdullah, the ruler of Transjordan, was the exception. A plausible explanation for his unique stance, writes Ilan Pappè, "is his lack of anti-semitism – unlike some of his contemporaries." Pappé, *Making*, 114.
91 Third Section of the Resolutions of the Anshas Summit of 29 and 29 May 1946, as cited by Zvi Elpeleg, *Through the Eyes of the Mufti. The Essays of Haj Amin, Translated and Annotated*, London 2009, 194.
92 E. Sasson's report on "Attempts for Agreement with Arabs" (Jerusalem), 5 March 1946, in "E. Sasson's Private Papers (T.A.)", cited after Thomas Mayer, "Egypt's 1948 Invasion of Palestine", *Middle Eastern Studies*, Vol. 22, No. 1, January 1986, 20–36, here 24. On the British policy that, whether deliberately or not, encouraged the Arab intervention, see Karsh, *Palestine*, 83–86.
93 Thomas Mayer, *Egypt and the Palestine Question: 1936–1945*, Berlin 1983, 191. This incident occurred in September 1944.
94 Mayer, *Egypt and the Palestine Question*, 298, and El-Awaisi, *Muslim Brothers*, 177.
95 El-Awaisi, *Muslim Brothers*, 184.
96 Ibid., 195.
97 Gudrun Krämer, *Minderheit, Millet, Nation? Die Juden in Ägypten 1914–1952*, Wiesbaden 1982, 410.
98 El-Awaisi, *Muslim Brothers*, 155, 207.

99 Rubin, *Arab States*, 182, 196, 199. "The fanatical content and bellicose tone of Arab broadcasts" further inflamed the situation; see Gelber, *Palestine*, 133. See also Pappé, *Making*, 105.
100 Rubin, Ibid., 175.
101 Report by Pinkney Tuck, US-ambassador to Egypt, to Secretary of State, 30 April 1948, cited after Herf, *Nazi Propaganda*, 254, see also Morris, *1948*, 183.
102 Fawaz A. Gerges, "Egypt and the 1948 War", Eugene L. Rogan und Avi Shlaim (eds.), *The War for Palestine. Rewriting the History of 1948*, Cambridge 2001, 151–177, here 154.
103 Rubin, *Arab States*, 161. See also Morris, *1948*, 66, 181.
104 According to the report on this conference by the British Arabist I. N. Clayton. See Issa Khalaf, *Politics in Palestine. Arab Factionalism and Social Disintegration, 1939–1948*, Albany, NY 1991, 273.
105 Ibid. 196, and "Mit deutschem Gruß für Palästina", *DER SPIEGEL* 51–52/1947, 20. Dezember 1947, 11.
106 Ibid.
107 Arab League Chronology, *The Middle East Journal*, Vol. 2, No. 2 (April 1948), 204–204, here 204; Thomas Mayer, "The Military Force of Islam. The Society of the Muslim Brethren and the Palestine Question, 1945–48", Elie Kedourie and Sylvia G. Haim (eds.), *Zionism and Arabism in Palestine and Israel*, London 1982, 100–117, here 109.
108 See Penkower, *Palestine to Israel*, 647–648. The most detailed account of the events in Deir Yassin is Uri Milstein, *The Birth of a Palestinian Nation. The Myth of the Deir Yassin Massacre*, Jerusalem and New York, 2012.
109 Khalaf, *Politics in Palestine*, 192.
110 Marilyn Stern, Eliezer Tauber on Deir Yassin: The Massacre That Never Was, Middle East Forum Webinar, 21 November 2022.
111 Mayer, "Military Force", 110–111.
112 See the "Report of the United Nations Palestine Commission, 10 April 1948" in T. G. Fraser, *The Middle East 1914–1979*, London 1980, 62–63. See also Meir Zamir, *The Secret Anglo-French War in the Middle East. Intelligence and Decolonization, 1940–1948*, London and New York 2015, 174 and 179; Rubin, *Arab States*, 188–189.
113 Helmut Mejcher, *Der Nahe Osten im Zweiten Weltkrieg*, Paderborn 2017, 282.
114 Elpeleg *Through the Eyes*, 26.
115 Cohen, *Army*, 10.
116 Herf, "Dschihad", 285.
117 Litvak and Webman, *Empathy*, 25–30.
118 Israel Gershoni, "Demon and Infidel. Egyptian Intellectuals Confronting Hitler and Nazis during Wold War II," Francis R. Nicosia and Bogac A. Ergene (eds.), *Nazism, the Holocaust and the Middle East*, New York 2018, 77–104, here 86.
119 El-Awaisi, *Muslim Brothers*, 189ff.
120 Rubin, *Arab States*, 165.
121 Elpeleg: *Through the Eyes*, 11.
122 Schechtman: *The Mufti*, 196.
123 Strawson, *Partitioning*, 117.
124 Bundesamt für Verfassungsschutz, *Antisemitismus im Islamismus*, Cologne 2019, 17.
125 Senator Robert F. Wagner et al., "To the United States and the United Nations", PM, 19 January 1948 cited after Herf, *Israel*, 299. The signatories included Senators Owen Brewster, Edwin C. Johnson, James E. Murray, Charles W. Tobey and Robert F. Wagner. I am grateful to Prof. Jeffrey Herf for providing me with a copy of the original statement.
126 Juliane Wetzel, "Judenfeindschaft unter Muslimen in Europa", Wolfgang Benz (ed.), *Islamfeindschaft und ihr Kontext. Dokumentation der Konferenz "Feindbild Muslim – Feindbild Jude"*, Berlin 2009, 45–61, here 52.

127 Michael Kiefer, "Islamischer, islamistischer oder islamisierter Antisemitismus?", *Die Welt des Islam*, Vol. 46, No. 3, 2006, 277–306, here 298.
128 Peter Wien, *Arab Nationalism. The Politics of History and Culture in the Modern Middle East*, London and New York 2017, 180.
129 Esther Webman, "From the Damascus Blood Libel to the 'Arab Spring': The Evolution of Arab Antisemitism", *Antisemitism Studies*, Vol. I, No. 1, Spring 2017, 157–206, here 165; Emphasis – M.K.
130 Michael Kiefer, *Antisemitismus in islamischen Gesellschaften. Der Palästina-Konflikt und der Transfer eines Feindbildes*, Düsseldorf 2002, 80. Emphasis – M.K.
131 UNESCO Document 82 EX/8, annex II, p. 9, section III, paragraph 6 and annex I, p. 3, section III, paragraph 4, cited after Lewis, *Jews*, 187.
132 Mejcher, *Die Palästina-Frage*, 211; Mejcher, *Naher Osten*, 282. Exceptions to this rule are the monograph by von Cüppers and Mallmann and the recent study by David Motadel.
133 Kiefer, *Antisemitismus*, 122; Alexander Flores, "Judeophobia in Context: Anti-Semitism Among Modern Palestinians", *Die Welt des Islam*, Vol. 46, No. 3, 2006, 307–330, here 329; Gilbert Achcar, *Die Araber und der Holocaust. Der arabisch-israelische Krieg der Geschichtsschreibungen*, Hamburg 2012, 242; Stefan Wild, "Importierter Antisemitismus? Die Religion des Islam und Rezeption der 'Protokolle der Weisen von Zion' in der arabischen Welt", Dirk Ansorge (ed.), *Antisemitismus in Europa und in der arabischen Welt*, Paderborn 2006, 201–216, here 202.
134 El-Awaisi, *Muslim Brothers*, 69.
135 Comment on a report of 29.09.1933 in AA Abt. III Po2–03588, cited in Krämer, *Minderheit*, 278.
136 Jean-Paul Sartre, "Betrachtungen zur Judenfrage", Jean-Paul Sartre (ed.), *Drei Essays*, Berlin 1970, 111.
137 Edwin Black, *The Transfer Agreement. The Dramatic Story of the Pact between the Third Reich and Jewish Palestine*, New York 2001.
138 David Motadel, *Für Prophet und Führer. Die Islamische Welt und das Dritte Reich*, Stuttgart 2017, 121.

5

IN THE NAME OF ISLAM

In 1948, Seth Arsanian had predicted that Radio Zeesen's hate campaigns would have "their subtle effect for some time to come," leading to the devaluation of "Western civilization in general" and "tending to strengthen traditionalist, conservative groups in the Middle East." He was proved right.[1] For the Arab peoples, the massive dissemination of the Nazi ideology in the 1930s and 1940s marks a cesura dividing their history into a "before" and "after."

In the preceding decades, a more modern approach to Islam seemed to be gaining the upper hand in many Muslim countries. The lack of attention that is currently paid to this phase is astonishing, given its evident relevance to contemporary debates about Islam. While right-wing populists like to insist that "the Muslim" is bound to the literal word of the holy texts, these decades show how in lived reality Muslims can emancipate themselves from the dogmas of their religion.

Thus, in 1839 the Ottoman Sultan called for equal rights for Jews and Christians, and in 1856 this was legally established. In 1909, with the granting of permission to Jews and Christians to perform military service, the last discriminatory barrier fell. Admittedly, the humiliating attitude to Jews did not disappear everywhere or immediately. Nonetheless, in the urban centers, they could become elected representatives and hold government posts.[2] This development was not only due to pressure from the European colonial powers. An even stronger motive was the wish of the Ottoman elite to draw closer to European civilization.

In the 1920s, sharia law ceased to apply in significant parts of the Muslim world. In 1924, it was abolished in Turkey by Kemal Atatürk. Iran began to secularize in 1925 under Reza Shah Pahlavi. In both Turkey and Iran, the nation was no longer treated as subordinate to Islam, but Islam as subordinate to the nation.

In Egypt, sharia was by then only applicable to personal affairs, with everything else being subject to European-style legislation.[3] The Zionist movement too

DOI: 10.4324/9781003369110-6

was initially greeted with a corresponding lack of inhibition. "The Zionists are necessary for this country (Palestine)," wrote the editor of the Egyptian newspaper *Al-Ahram*. "The money that they will bring in and the intelligence and energy that characterizes them will without doubt contribute to reviving the country."[4] Egyptian Prime Minister Ahmed Zaki expressed himself in the same vein in 1922, writing that "The victory of the Zionist idea is the turning point for the fulfilment of an ideal which is so dear to me, the revival of the Orient."[5] In the same year, Egyptian woman's rights activist Huda Sha'rawi decided to discard her veil; in 1923, she founded the Egyptian Feminist Society. In 1927, the fatwa committee of Al-Azhar Mosque determined that it was not obligatory under Islamic law to wear a headscarf.[6]

Just a few years previously Mustafa Kemal – known as Atatürk ("father of the Turks") – had revolutionized Turkish civil law: instead of polygamy, civil marriage; instead of the repudiation of the woman by the man, a divorce law that granted equal rights to both parties. Muslim women were permitted to marry non-Muslims, and every adult was allowed to change their religion without hindrance.[7]

Nazi interventions in the region and the subsequent aggravation of the conflict in Palestine ended this liberal phase. The clearest expression of this shift was the exodus of the Jews from the Arab world. Of the more than 800,000 Jews who had lived in Arab countries before 1948, all but a few thousand had departed.

> Of the over 250,000 Moroccan Jews only about 2,000 remained in the country. 100,000 Jews lived in Tunisia, today there are 1,000. In 1948 75,000 Jews lived in Egypt and in Iraq 135,000. Now there are fewer than 20. In Yemen there were about 60,000, now it is an estimated 50. The Syrian Jewish community was reduced from 30,000 to fewer than 15. In 1948 140,000 Jews used to live in Algeria and 38,000 in Libya. Today there are none at all left.[8]

This loss changed the character of the societies the Jews had left behind. The relationship between Arabs and Jews always involved "the broader question of the emancipation of the subject" or, to be more precise, "the question of the confrontation of the Arab-Muslim world with the modernity of the Enlightenment," emphasizes Georges Bensoussan, a historian of Moroccan origin.[9]

The middle of the twentieth century marks the end of the modernizing trend. In Egypt, since the beginning of the 1950s, a series of military leaders starting with Gamal Abdul Nasser have tried to keep the influence of the Muslim Brotherhood at bay. At the end of the 1970s, Shiite Islamists came to power in Iran, and in the new millennium, Sunni Islamists have been on the advance in Turkey and Indonesia. It is also true that at the same time a series of Arab intellectuals have reached the conclusion that the exodus of the Jews also meant the end of social progress and that dogmatic enmity towards Israel has harmed their countries. It will, however, require a tremendous effort to overcome the current reactionary phase of Islam. Algerian writer Boualem Sansal speaks of a

> titanic task that equates to a 'cleaning out of the Augean Stables', in order to get rid of all this magical-religious-cultural-political junk that has been implanted in the genes of the Arab peoples over decades of tyranny and centuries of humiliating religious teaching.[10]

Any change for the better requires a new definition of the Arab relationship with Israel and Judaism and the repudiation of the lasting effects of the Nazi ideology.

What Do You Think of Adolf Hitler?

In autumn 2018, I met with my friend and colleague Dr. Edy Cohen in Tel Aviv. Edy's mother tongue is Arabic. He grew up in a Jewish family in Beirut and then in 1995 came to Israel where he works as a researcher at the Begin-Sadat Center for Strategic Studies writing books and articles on the history of the Middle East conflict. His brief commentaries are especially popular in the Arab world: at that time, 158,000 Arabs followed his Arabic-language Twitter account, and his tweets were getting between 800,000 and a million views per day.[11] Edy had his laptop with him. On the spur of the moment, I asked him to conduct a test: what would happen if he asked his followers the question: "what do you think of Adolf Hitler?" He typed in the question. After five minutes, there were 37 responses and after 20 minutes 120. During this time, 5,800 of Edy's followers had clicked in.

So what did we find? Edy translated the first 40 tweets for me, yielding the following results: 10 were clearly against Hitler, six were neutral or incomprehensible and four equated Hitler with Israeli politicians. Of the remaining 20, 1 praised Hitler with certain reservations, while the other 19 were totally pro-Hitler. Among the last group were answers such as "The bravest man in the world. He made one mistake: he did not burn all of you." "A great hero. He tried to wipe out the Jews to save the world." "Hitler knew that no peace with you will work. So he treated you as was necessary." "I love this guy, but I don't know why. Tell me why?" "The best thing he did was the Holocaust." "A man of honor. He gave the Jews what they deserve." "Someone asked Hitler, 'why did you not kill all the Jews, although you were in a position to do so?' His answer, 'So that all the world could see why I killed them.'"

So nearly half the responses were unreservedly pro-Hitler. In Europe, any poll yielding such results would be a scandal. In the Middle East, however, the scale of the admiration for Hitler is an open secret; it is considered normal. Thus, the fictional Hitler quote – "I could have annihilated all the Jews in the world, but I left a few so that you would know why I annihilated them" – was displayed on the official Facebook pages of two girls' high schools in the Palestinian Autonomous Territories together with big portraits of Hitler.[12] The online news monitoring service

Palestinian Media Watch provides many further examples of such sentiments under the rubric *Admiration of Hitler and Nazism*.[13]

This support for Hitler shows that since 8 May 1948 the world has experienced two binary divisions. The first, between politico-economic systems, is known as the Cold War. The second, hidden from view for decades by the Cold War, relates to the attitude to National Socialism. Almost everywhere else in the world, both at the official level and in the wider society, Adolf Hitler and his regime are considered the epitome of evil. The Arab world, however, is not part of this consensus. Here, no one was or is surprised or disturbed by the expression of a liking for Hitler. One of the few people to recognize this was Hannah Arendt, writing about the trial of Adolf Eichmann in 1961:

> The papers in Damascus and Beirut, in Cairo and Jordan did not hide their sympathy for Eichmann nor their regret that he "did not complete his business". A radio broadcast from Cairo on the day of the trial's opening even took a little sideswipe at the Germans, reproaching them for the fact that, "in the last war not one German airplane had flown over and bombed a Jewish settlement."[14]

Contemporary Middle East experts can also tell us a few things about this pro-Nazism. An example is the pioneering work by Israeli researchers Meir Litvak und Esther Webman, *The Arabs and the Holocaust*, published in 2009. In it they dealt with the widespread defense of the Holocaust in the Arab world.

> Justification of the Holocaust was less prevalent than its denial. Still its very existence, scope, bluntness and the argumentation it contained had no parallel in any other post-war societies. Even old or neo-Nazi groups in Europe that sought to rehabilitate the image of Hitler and his regime tended to deny the Holocaust and minimize Nazism's other crimes, rather than to openly and explicitly justify and defend them. As was the case with Arab denial, justification was not confined to marginal or radical circles and media, but appeared among mainstream producers of culture, and did not arouse any significant criticism or condemnation in the Arab public discourse, even from those who did not espouse it.[15]

It is bad when some people justify the murder of millions and shocking when the rest of the society takes no offence at this, thereby suggesting that denial or defense of the Holocaust is part of their cultural identity. The all-consuming, annihilatory hatred that we find here can be neither justified nor explained by the territorial conflict over Palestine. Nevertheless, the West refuses to take this hatred and the related Hitler-love seriously. Instead, still today "the totally interchangeable travelers' tales from Casablanca, Cairo, Damascus or Baghdad in which tourists identified as German are greeted with a 'Heil Hitler' are considered bizarre eccentricities."[16] Would an identical "Heil Hitler" be taken so lightly if encountered in Germany or France? Certainly not!

It borders on racism to apply a different standard to an Arab than a European. It not only means that one does not take them or their statements seriously but also renders one incapable of challenging them. But that is precisely what ought to happen. Not only *ought* the Arab world to adopt a clear anti-Nazi position in line with universal human rights. If it wishes to overcome stagnation and regression, it *must* do so.[17]

In Germany, the inclination to make excuses for Arab Hitler lovers and Holocaust deniers is not confined to tourists. Thus, the prominent German Islam expert Gudrun Krämer refuses to "interpret" Arab statements about the Holocaust "in the light of European experiences." For many Arabs and Palestinians, "the recognition of the Shoah equates to the recognition of the State of Israel, which presents a dilemma."[18] So, because Arabs cannot be expected to consider the foundation of Israel legitimate, one must show a degree of understanding for Holocaust denial. Her younger colleague René Wildangel goes further. For him, from the Arab point of view, Holocaust denial is almost a must. Wildangel writes, "the more insistently the Holocaust is used to justify the Israeli state's legitimacy, the less possible does it become for Arabs to accept its reality."[19]

It is correct to say that there is a connection between the recognition of the Holocaust and Israel's right to existence. One is indeed obliged to deny or justify the Holocaust if one wishes to deny Israel's right to exist and eliminate Jews as the evil of the world. Holocaust denial, liquidation of Israel and demonization of Jews – these are three sides of an ideological triangle that vanishes if one of the sides is removed. They have to be rejected or accepted as a whole. Krämer and Wildangel seem to find the denial of Israel's right to exist understandable. The logic of their argument therefore obliges them to find Holocaust denial understandable too.

Gilbert Achcar, a professor at the London School for Oriental and African Studies, finds other grounds for defending Arab Holocaust deniers.

> Are all forms of Holocaust denial the same? Should such denial, when it comes from oppressors, not be distinguished from denial in the mouths of the oppressed, as the racism of ruling whites is distinguished from that of subjugated blacks?[20]

Here, Achcar supplies Holocaust deniers, just as long as they belong to the "oppressed," with a moral free pass. What would be scandalous if others did it, is found acceptable in their case. He treats them as idiots who do not know what they are doing. When Arabs deny the Holocaust, he has stated in an interview, "It has nothing to do with any conviction. It's just a way of people venting their anger, venting their frustration, in the only means that they feel is available to them."[21] This is a kind of racism that feigns benevolence. British author Majid Mawaz has described it as the "racism of low expectations."[22]

This "racism of low expectations" is also virulent in Germany. It finds expression in the belief that Muslims living here cannot be expected to concern themselves with the Shoah. Thus, in an article in the *Jahrbuch für Antisemitismusforschung*

(Yearbook for Antisemitism Studies), Islam expert Jochen Müller calls for greater respect to be shown for "Arab" or "Muslim" perspectives in school classes:

> This also includes a revision of politics and history teaching: while in this country for example the Holocaust is presented as a civilizational break and the moment of birth of a new Europe, it cannot have this central meaning for migrants from the Arab-Muslim world. For them – and Arab scholars also say this – the colonial period and its consequences play a much greater role in their collective historical consciousness. In this situation we must reassess how a contemporary 'Holocaust education' should look when 70, 80 or 90% of students are of migrant background.[23]

Juliane Wetzel from the Center for Research on Antisemitism goes further. She believes that dwelling on the Holocaust might strengthen antisemitism among Muslims. While the antisemitic stereotypes found among young people with or without a migrant background are similar, the differences are, Wetzel claims,

> to be sought more in the motives. Migrants who feel themselves to be underdogs, who are excluded from the society … feel themselves to be treated differently to the Jewish minority. Not without influence is the presence of Holocaust memorializing in public discourse, which, among Muslims of migrant background, leaves behind the justified impression that the post-colonial history of persecution of their own family is being largely overlooked.[24]

The author does not explain in this text from 2009 what precisely she means by a "post-colonial history of persecution" in relation, for example, to German-Turks who form the majority of Muslims of migrant background in Germany, given that Turkey was never a colony. Nor does she cite any research to back up her contention that Muslims do not want to learn about or discuss the Holocaust. Perhaps she believes she is doing Muslims a favor by confining their education within an "Arab" or "Muslim" perspective. Underlying all this, however, is a refusal to treat them as mature citizens who as part of German society share responsibility for the common struggle against antisemitism.

The same "racism of low expectations" is also found in a study published in 2014 by the Center for Research on Antisemitism. "Immigrants from the states bordering on the Israeli-Palestinian conflict as well as from Turkey, which is also Muslim" are "less likely to be ready" to combat antisemitism. Students "from families with a migrant background" display a "migrant distance" from German history so that an emphasis on the Holocaust, in particular, "can be the starting point for racist exclusion when dealing with heterogeneous populations with different points of origin."[25]

Take note: whoever raises the Holocaust in mixed school classes is possibly acting in a "racist" manner. So please, no more efforts to integrate immigrants from the Middle East and Turkey at the historical–political level. Instead: perpetuation unto eternity of the "migrant distance."

I find the call that Arab and Turkish migrants should not be confronted with the reality of the Shoah bizarre. To heed it means extending the reach of the Arab world's pathological Hitler worship, Holocaust denial and antisemitism into Europe, rather than striving to combat it from here outward. Dealing with the Shoah is of central importance not only for native Germans but also for everyone – Muslim or non-Muslim – who has been born in or migrated to the country. Indeed, it is the necessary starting point for any pedagogy against antisemitism and the linchpin for challenging the other two components of the triangle – antisemitism and hatred of Israel.

There is not the slightest reason to believe that Muslim immigrants in Germany are uninterested in Hitler and the Shoah. In my 28 years, as a teacher of politics in a Hamburg technical college, I have never come across a single student from a Muslim background who was not interested in these matters. Any resistance to dealing with the Shoah in class has come from native Germans who have not wanted to hear about it because of the involvement of family members in the Nazi period or because they feel that bringing this topic up threatens their longing to be "proud of Germany." Such resistances play no role when it comes to students from Muslim backgrounds. On the contrary, as a rule they have shown a keen interest in everything to do with "Jews" – even if sometimes for dubious motives.

We observed above that after World War II, radical antisemitism gained a resonance in the Arab world that was found nowhere else. To resign oneself to this and "spare Arabs, the responsibility of Holocaust remembrance actually exposes the soft bigotry of our own low expectations," writes Robert Satloff.[26] Instead, we should do more.

Antisemitism in the Arab world should long since have been made an explicit theme in German foreign policy. With the coming of Arab migrants to Germany, it has now also become a domestic issue. The more is known about the Nazis' influence on the Middle East, the more we understand about Goebbels's instrumentalization of Islam, the more self-evident it should be that this partial symbiosis between Nazism and the Arab world should become not only part of the curriculum of German schools but also an important aspect of Shoah remembrance. Of course, as part of this German–Muslim "reckoning with the past," the stories of heroic Muslim rescuers of Jews would also be rediscovered and due tribute paid to the many Arab Palestinians who fought on the Allied side.[27]

However, it is not only the racism of low expectations that hinders an active approach to German–Muslim history and antisemitism but also a dishonest attitude to Islam.

Active Ignorance

I don't often turn on the TV, but I did not want to miss the on-screen duel between Chancellor Angela Merkel and her main opponent Martin Schulz that took place on 3 September 2017, shortly before the German federal elections. Twenty minutes after the start of the debate, things got lively.

"In the name of Islam," declared the Chancellor,

> dramatic terrorist attacks are being committed at the present time. How can one invoke the religion in this way is something that many people do not understand at all and so I have made it clear that the spiritual leaders of Islam must say very much more strongly still that this has nothing to do with Islam.[28]

A contrary view was put by Yemeni historian Arwa al-Khattabi in answer to the question of whether the Islamic State in Iraq and Syria (ISIS) represents Islam:

> Yes. This is the truth, and we must discuss this in full honesty and fairness. We must confront our [problems]. ISIS has come to implement Islam as it is, by the book. It has not come up with anything of its own. It evoked the religious texts exactly as they are. It did not distort, change, or replace anything on its own. … It is very unfortunate that we want to deny this. … We have a huge problem and we must recognize this before [we do] anything else, and we must take responsibility for it before we blame others for what is happening in the world. We cannot shut our eyes and deny this.[29]

Al-Khattabi forcefully draws attention to the fact that Islamists are able to refer to Koranic commandments to justify their atrocities. Thus, even some of ISIS's worst atrocities can be justified on the basis of Sura 47, Verse 4 – "when you meet the unbelievers … strike off their heads and, when you have laid them low, bind your captives firmly."[30]

This state of affairs has also been implicitly recognized by Cairo's Al-Azhar University. In December 2014, it organized an international anti-terrorism conference. The demand to excommunicate ISIS as "unislamic" hung in the air. Al-Azhar, the world's most prestigious Sunni Muslim educational institution, did indeed criticize ISIS's terrorism and designate it as a deviation from the correct Islamic path. However, it shrunk back from condemning the Islamic State as "unislamic."[31]

Not so the German Chancellor. Instead of supporting those Muslims such as Al-Khattabi who have had the courage to speak out about the problematic side of Islam, she stabbed them in the back. She denied that Islamist terrorists refer to Koranic verses and even called on Islamic spiritual leaders also to deny this constantly reconfirmed link "more strongly still" than previously. "One must see what one sees," writes Georges Bensoussan. "In fact, however, the eye only sees what the mind is ready to understand."[32] This seems to be the motto of the Chancellor's office.

Meanwhile, the opposition candidate from the Social Democratic Party, Martin Schulz, was not to be outdone by Merkel in the naivety stakes. "Islam is a religious community like any other," he declared in front of an audience of millions. "Don't let's be pushed into allowing the five or three percent of fanatical Islamic fundamentalists to be used to discredit or slander Islam in this country."[33] If only it were so! As long as this religion is interpreted by Islamic organizations in the conservative way that it currently seems to be in Germany, it is not a "religion like any other" but a faith movement that differs from others through its absoluteness, its alleged superiority and its promotion of a definite social model.

Absoluteness: Only Islam makes the claim that every word of the Koran comes directly from Allah and was whispered into the Prophet Muhammad's ear by the Archangel Gabriel. As a result, for conservative believers, the Koran is considered the absolute truth and measure of all behavior. Following the logic of this doctrine, the space and time-bound Koranic account of Muhammad's relations with Medina's Jews is torn out of its historical context and turned into the only true and eternally valid revelation about Jews as a whole.

Superiority: According to the Koran, Noah, Abraham, Jesus and all the other prophets were already Muslims. From the very beginning, Allah is deemed to be in possession of the "Eternal Book" (43/4), the Koran. Following the faulty interpretations of this book by Jews and Christians, it fell to Muhammad to succeed in promulgating it correctly. Thus, traditional Islam bases itself on a historical construction that elevates it over Judaism and Christianity.

Social model: Unlike Christ, Muhammad did not suffer martyrdom but gained power. He was Head of State, commanded armies, raised taxes, administered justice and promulgated laws. While Christianity distinguishes between state and faith, in canonical Islam the two coincide. Traditional Islam views itself, therefore, not only as a religion but also as an all-encompassing political and social system. Conservative Muslims are unshakably convinced that the course of history will finally prove the superiority of this system: "In essence Islamic history is the fulfilment, under divine guidance, of the purpose of human history."[34]

That another understanding of Islam is possible is shown by the Turkey and Iran of the first half of the last century. Today, however, the hurdles standing in the way of the rollback of Islamic antisemitism are high. Abdel-Hakim Ourghi, a scholar of Islam who teaches in the German city of Freiburg, has explained how deeply the hatred of Jews is rooted in this religion:

If they perform daily prayers, Muslims recite seventeen times each day the first sura of the Koran, 'The Exordium', praying thus: "Guide us to the straight path, The path of those whom You have favored, Not of those who have incurred Your wrath, Nor of those who have gone astray" (6:7). All schools of Koranic exegesis agree that the second part of the prayer refers to the Jews and Christians.[35]

Already from this ritual, it becomes clear that, unless Islam is confronted by Enlightenment thinking, the anti-Jewish resentment contained in it will find expression. A conscious effort is needed to remain unmoved by this suggestive influence, let alone positively oppose it.

Martin Schulz's statement that only some "five percent or three percent" of fanatical Islamists are the problem is also misleading. It is true that only a handful of the five million people considered to be Muslims in Germany are potential terrorists or Islamist cadre. Thus, in 2018, in Germany a mere 2,240 persons – or 0.05% of the five million – were classified as "Islamist-terrorist personnel." In 2019, in Germany there were an estimated 11,500 Salafists, a share of 0.23%.[36] However, this minority emanates an unhealthy influence. "The main problem of radical Islam," writes Jehuda Bauer, "is that their ideas have penetrated into everyday Islam."[37] The German security services share this view.

"The ideas of the Salafists [have] by now seeped into the everyday culture of many Muslims," explains Marwan Abou-Taam, who works as an analyst for the State Criminal Police Office of Rhineland-Palatinate.[38] Of special concern is the growing influence of the Muslim Brotherhood, which

> acts with ever increasing confidence in Germany. The authorities believe that a whole series of new associations and mosque communities belong to the network of this movement that arose in 1928 in Egypt. … Internal security officers have for a long time feared that the Muslim Brotherhood would ultimately profit from the fact that, after the defeat of the IS, the faithful no longer see the armed struggle as viable, while conservative Islam on the other hand advances through intensifying the cultural struggle.[39]

The greater these advances are, the smaller the chances of defeating Islamic antisemitism. So long as the political class refuses to see what is in front of its eyes, and so long as Islam is not held responsible for Islamism because the latter allegedly has nothing to do with the former, Islam will continue to be "the best defense of Islamism."[40]

An estimated 25.7 million real or alleged Muslims lived in Europe in 2016 – about 4.9% of the total population. If immigration continues as predicted (medium scenario), the proportion in 2050 will be 11.2%.[41] The answer to the question of the future of Islam is, at least for Europe, a matter of great importance.

We must therefore go beyond observing that different interpretations of Koranic verses are possible. "If my liberal interpretation is right, then that of Abu Bakr al-Bagdadi, the Caliph of IS, can also be true," comments the Turkish scholar of Islam, Ednan Aslan.

> We Muslims today dissociate ourselves from the Islamic State. But if we don't also dissociate ourselves from the related theology, we lack credibility. We Muslim theologians must finally find the courage to say that some interpretations of Islam are wrong. Unacceptable. But we do not do this.[42]

Abdel-Hakim Ourghi agrees.

> It is not enough to understand the revelation of the Koran in its historical situation of origin. In addition to this a method must be developed that, on the basis of critical reflection, frees Islam from the power of the contested Koranic verses.[43]

"Freeing Islam from the power of contested Koranic verses" – such a discussion has not even begun in Germany. So far the buds of a liberal Islam have been nipped by the conservative Muslim organizations that have the ear of the political establishment. Today, it is these organizations that control the selection, education and appointment of Imams (mosque leaders) in Germany.

There are between 2,000 and 2,500 such Imams in Germany. About 80%–90% of them come from abroad. They have been trained, for example, in Turkey or Iran, get their funding from those countries, know little about German society and speak no German. This strong external influence is "often connected to a conservative and sometimes reactionary and anti-democratic interpretation of the faith," we read in a study by the Konrad Adenauer Foundation. "Moreover, there is mounting evidence of propagandistic activities by Salafist preachers and recruiters in Germany."[44]

In France, home to both the largest Muslim (eight million) and the largest Jewish (460,000) populations in Europe, matters are somewhat further forward. In that country, Imams must accept Republican values, disclose their sources of financing and demonstrate that they are familiar with the country and speak French.[45] Moreover, in France, where radical Muslims have murdered 11 Jews in recent years, there has at least been a public discussion about Islamic antisemitism. Thus, on 21 April 2018, the *Le Parisien* newspaper published a *Manifeste contre le nouvel antisémitisme* (Manifesto against the New Antisemitism). The Manifesto called on Islamic authorities in France to declare specific Koranic verses that call for the murder of Jews, Christians and unbelievers obsolete "so that no Muslim can appeal to a holy text to justify a crime."

As a precedent, the signatories cited the Second Vatican Council that reinterpreted the relationship between Jews and Catholic Christians without changing the Biblical wording. Among the signatories were former President Nicolas Sarkozy, former Socialist Prime Minister Manuel Valls, and other prominent politicians as well as artists (e.g. Charles Aznavour, Gérard Depardieu, Francoise Hardy), writers (e.g. Elisabeth Badinter, Pascal Bruckner, Boualem Sansal, Pierre-André Taguieff) and Muslims such as Hassen Chalghoumi, Imam of the Drancy Mosque in Paris, and the Palestinian blogger Waleed al-Husseini.[46]

The initiative met with little immediate success: Al-Azhar reacted indignantly, deeming the Manifesto "insolent,"[47] while Turkish President Recep Tayyip Erdogan declared the signatories to be "disgusting" and compared them to Islamic State.[48] Within France itself, the appeal was criticized by leading representatives of Islam.[49] In this respect, the fact that it had been initiated by non-Muslims may well have played a role.

In Britain, Fiyaz Mughal, Director of the inter-religious Faith Matters association, founded the group Muslims Against Antisemitism (MAAS), which went public in May 2018 with whole-page adverts in three British daily papers. Under the headline, "We Muslims have one word for Jews. Schalom," the text called on British Muslims to stand up against antisemitism.

According to Mughal, "all modern editions of the Koran [must] have commentaries that historically contextualize the texts [about the Jews]." If this is not done, the harm to Islam will be immense, because organizations such as Islamic State will use this silence for their own ends.[50]

It is true that modernizing changes in Islam can, at the end of the day, only be brought about by Muslims themselves and that "radical Islam can only be combated by non- and anti-radical pious Muslims," as Jehuda Bauer puts it.[51] It is nonetheless necessary for the non-Muslim society to participate and take sides in this intra-Muslim controversy. Women's rights activist Seyran Ates, for example, is correct and deserves support when she demands a "change of direction" in German policy towards Islam and lambasts "ignorance regarding the implications of the advance of anti-Enlightenment ideas."[52]

However, it is precisely in the Arab–Muslim world, where Adolf Hitler still enjoys a good reputation among so many, that there are encouraging signs of change. These relate to the core issue in the region – the attitude of Arabs to Israel and the Jews. The realization is gradually dawning among moderate Arab nationalists that the uncompromising approach pioneered by Amin el-Husseini was a mistake and has failed to achieve anything. The more energetically the Arab side has tried to destroy Israel, the stronger it has become. It is today apparent that the erstwhile Jewish "homeland" has become one of the region's strongest and most stable states. In this context, individual Arab politicians and writers are increasingly ready to recognize the truth about, and so too the failure of, the militant all-or-nothing strategy and seek the reasons for this failure no longer solely in Israel or "imperialism," but on their own side. Regrettably, these brave politicians and intellectuals get no coverage in the German language media even though they could exert an influence on, and perhaps even serve as models for, Muslims in Germany. We will therefore quote some of these voices.

Sami Abdullatif Al-Nesf, former Information Minister of Kuwait:

> In 1917, just as there were extremists, there were also wise, reasonable people. One of them was [Lebanese politician] Shakib Arslan. He said: When I visited the [Jewish] settlements, I realized that they were like an advanced locomotive, which could pull us out of our ignorance, poverty, and so on. ... There were Palestinians who said the same thing. Some Palestinians said: [The Jews] have been here since 1700–1800 and throughout history. The Israelites and the Land of Israel are mentioned in the Koran.... Let's reach understandings, those people said. Extremists like Amin Al-Husseini, Arafat, Ahmad Shukeiri, and all the people who held the banner of extremism, have harmed the Palestinian cause and the cause of the Arabs.

As an example, Al-Nesf cites the 1937 Peel Plan. It had offered the Palestinians 80% of the territory and the Jews a mere 20%. "The loud and empty slogans by Mufti Amin Al-Husseini thwarted the [1937] two-state plan. … Historically speaking, the Palestinian cause has lost time and again because of the extremists, not because of the moderates."[53]

Mish'al Al-Sudairy, a Saudi author who writes for the daily newspaper *Al-Sharq Al-Awsat*:

> We must admit frankly that the ones who damaged the [Palestinian] cause more than anyone else were some Palestinian leaders and some Arab leaders. … Amin Al-Husseini was the one who tried to combine the ideology of the Muslim Brotherhood and the Nazi ideology. … According to the popular saying, "he who wants everything loses everything", ultimately, nothing came of the boastful slogans.[54]

Nabil 'Amr, Fatah member and former minister in the Palestinian National Authority:

> Seven decades after the Arabs and Palestinians rejected the [1947] Partition Plan, the question is whether they were right or wrong in doing so. … Those who believe in agreements and in the principle of "saving what can be saved" consider this a bitter mistake that led to losses and no gain. … The best proof that the opponents [of the Partition Plan] were wrong is that, today, [the Palestinians] are demanding less than a quarter [of the territory] that they rejected at the time.[55]

Zakariya Al-Muharrami, Omani intellectual:

> The Jews are among the original inhabitants of this region. They lived in this region and there are no problems between us and them. Our religion does not prohibit us from opening up to the Jews or from interacting with them. The Israeli-Palestinian problem is not a religious one, but a problem of justice.[56]

Anwar Gargash, Foreign Minister of the United Arab Emirates: "Many many years ago, when there was an Arab decision not to have contact with Israel, that was a very, very wrong decision, looking back."[57]

> Abdulhameed Hakkem, Director of the Middle East Center for Strategic and Legal Studies in Jeddah: The Arab mentality must be liberated from the Nasserist heritage, and from the heritage of political Islam – both Sunni and Shiite – which, for purely political reasons, have sown the seed of the culture of hatred towards the Jews, and of denial of their historic rights in the region.[58]

It is not possible to overestimate the courage of these people. They have been fiercely attacked by protagonists of Islamic antisemitism such as Yemeni politician Tahir An'am:

> The hatred of the Jews comes from the Koran. The Koran teaches us in many verses... More than 40 or 50 Koranic verses warn us against the Jews, their evil and their malice, and state that they are the enemies of Allah.[59]

The fact that significant Arabic opinion leaders are beginning to turn away from the hate discourse against Israel that has dominated Arab life for some 80 years gives us hope that the vicious circle of antisemitism and Middle East crisis may eventually be broken. To the murderous fantasies of jihad, they are opposing a pragmatic alternative that promotes normal international relations with Israel instead of hatred of Jews. This development, fragile though it be, once again makes it clear that Muslims are not doomed to adhere to a literal interpretation of the Koran that plays into the hands of forces like ISIS. The fact that the currently dominant forces in Saudi Arabia, the birth place of Islam, are now attempting to normalize relations with Israel proves that it is not the religion as such that inevitably blocks such normalization but its antisemitic and Islamist interpretation.

How to Combat Islamic Antisemitism?

But back to Europe, where there is little sign of any positive developments within Islam. Antisemitism researcher Günther Jikeli interviewed 117 young Muslims in London, Paris and Berlin. In the process, he encountered several patterns of antisemitism, including conceptions in which fragments of a – sometimes rather vaguely – Koran-related Jew-hatred were combined with clichés of European anti-semitism.[60] Some excerpts from Jikeli's interviews are as follows:

"Generally-speaking Muslims of course have a problem with the Jews," says 25-year-old Ümit from Berlin, "because they have obviously been cursed by God." Twenty-three-year-old Agantuk from London is more specific. "It is written in the Koran and has been shown that now a Holy War is coming. The [Jews] want to kill all the Muslims." Khalil from Paris (20) affirms that "In Israel the Jews are waging war on the Muslims. ... So we see that they [the Jews] want to kill all Muslims." Sixteen-year-old Beyar from Berlin is not altogether clear: "Well, there were also Jews earlier ... War with the Muslims and so on. Because of this it is now forbidden by Islam to be friends with Jews." Bilal from Paris (15) claims that "all Muslims hate the Jews because the Jews have killed Muslims," while 21-year-old Bashkar from London is indignant that "they [the Jews] are trying to say that Al-Aqsa, one of Islam's main mosques, belongs to them." He believes that Jews wish to take over "the whole Middle East, all the main Islamic centers."[61]

It must be emphasized that Jikeli's survey is not representative and that some of his interviewees showed no sign of antisemitic thinking or consciously distanced themselves from Jew-hatred. Most of those interviewed also reported experiences of discrimination and prejudice against their own ethnic or religious community. Some felt themselves discriminated against on the jobs market, others complained about racially motivated police checks and most mentioned getting hostile looks when they were outside their neighborhoods. However, no relationship between the scale of perceived discrimination and the level of Jew-hatred was found. Jileki concludes: "experiences of discrimination by the ... majority society ... are decisive neither for the adoption or rejection of antisemitic ideas."[62]

But if discrimination is not the key, what might be the reason for the presence of antisemitic ideas? In the search for an answer, I came across a remark by the Jewish art historian, Ernst Gombrich (1909–2001), who analyzed Nazi broadcasting while working for the BBC during World War II. Gombrich wondered why Nazi propaganda, despite its obvious absurdity, was still effective. His answer makes a point that is still relevant today.

> What is characteristic of Nazi propaganda is less the lie than the imposition of a paranoiac pattern on world events. ... Paranoia ... is the pathological magnification of a reaction to which we are unfortunately only too prone, because it is rooted in the given contrast between me and them. It is they who thwart me and do me down. Every frustration may produce such irrational reactions in all of us. If we can also laugh at our fantasies this is due, I believe, to our knowledge that others would laugh at us. But remove this safeguard, forbid any expression of doubt in the paranoiac myth [and] ... it becomes self-confirming. Once you are entrapped in this illusionary universe it will become reality ... When you have been caught in this truly vicious circle there is really no escape.[63]

Gombrich is talking here about the paranoid framework of the Third Reich's Jewish policy. His remarks can, however, also be applied to the echo chamber of Islamic antisemitism. The escape route he suggests is the capacity to laugh at irrational myths. If there are people ready to openly mock ridiculous claims such as that Jews wish to destroy Islam, the antisemite's cause is in the long run doomed to failure. If, on the other hand, no one says anything, the antisemite's fantasy is validated. If this nonsense is constantly reiterated by family, friends, the TV and the Internet, then there is no longer any way out of the vicious circle that constantly reproduces and reinforces the paranoid myth.

It is a cogent argument. Laughter is foreign to Muslim zealots. When Khomeini, the leader of Iran's Islamic Revolution, returned to Iran in 1979, one of his first decrees was a ban on the publication of photos that showed him laughing or looking happy. "All this is utterly serious and no jest, for those who are fighters do not jest," asserts article 19 of the Hamas Charter.[64]

It is clear that peer groups offer especially fertile soil for instilling anti-Jewish ideas as a kind of common sense. Such ideas have "an especially strong influence among friends," states Jikeli, "where they are the norm or where the social hierarchy is upheld by the use of antisemitic language, such as the derogatory labelling of individuals as 'Jewish' inside groups of young people."[65] The cognitive scientist Monika Schwarz-Friesel affirms that "the human mind quickly constructs thought and classificatory channels and then resorts in preference to known and fixed schemata in which experiences are automatically classified. ... Moreover, the human cognitive apparatus believes above all what it wants to believe."[66]

Certain factors foster fixed antisemitic schemata. Among them are segregation, essentialism and a lack of democracy.

Segregation: Islamic antisemitism thrives above all where European Muslims live in parallel societies. So long as people stay among their own kind in mosques, neighborhoods, social circles and linguistic communities where conservative interpretations of Islam dominate, the chances of "doubt about the paranoid myth" are even slimmer than otherwise. One of the reasons for this ghetto-building is the feeling of being excluded, discriminated against and perceived as "other" by the majority society. At the same time the segregation of Muslims and the prevention of their integration is a deliberate policy goal of the Muslim Brotherhood and other conservative Islamic organizations.[67]

Essentialism: Indiscriminate references to *the* Muslims or *the* Arabs characterize the delusion of a general and hereditary enmity against *the* Jews. "In any case, we, the Arabs, never get along with them [the Jews]," explained 17-year-old Hafid from Paris to his interviewer.[68] But who are "the Arabs" or "the Muslims"? That they do not and cannot exist was once again made clear in June 2019. That was the month in which Saudi journalist Sukina Al-Meshekhis asked on Twitter: "Do you support Gulf countries cultivating good relations with Israel and treating it as [just another] country in the Middle East?" Of the 5,300 answers, 33% were positive, 47% negative and 20% neutral.[69] So are the 47% or the 33% "the Arabs"? Regrettably, diversity of opinion in the Arab world is seldom acknowledged. While the media are keen to report on the manifold views of Jews in relation to Israel, they present the "Arab world" as a single anti-Israeli bloc. This is a distortion of reality that fosters essentialization and so too exclusion.

Freedom of expression and democracy: In his argument, Gombrich identifies a connection between antisemitism and political oppression. So in a country like the USA, where freedom of expression is politically and culturally secured, jokes are made about Donald Trump. This is not only to do with the character of Trump but also and above all to do with the fact that it is allowed. For this very reason, mass antisemitism has less of a chance in the USA. In, for example, Turkey the situation is different. Anyone who lets drop a critical word about President Recep Tayyip Erdogan has one foot in jail. Where freedom of expression is curtailed, the capacity for self-awareness that Gombrich calls for is eliminated.

Europe is a special case. Here freedom of expression is unrestricted when it comes to criticism of government actions. When it comes to Islam, however, it is a different matter. In January 2015, Islamists killed five prominent cartoonists and almost the entire editorial team of the magazine *Charlie Hebdo* in Paris. In doing so, they destroyed a group of courageous people who formed a kind of vanguard of freedom of expression for Europe. This attack on the freedom to laugh and to think has practical effects.

Thus, in Germany, Muslims who want to reform Islam can publish books. However, they are unable to go out in public without police protection. This restriction of freedom of movement – and so also expression – applies, for example, to Seyran Ates, founder of the liberal Ibn-Rushd-Goethe Mosque in Berlin. Other cases are those of Hamed Abdel-Samad and Ahmad Mansour, two advocates of a modern Islam; Mouhanad Khorchide, Professor at the University of Münster's Center for Islamic Theology; and the Freiburg-based researcher of Islam Abdel-Hakim Ourghi.[70]

It is disgraceful and wrong that the majority society accepts this state of affairs. The distancing of the political left from critics of Islam is of special importance. "The progressive thinking intellectuals are more scared of Islamophobia than of Islamism," complains the American philosopher, Michael Walzer.[71] As long as calls for the murder of liberal Muslims are accepted without demur and not punished with anything remotely like the severity meted out to those engaging in similar incitement against politicians, the struggle against Islamic antisemitism, which in the last analysis can only be waged by Muslims, is undermined.

In particular, liberal dissidents in the Arab world, where their lives are in constant danger, need greater protection and attention. TV journalist Samuel Schirmbeck has identified over 60 cases of freedom seekers who "have been killed by Islamic State or murdered by religious fanatics because they 'caused dissension' or 'weakened the faith.'"[72]

But let us return to Ernst Gombrich and his proposal to puncture the "delusional universe" of antisemitism through open disagreement and reflection. One can relate this imperative to both the microcosm of education and the macrocosm of official foreign policy. Let us look first at the situation in the schools and focus on the use of the word "Jew" as an insult.

When a teacher overhears this insult and does not react, the pupils will "feel more or less compelled to accept antisemitic language or feel themselves excluded since calling someone a 'Jew' has the group-dynamic function of exclusion."[73] The website *stopantisemitismus.de*, which monitors anti-Jewish abuse in everyday life in Germany and advises on how to respond to it, makes the same point. "Using 'Jew' as a term of abuse causes harm," they say,

> even when the user is not doing so consciously. Even when no Jew is present! Even unintentional and unconscious speech acts can cause antisemitism to spread. Thoughtless remarks of this kind help shape social consciousness, since they give the word "Jew" a negative connotation and keep this connotation in circulation.

stopantisemitismus.de recommends:

> React, make it clear that a boundary is being crossed here! If you ignore words, the speakers and hearers of these words will probably use and spread their use again without hesitation. ... The most important thing is to display some kind of reaction.

But what should we do with people young or old who are not amenable to argument? For them the recommendation of Theodor W. Adorno from 1962 should apply that "the actually available means of power should be used without sentimentality ... to show them that the only thing that impresses them, namely real social authority, is on this occasion against them." And, Adorno reiterates, "antisemitic expressions must be countered very energetically, they must see that the person who opposes them is not afraid."[74] This too ought to be a guiding principle in schools, universities and other educational institutions, regardless of whether we are dealing with pupils of Muslim or non-Muslim background. Educators who are not in a position to implement it must be helped. In 2019, French President Emanuel Macron promised to set up a national response unit able to come to the help of teachers in Islamist-affected neighborhoods "within 24 hours" in cases of trouble in the classroom. "All headteachers have been instructed to report 'even the slightest problem' and not sweep anything under the rug. 'The school must once again play its full role as the bulwark against prejudice and hate,' Macron declared."[75]

Similarly, energetic steps would also be welcome in Germany. However, educational measures can only have a limited effect so long as the flood of Islamic antisemitism is not cut off at source: in Ankara, Tehran, Beirut or Gaza. Day in, day out TV stations based in these places pour antisemitism, incitement to murder and conspiracy theories into children's rooms and the living rooms of families living here. An example is Al-Aqsa TV, the station of the Sunni Hamas movement, which is notorious for its anti-Jewish broadcasts. In one such, a certain

> 'Uncle Hassan' summons little "Alloush" and the watching children to engage in resistance against the Jews and liberate Jerusalem. [...] In a report entitled "Holocaust in Palestine" Al-Aqsa claims that the Holocaust is a conspiracy of the Jews, who got rid of their old and sick people in this way.[76]

One can watch Al-Aqsa TV in Germany on Livestream, on the Internet or via NileSat, an Egyptian satellite operator.[77] No less influential is the Shiite Hezbollah movement's Al-Manar TV, which, according to the German government, "presents cleverly edited propaganda inciting hate against those of Jewish faith and the State of Israel," which "is consumed by many Muslim immigrants in the Federal Republic of Germany."[78]

In 2004, Al-Manar was banned by France's highest administrative court and removed from the French satellite Eutelsat. In 2009, it was also banned in Germany, but could still be viewed via Arab satellites such as NileSat and Arabsat. Al-Manar is now no longer available via these sources but can still be accessed in Germany on the Russian satellite Ekspress-AM08.[79] Al-Manar and Al-Aqsa perpetuate the "paranoid framework through which every world event is interpreted" referred to by Gombrich. However, neither statistical information about nor a counterstrategy to the use of these stations in Germany exists. Who can stop Russia from broadcasting Al-Manar? Such matters can only be dealt with at the level of governments, which have the necessary instruments of pressure at their disposal. In this respect, the struggle against Islamic antisemitism has a specific foreign policy dimension. German foreign policy must, therefore, focus as a priority on the current headquarters of Islamic antisemitism – Ankara and Tehran.

Ankara and Tehran

Only inadvertently did we learn in August 2016 about how the German government assesses the situation in Turkey under Recep Tayyip Erdogan. "Turkey," declared the Federal Interior Ministry in reply to a parliamentary question from the Left party, "has developed into an operating platform for Islamist groups in the Middle East." Erdogan and his ruling party *Adalet ve Kalkinma Partisi* (AKP) show "an ideological affinity with the Muslim Brotherhood," which finds expression in "many statements of solidarity and acts of support" for the Egyptian Muslim Brotherhood and Hamas. These statements, the truth of which no one doubts, are based on an assessment carried out by the Federal German Intelligence Service. They carry weight.

A member of the North Atlantic Treaty Organization (NATO) that operates at the same time as an Islamist base? A ruling party that is especially close to the antisemitic Hamas movement, which the European Union has placed on its list of terrorist organizations?

In summer 2016, however, it was not these questions that caused uproar but the fact the publication of this information was due to an internal government slip-pup. The report should never have been made public. The Foreign Office, at that time headed by Frank-Walter Steinmeier, was especially indignant. His ministry had not been "brought in" on the response to the parliamentary question, meaning that he had not been in a position to do a "clean tackle" to prevent the leak.[80] The really important question of what conclusions should be drawn from the assessment remained unasked.

This omission is a serious matter. The Islamization of Turkey had already begun back in 2002 with the AKP's first electoral victory. This gave "the Muslim press which is notorious for its antisemitic rhetoric a powerful boost in self-confidence and aggressiveness."[81] Since then Jew-hatred has grown ever stronger in Turkey. A survey conducted in 2004 by the American Pew Research Center revealed that 49% of the Turkish population held negative views about Jews. In 2006, the proportion had risen to 65% and by 2008 to 76%.[82]

This development has had an impact on the three million people in Germany of Turkish extraction. They have cable and satellite access to some 70 Turkish-language stations.[83] The new Turkish antisemitism is also conveyed via the Internet, by newspapers and books and by lurid films such as *Valley of the Wolf – Palestine*.[84]

According to a survey published in 2007, some 30% of the Turks in Germany – so around 900,000 people – exclusively or mostly watch Turkish TV and read Turkish newspapers. A further 30% get their information in equal measure from Turkish and German media, while 40% rely predominantly on German media.[85]

It is therefore no wonder that in the estimation of the German government's antisemitism commissioner, Felix Klein, the policies of the Turkish leadership "have led to a marked rise in antisemitism among Turkish immigrants and in particular among Erdogan's supporters."[86]

It is possible to calculate the number of these supporters. In November 2016, 574,000 Turks living in Germany participated in the Turkish parliamentary elections. Sixty percent – 343,000 people – voted for Erdogan.[87]

Their idol may superficially reject antisemitism, but he at the same time promotes it where he can. "The Jews ... print money wherever they happen to be," Erdogan declared in one statement. On another occasion, he has said that "there is a world press under Israeli control."[88] Israel is a special obsession. He has called Zionism "a crime against humanity" and Israel "a festering boil in the Middle East that spreads hate and enmity." He equates Israeli policy towards the Palestinians with Nazi policy towards the Jews and describes Israel as "a fascist and racist country where the spirit of Adolf Hitler has re-emerged."[89] Erdogan's supporters in Germany at least passively accept these hate messages.

A central theme of his agitation is religion-based and focused on Jerusalem. "We will not abandon Jerusalem, our first qiblah [Islamic direction of prayer], to invaders," he pledged in a speech in New York, setting the tone for others.[90] Thus, according to the Mufti of Istanbul, Hasan Kamil Yilmaz, the "liberation" of the Al-Aqsa Mosque must become the shared goal of all Muslims. Ali Erbas, President of Turkey's religious authority, Diyanet, was not far behind. He called on the Islamic *umma* to end the "barbaric occupation" of Jerusalem. "One seeks in vain in his [Erbas'] statements as in the whole Islamist scene for any recognition that Jerusalem might also have something to do with Jewish history," writes Joseph Croitoru in the *Frankfurter Allgemeine Zeitung*. Diyanet has its own TV station and website which "can be easily accessed in Germany via various electronic means."[91]

Of particular significance is the fact that the "ideological affinity" between the AKP and the Muslim Brotherhood seems to be growing over into a kind of symbiosis. Thus, in June 2019, one day after the sudden death of Mohammad Morsi, mourning ceremonies took place throughout Turkey. Morsi had been a leading member of the Brotherhood and President of Egypt between June 2012 and July 2013. At these events, during which both Erdogan and Diyanet President Ali Erbas made speeches, the crowd chanted not only the well-known battle cry of Islamic antisemitism – "Khaybar, Khaybar, Muhammad's army will soon return" – but also, and to my knowledge for the first time, the founding manifesto of the Egyptian Muslim Brotherhood: "Allah is our goal, the prophet our model, the Koran our constitution, the Jihad our path, and death for the sake of Allah the loftiest of our wishes." The fact that Diyanet covered the events on its YouTube channel underlines the significance of this step.[92]

In order to spread the word beyond Turkey, in January 2019, Diyanet in association with its German offshoot Ditib organized a conference with 100 participants. The event took place at the Central Mosque in Cologne with several Muslim Brotherhood representatives in attendance.

This "2nd Meeting of European Muslims" – only made public by Ditib after it was over – decided to establish a Secretariat "under the auspices of Turkey's Religious Affairs Directorate [Diyanet]"[93] and to organize further such gatherings. In his closing speech in Cologne, Erbas explicitly rejected the idea of a "German" or "European" Islam.[94] Instead, he advocated a shift towards a Muslim Brotherhood-style Islamism. This shift, which runs counter to the integration of Muslims and throws open the doors for Islamic antisemitism, would apply to the 900 religious mosques in the Ditib network, the largest in Germany. Ditib is controlled by the Turkish religious authority, Diyanet, which supports the Erdogan government and has sent almost 2,000 preachers to other countries, and half of them to Germany.

How did the German Foreign Office react to all this? It was indeed indignant that the teamwork between Islamism and the Turkish government had been exposed through a "slip-up." It made, however, no public protest against the promotion of antisemitism by the Turkish state or the latter's cooperation with the Muslim Brotherhood.

Turkey has only, in recent years, established itself as the new center of Sunni Islamism; Iran has been playing that role for Shiite Islamism since the Islamic Revolution of 1979. As we have seen, even in the 1960s that revolution's leader, Ayatollah Khomeini, had based his antisemitism on religious arguments.[95] He "Islamized" the Arab–Israeli conflict, describing the Jewish state as the "seed of corruption … whose destructive impulses threaten the whole Islamic world every day."[96] Through such language, he transformed the political conflict into a religious test of strength between Good and Evil. "Any relations with Israel and its agents … is forbidden by the religion and signifies enmity towards Islam."[97]

There is nothing self-evident about such hatred of the Jewish state in Iran. There are no disputes between Israel and Iran over territory or refugees. Before 1979, relations between the two countries were good, and there were lively economic relations, notably in the spheres of agriculture and water management. Historically, Iranians had been apt to show hostility towards Arabs, not Jews, with whom they had lived together for over 2,500 years. Nor do Tehran's constant proclamations of solidarity with the Arabs of Palestine explain the vehemence with which the Iranian regime strives for the destruction of Israel. Muslims are oppressed in many parts of the world without Tehran responding in this way. Where does the special hatred of the Iranian rulers for Israel come from? The key driver here remains the antisemitic fantasy. It is because "Jews" are in conflict with the Arabs and allegedly occupy Arab land that Tehran calls for action. And because Islam allegedly requires this jihad and prophesies the defeat of Jews, the rulers in Tehran are confident of victory.

The current Supreme Guide and Khomeini's successor, Ali Khamenei, maintains the former's approach. In his statements regarding Palestine, Khamenei inflates the significance of this small country immeasurably, in order to underline what for him is really at stake: "Today the issue of Palestine is the most fundamental issue of the world of Islam," he has declared. "The war over Palestine [is] a war over the existence of Islam." "The fate of the world of Islam and the fate of all Islamic countries depend on the fate of Palestine."[98] We are dealing once more with a "paranoid framework" at which no one is laughing.

Tehran's war for Palestine is characterized by the glorification of suicide bombings.[99] "We did not join the Revolutionary Guards in order to stay alive. We have come here to sacrifice our lives and to be torn to pieces, so that our religion remains," declares Ali Shirazi, Khamenei's representative to the Quds brigades.[100]

In an article in an Iranian specialist journal, political scientist Mahdi Mohammad Nia vividly explains the difference between the philosophy of a martyrdom-war and Western behavior:

> According to the Holy Koran, a martyr has a guaranteed place in Paradise. Martyrdom-seekers and Jihadists are not afraid of death at all in a battle or front. The fear factor is a serious dilemma in mundane and materialistic societies in which life is defined solely within the boundaries of the physical existence. They regard the happiness and well-being within the short span of life on earth. This culture is completely opposite to the cult of martyrdom. ... In this context defeat is not necessarily equated with failure. This emphasis on continuing the struggle against oppression and injustice (as an Islamic duty) rather than on achieving 'victory' is seen as producing a high tolerance of pain in Iran. The cult of martyrdom inherent in Shi'ism, specifically, the honor accorded those who give their life to defend the faith, may give Iran certain practical military advantages.[101]

According to Nia's analysis, Tehran's policy towards Israel is motivated not so much by a wish to bring "happiness and well-being" to the Palestinians but by the impulse to fulfill a religious duty through a religious war, in order, even in the event of defeat, to gain a place in paradise.

It is no accident that to this day Ali Khamenei continues to rely on religion in order to torpedo Arab attempts at a rapprochement with Israel. "Normalizing relations with Israel breaks with the Koran and Islamic faith," he stated in April 2019. "The Koran says, 'Be stern with the disbelievers.' Some Muslims forget that."[102]

Here we see how differing interpretations of the Koran can decide between war and peace. In Germany, however, we are far from any understanding of what "religious war" means. Here people prefer to perceive only those aspects of life in the Islamic Republic that correspond to their own idea of normality. As Bensoussan has said, "the eye only sees what the mind is ready to understand."[103]

Germany's government seems unwilling to take the religious dimension of the Iranian regime's policy and its antisemitism seriously. So, at the very time that Germany's parliament was verbally condemning the burning of Israeli flags on German soil, senior German Foreign Office officials were participating in the celebrations of the 40th anniversary of the Iranian revolutionary regime, which is forever burning Israeli flags.[104]

The Bundestag may have committed itself in words to "fighting antisemitism in all its forms" and "decisively oppose the BDS movement," but this has changed nothing when it comes to German pride in relations with a Tehran that not only boycotts Israel but desires to destroy it. "Let us work together to further strengthen our good relations," said the German Ambassador in Tehran at the same time as the Bundestag resolution was being adopted.[105]

This gulf between word and deed is equally apparent in the Government's treatment of Shiite organizations. Berlin may have noted that the Iranian regime's constitution "makes the worldwide 'export' of the Iranian revolution and so the Islamization of other countries on the Iranian model a goal of state policy," but the insight has remained without consequences. Just as Erdogan uses Ditib to assert his influence over the majority of Germany's Sunni Muslims, Khamenei uses the Islamische Zentrum in Hamburg (IZH) to promote his influence over Germany's Shiites. The financing of the IZH is assured by Khamenei's office, *Beyt-e rahbari*, which has a staff of thousands.

According to the German government, along with the Iranian embassy in Berlin, the IZH is

> The Islamic Republic's most important agency in Germany and one of its most important propaganda centers in Europe. With the aid of the IZH, the regime of the Islamic Republic of Iran attempts to influence Shiites of various nationalities and disseminate in Europe the basic social, political and religious values of the Islamic Revolution.[106]

Islamic antisemitism is one of these basic religious values. Thus, the IZH has published a translation of a speech by Ali Khamenei in which he calls on the Islamic world to "focus all our energy on the confrontation with the conspiracies of the Zionist regime and the acts it has committed against Holy Quds (Jerusalem) and the Al-Aqsa Mosque."[107]

In 2009, the IZH set up the *Islamische Gemeinschaft der schiitischen Gemeinden in Deutschland* (IGS – Islamic Association of Shiite Communities in Germany). The IZH plays a decisive role in financing the IGS and is personally represented on its management. Through this link, the Mullahs' regime is in a position to control and lead Germany's 150 or so Shiite communities.

Joachim Wagner relates an example of the extent of Tehran's reach: a Round Table was set up in Berlin's Neukölln district to discuss the matter of the Ramadan fast in Berlin's schools with three Shiite Mosque communities. The Shiite groups first had the draft agreement checked by the IZH, which then, however, had to ask religious scholars in Iran for approval. In the event, it was these Iranian scholars who torpedoed the proposed agreement.[108]

Despite the fact that the IGS is controlled by Iran, between 2016 and 2019, the Federal Government provided it with hundreds of thousands of euros in subsidies. In return, the IGS was supposed to assist with preventive measures against religiously motivated extremism.

Here, to put it mildly, the fox had been set to guard the henhouse. For the IGS differs from Ditib in one important respect. According to government information, "There are real indications that some of the [IGS'] branches have links with the IZH and/or the Islamist/terrorist *Hizb Allah* [Hezbollah] organization."[109]

The Lebanese Hezbollah ("Party of Allah") movement operates as Tehran's terrorist long arm in the global war against the Jews. Thus, in 1994, it was Hezbollah cadre who, at the behest of the Iranian leadership, blew up the Jewish Center in Buenos Aires, killing 85 people. Further attacks or attempted attacks were carried out in Thailand, Georgia and India. After five Israeli tourists were slain by Hezbollah killers in Bulgaria in 2012, the European Union placed the organization on its terrorism list. This measure, however, applied only to Hezbollah's "military wing"; its "political wing" remained legal. The distinction is totally artificial. As the organization's founding manifesto explains, "Our military apparatus is not separate from our social structures. Every one of us is an active combatant."[110]

Of these "active combatants," 950 lived in Germany in 2017; by 2018 their number had risen to 1,050, an increase of 10%.[111] Hezbollah uses Germany as a base for retreat, recuperation and recruitment. Here they have access to funds raised through collections or derived from organized crime, recruit to their organization and maintain active-service-ready units. According to the German internal security service, some 30 mosques and cultural centers serve as meeting points for local Hezbollah supporters.[112]

In 2019, it was not only Germany's Jewish Central Council that called on Berlin to ban Hezbollah in its entirety. Adding weight to their call, the governments of Israel and the USA as well as congressional representatives of both the main political parties in the USA appealed to Chancellor Angela Merkel. "The growth of support for Hezbollah will contribute to the rise of anti-Semitism in Europe, which has already resulted in deadly attacks against Jews," as the US congressional resolution put it.[113]

However, although not only all the Arab League states but also the USA, Canada, the Netherlands and Britain had by now designated Hezbollah as a whole as terrorist, Germany refrained from following suit. The terror group is "a relevant social factor ... in Lebanon," Nils Annen, a junior minister at the Foreign Office declared.[114] This is an absurd argument – unless Germany is also going to legalize the Taliban or Al-Qaeda, who are also quite influential in certain parts of the world.

Only in April 2020 did the German government at least partially yield to the pressure by imposing a "ban on activity" on Hezbollah in Germany.[115] So, for example, in the future the organization cannot display its flag in public. However, in order to destroy its organizational structure, a "ban on organization" would be required. In the absence of this, the structure has remained intact, as the government admitted in May 2021, a year after the imposition of the "ban on activity":
As before,

> the supporters of Hezbollah in Germany maintain organizational and ideological cohesion in local mosque associations that are primarily financed by donations. ... The individual associations continue to exist, since no ban on organization was imposed ... No property belonging to "Hizb Allah" in Germany has been confiscated.[116]

Germany's half-hearted policy towards Hezbollah continues to present a threat to Jews. There is a real danger of Jewish and Israeli organizations and individuals becoming the target of terrorist attacks should there be a confrontation between Hezbollah and Israel or a war between Israel and Iran. In 2019, Federal German Supreme Court prosecutors charged 11 Shiites with spying on Israeli and Jewish organizations,

> Allegedly [in preparation] for attacks on a 'Day X', according to sources in the security services. The [Iranian] Revolutionary Guards are preparing to respond to an Israeli attack on Iran's nuclear installations with attacks, sources say, in Germany and worldwide.[117]

All the 11 accused Shiites belonged to the Al-Quds Brigades, a special unit of the Iranian regime. In 2017, Berlin's Supreme Court sentenced one of its members, the Pakistani Haider Syed M., to over four years in jail. He had been spying on the President of the German-Israeli Association, Reinhold Robbe, with an eye to the very same "Day X." However, the German government wanted to avoid upsetting the Iranian rulers. "We wager on dialogue," explained Nils Annen in 2019, repeating a mantra we have heard for the past 40 years.

But what has all this dialogue achieved? Has it prevented a single execution of a gay man, because he is gay? Or a single test of missiles able to deliver nuclear warheads? Or a single terrorist attack by Hezbollah?

My short comments on the centers of contemporary Islamism show that the fight with Islamic antisemitism can be neither confined to the educational sphere nor limited to Germany. The sources of this ideology of hate lie in the Islamic world. It must be stopped at source.

EPILOGUE

Why do many Muslims hate Jews? Felix Klein, the German government's antisemitism commissioner, gives the following answer:

> Although antisemitic propaganda has roots going back centuries, its causes lie in the present: anyone who is able to live contentedly in, accepted by and integrated into the host society has little reason to join movements of the frustrated and embittered that call for the hatred of others.[118]

The cause-and-effect schema that Felix Klein uses here is attractive because it seems reasonable and promises a solution: If the causes of the frustration and bitterness disappear, then so will hatred of Jews. It would be nice if it were true. However, it does not work as an explanation of antisemitism, as a brief glance at history shows. Six million Jews were murdered without there being any such "reason" for it. When the mass murder program began in 1941, everything was going splendidly for the Germans: it was not a time of frustration or bitterness. And what about antisemitism in the German majority society today? It exists also among those who are "contented," as we all know.

Felix Klein applies his cause-and-effect schema to Germany. It is even more frequently applied to Israel. If the Palestinians could live "contentedly" and "accepted" in their own state, so it is said, they would have no further reason to hate Jews. This idea is endlessly repeated because it appears logical and reasonable: Israel the cause, Jew-hatred the effect. In reality, however, even if Israel disappeared, antisemitism would remain. The very existence of the 1937 pamphlet *Islam and Judaism*, which repeatedly refers to an essential hostility between the Jews and Islam, disproves the idea that Arabs would get along with Jews after a victory over Zionism. Even then, the pamphlet's Arab version explains, Allah will

DOI: 10.4324/9781003369110-7

"break their spines." Seventy-two years later, Muslim religious leader Mohammad Hussein Ya'kub came to the same conclusion. "If the Jews give us back Palestine, will we then begin to love them? Of course not," he declared on the Egyptian TV channel, Al-Rahma TV. "We will fight, conquer and destroy them until not a single Jew remains on Earth."[119]

Here Ya'kub expresses the quintessence of antisemitism. It is a pure, projective hatred, a delusion that takes possession of people, regardless of what Jews do or do not do and regardless of their actual material situation.

Ya'kub's idea of killing Jews "until not a single Jew remains on Earth" is not to be found in the Koran. A hundred years ago, no Muslim religious authority would have thought of saying such a thing. What we are dealing with here is a late echo of the Nazi propaganda. While we cannot precisely measure its impact on Arab thinking, three things are nonetheless clear: first, from 1937 onward, the Mufti's faction and their German friends pursued the goal of instilling Islamic antisemitism on a mass scale. Second, from 1945 to 1948, Arab leaders repeated many of the anti-Jewish and anti-Zionist slogans that had been disseminated by Radio Zeesen in the immediate past. Third, Jew-hatred is particularly prevalent in the regions that had once been subject to the waves of hate from Zeesen. In 2014, the Anti-Defamation League released a study showing that 75% of Muslims surveyed in the Middle East and North Africa agreed with antisemitic statements. In parts of Asia that Zeesen had never reached, the figure was 37%.[120] In post-1945 Bosnia–Herzegovina too, where the radio propaganda was not been available during the war, antisemitism has been far less prevalent than in the Middle East, where it had. Everything supports the view that the years of relentless propaganda made a huge contribution to the creation of a mass antisemitic consciousness. And not only that: the few years of exposure to Nazi ideology brought about a long-lasting change in the Arab world.

To this day the anti-Jewish passages in the Koran are incessantly repeated there, to this day the course of events is interpreted through the lens of the *Protocols of the Elders of Zion* and to this day the Palestinian Authority views every attempt to normalize relations with Israel as high treason.

It is, of course, true that fundamentalist positions have always existed in the Zionist camp too. They have, however, remained socially marginal, unlike in the Palestinian camp, where many of the Mufti's instructions remain effective. So in 2018 the current Mufti of Jerusalem refused a Muslim burial to a believer because he had allegedly sold a piece of land to Jews. In doing so, the Mufti referred explicitly to a fatwa issued by Amin el-Husseini in 1935.[121]

El-Husseini was never a mere tool of the Nazis. As an active partner of the Germans, he was extremely creative. Indeed, he played a decisive role in the formulation of Islamic antisemitism. It was he too who in 1938 pressurized Berlin into setting up its Arab-language broadcasting service. This shows that a substantial proportion of the Palestinian Arabs were involved in what happened between 1939 and 1945.

Today there is no conspicuous worship of the Mufti in the Palestinian territories. Only one school – the Amin Al-Husseini Elementary School in El-Bireh – is named after him. Nevertheless, the Palestinian leadership remains committed to his legacy. Yasser Arafat himself extolled the Mufti as a hero whose soldier he had been. His successor, Mahmoud Abbas, has referred to El-Husseini as a "hero" and "pioneer." In July 2019, Mahmoud al-Habbash, one of Abbas's closest advisers, posted a photo of the Mufti on his Facebook page and praised him as "leader and example."[122] So long as the Palestinian leadership adheres to this tradition, peace is hardly possible.

Once, however, we accept the fact that Nazi propaganda made a crucial contribution to antisemitism in the region, then our view of the Middle Eastern conflict has to change. Because then it is not Jewish settlement blocks but Palestinian ideological blocks that present the biggest obstacle to a peace settlement.

Then, the Jew-hatred in the region can no longer be dismissed as a kind of local color. Then, in the manifestations of antisemitism that are spreading from the Middle East into Europe, we look into the grisly face of our own European past.

Did everything in 1945 point inevitably to the 1948 war? Not at all. Another course was possible that would have spared both sides much pain and grief. Let us do a thought experiment: if the Egyptian government had banned the Muslim Brotherhood not in December 1948, but after the anti-Jewish outrages of 2 November 1945 three years previously, the Brotherhood's subsequent pro-Mufti campaigning might never have occurred. In that case, the Egyptian government might not have felt obliged to hoist El-Husseini back into the leadership of the Palestinians. Without the Mufti and the Brotherhood, it would scarcely have been possible to whip up the mass war hysteria against the UN partition plan. If Egypt, and so the Arab League, had stuck to their original reluctance to go to war, there might have been no flight or expulsion of the Palestinian Arabs. Then perhaps in 2023 we might have been able to celebrate the 75th anniversary of the establishment of a Palestinian state.

As we know, history took another path. Not because it was inevitable but because the Arab world including its elites allowed itself to become infected by Jew-hatred, instead of resisting it.

Accommodating Jew-hatred rather than opposing it: this pattern had already marked Allied behavior in World War II. Thus, the British government did all it could to avoid giving the impression of sympathizing with Jews. "Even the fact that the Nazis were persecuting Jews was to be kept as far as possible secret, as likely to awaken Arab sympathies for the former," remarked Arthur Koestler in 1949.[123] The USA adopted the same tactic, as we have seen. After 1945, the West maintained this approach. To this day it does not want to know too much – or even anything at all – about antisemitism in the Arab world. Thus, in 1990, the call by Herbert A. Strauss, the Jewish founding director of the Berlin Center for Research on Antisemitism (ZfA), for "the Arab-Islamic world [to] be included in antisemitism research" fell on deaf ears.[124] The Center continues to ignore the Hamas Charter, which has never been taken into account by German politicians.

Accommodating antisemitism rather than opposing it: history shows where that leads. Nevertheless, German foreign policy remains ambivalent precisely where a clear stand must be taken. Germany is always "for the security of Israel on the one hand and the legitimate rights of the Palestinians on the other," a junior Foreign Office Minister Niels Annen has stated. "Every attempt," he goes on, "to shift the balanced German and European position to the advantage of one side is essentially problematic."[125] Balance rather than commitment, ambivalence instead of clarity – it seems that Berlin too does not want to be seen to be on the side of the Jews. In a debate on banning Hezbollah, Roderich Kiesewetter, a leading member of the CDU/CSU group in the Bundestag, defended Germany's "more balanced position as mediator" that would be endangered by such a ban.[126] This reminds me of a well-known cartoon by A. F. Branco in which Benjamin Netanyahu and a grim-looking Hamas cadre sit facing one another. The latter has a paper with the words "Death to all Jews" in his hand. In the middle sits the "mediator", former US Secretary of State John Kerry, addressing Netanyahu with the words, "could you at least meet him half way?"[127]

"Balance" and "the mediator position" are not appropriate when it comes to antisemitism. This is especially true in the country that once initiated the Shoah and did its utmost to whip up Jew-hatred among Muslims too. The partiality called for by Thomas Mann in 1941 is needed once more today: "Who is not against evil, passionately and with their whole being against it, *is more or less in favor of it.*"[128]

Notes

1 Seth Arsenian, "Wartime Propaganda in the Middle East", *Middle East Journal*, Vol. II, No. 4, October 1948, 428.
2 Yossef Bodansky, *Islamic Anti-Semitism as a Political Instrument*, Houston, TX 1999, 20–25.
3 Albert Hourani, *Die Geschichte der arabischen Völker*, Frankfurt am Main 2000, 420.
4 Stefan Wild, "Zum Selbstverständnis palästinensisch-arabischer Nationalität", Helmut Mejcher (ed.), *Die Palästina-Frage 1917–1948. Historische Ursprünge und internationale Dimension eines Nationenkonflikts*, Paderborn 1993, 75–88, here 79.
5 Abd al-Fattah M. El-Awaisi, *The Muslim Brothers and the Palestine Question, 1928–1947*, London 1996, 69.
6 Johanna Pink, *Geschichte Ägyptens. Von der Spätantike bis zur Gegenwart*, München 2014, 182f.
7 Bernard Lewis, *The Emergence of Modern Turkey*, Oxford 1961, 273.
8 Stephan Grigat, "Zweierlei Vertreibungen, zweierlei Integration", Foreword to George Bensoussan, *Die Juden in der arabischen Welt. Die verbotene Frage*, Berlin-Leipzig 2019, 12.
9 Bensoussan, *Die Juden*, 31.
10 Boualem Sansal, "Avant-Propos" to Matthias Küntzel, *Jihad Et Haine Des Juifs. Le lien troublant entre islamisme et nazisme à la racine du terrorisme international*, Paris 2015, 5.
11 In 2021 Cohen had 409,000 Arab Twitter followers – see, Eyal Levi and Edy Cohen, "A One-Man Hasbara Machine with 409K Arab Twitter followers", *Jerusalem Post*, 4 February 2021.

12 *PMW*, "Iktiba High School Posts Picture Presenting Hitler as Admirable", 22 May 2012, https://palwatch.org/site/modules/print/preview.aspx?fi=655&doc_id=15438.

13 https://palwatch.org/main.aspx?fi=655.

14 Hannah Arendt, *Eichmann in Jerusalem*, Munich 1986, 81.

15 Meir Litvak and Esther Webman, *From Empathy to Denial. Arab Responses to the Holocaust*, London 2009, 195.

16 Klaus-Michael Mallmann and Martin Cüppers, *Halbmond und Hakenkreuz. Das Dritte Reich, die Araber und Palästina*, Darmstadt 2006, 253.

17 Robert Satloff, *Among the Righteous. Lost Stories from the Holocaust's Long Reach into Arab Lands*, New York 2006, 187.

18 Gudrun Krämer, "Antisemitism in the Muslim World. A Critical Review", *Welt des Islam*, Jg. 46, Nr. 3, 2006, 243–276, here 272f.

19 René Wildangel, *Zwischen Achse und Mandatsmacht. Palästina und der Nationalsozialismus*, Berlin 2007, 403.

20 Gilbert Achcar, *Die Araber und der Holocaust. Der arabisch-israelische Krieg der Geschichtsschreibungen*, Hamburg 2012, 262.

21 "Gilbert Achcar Interviewed by George Miller: Israel's Propaganda War - Blame the Grand Mufti", http://mrzine.monthlyreview.org/2010/achcar120510p.html.

22 Maajid Nawaz, "The British Left's Hypocritical Embrace of Islamism", *The Daily Beast*, 8 August 2015.

23 Jochen Müller, "Zwischen Abgrenzen und Anerkennen. Überlegungen zur pädagogischen Begegnung von antisemitischen Einstellungen bei deutschen Jugendlichen muslimischer/arabischer Herkunft", Wolfgang Benz (ed.), *Jahrbuch für Antisemitismusforschung 17*, Berlin 2008, 97–103, here 100f.

24 Juliane Wetzel, "Judenfeindschaft unter Muslimen in Europa", Wolfgang Benz (ed.), *Islamfeindschaft und ihr Kontext. Dokumentation der Konferenz "Feindbild Muslim – Feindbild Jude"*, Berlin 2009, 45–61, here 57–58.

25 Michael Kohlstruck and Peter Ullrich, "Antisemitismus als Problem und Symbol. Phänomene und Interventionen in Berlin", Vol. 52 of the series *Berliner Forum Gewaltprävention*, Berlin 2014, 27, 67, 21.

26 Satloff, *Righteous*, 5.

27 Maya Margit, "When Palestinian Arabs and Jews Fought the Nazis Side by Side", *Jerusalem Post*, 12 June 2019.

28 https://www.daserste.de/information/nachrichten-wetter/ard-sondersendung/videos/tv-duell-merkel-schulz-2017-das-erste-100.html, from 19:50.

29 *MEMRI*, "Yemeni Academic Dr. Arwa Al-Khattabi: ISIS Represents Islam; We Must Discuss This Honestly and Take Responsibility for What Is Happening in the World", Clip No. 7113, 16 March 2019.

30 Further examples can be found in Koranic verses 2/191, 4/89, 8/12 and 9/5. In reply, some like to quote verse 5/32: "whoever killed a human being ... should be looked upon as though he had killed all mankind." However, this reads in full: "*We laid it down for the Israelites* that whoever killed a human being, *except for murder or other wicked crimes*, should be looked upon as though he had killed all mankind." So only the Jews are explicitly subject to this injunction. Moreover, in the very next verse (5/33), we get the following Koranic order to the Muslims: "Those who make war against Allah and his Apostle and spread disorders in the land shall be put to death or crucified or have their hands and feet cut off on alternative sides, or be banished from the country."

31 "Egypt's Al-Azhar Stops Short of Declaring ISIS Apostates", *Asharq Al-Awsat*, 14 December 2014; *MEMRI*, "Al-Azhar: The Islamic State (ISIS) Is a Terrorist Organization, But It Must Not Be Accused of Heresy", Special Dispatch No. 5910, 21 December 2014.

32 Bensoussan, *Die Juden*, 162.

33 https://www.daserste.de/information/nachrichten-wetter/ard-sondersendung/videos/tv-duell-merkel-schulz-2017-das-erste-100.html, from 22:20.
34 Ronald L. Nettler, *Past Trials & Present Tribulations. A Muslim Fundamentalist's View of the Jews*, Oxford 1987, 14.
35 Abdel-Hakim Ourghi, *Reform des Islam. 40 Thesen*, Munich 2017, 214.
36 "Haldenwang warnt vor Gefahr durch Rückkehrer", *FAZ*, 15 April 2019; Alexander Haneke, "Die Saat der Salafisten", *FAZ*, 11 June 2019.
37 Jehuda Bauer, *Der Islamische Antisemitismus: Eine aktuelle Bedrohung*, Berlin 2018, 34.
38 Haneke, "Saat".
39 Ibid.
40 Samuel Schirmbeck, *Der islamische Kreuzzug und der ratlose Westen. Warum wir eine selbstbewusste Islamkritik brauchen*, Zurich 2017, 4.
41 Julian Staib, "Europa wird muslimischer. Studie entwirft Szenarien für Zuzug", *FAZ*, 30 November 2017.
42 Evelyn Finger, "Diese Gewalt wird gepredigt". Ein Gespräch mit dem türkischen Islamwissenschaftler Ednan Aslan", *ZEIT*, 17 December 2014, 58.
43 Ourghi, *Reform*, 216.
44 Andreas Jacobs and Janosch Lipowsky, "Imame – Made in Europe?", *Konrad Adenauer Stiftung, Analysen & Argumente*, No. 346, March 2019, 6f; Sebastian Ehm, "Imam-Ausbildung in Deutschland noch am Anfang", *zdf.de*, 28 March 2019.
45 Ibid.
46 http://www.leparisien.fr/societe/manifeste-contre-le-nouvel-antisemitisme-21-04-2018-7676787.php.
47 Y. Graff, "French Manifesto Calling to 'Declare Obsolete' Violent Quranic Verses Sparks Fury from Islamic Religious Establishment, Writers in Arab Media", *MEMRI, Inquiry & Analysis Series*, No. 1413, 20 August 2018, 1.
48 "Erdogan Denounces French Manifesto Calling for Removal of Qur'an Passages", *Iran Daily*, 9 May 2018, http://www.iran-daily.com/News/214776.html.
49 *AFP*, "French Muslim Community Blasts Anti-Semitism Letter as Attack on Islam", 24 April 2018; Karina Piser, "Muslims Recoil at a French Proposal to Change the Quran", *The Atlantic*, 3 May 2018.
50 Daniel Zylbersztajn, "Dem Hass die Stirn bieten", *Jüdische Allgemeine*, 7 June 2018, http://muslimsagainstantisemitism.org.
51 Bauer, *Antisemitismus*, 71.
52 Seyran Ates, "Keine Toleranz mit den Feinden der Toleranz!", 15 June 2019 at: https://www.facebook.com/SeyranAtesBerlin/posts/459432431509826.
53 *MEMRI*, "Fmr. Kuwaiti Minister Sami Al-Nesf Blasts Palestinian Strategy in Past Century: The Arabs Have Lost the Wars and Must Pay the Price", Clip No. 6693, 11 July 2018.
54 *MEMRI*, "Saudi Writer: The Arab League Summits Are Completely Pointless: Palestinian Leaders – First and Foremost Jerusalem Mufti Al-Husseini and PLO Leader Arafat – Damaged the Palestinian Cause the Most", Special Dispatch No. 7499, 31 May 2018.
55 *MEMRI*, "Arab Writers: The Arabs and Palestinians Must Stop Rejecting Every Proposed Settlement with Israel; Sadat Was Right in Making Peace", Special Dispatch No. 8007, 17 April 2019.
56 *MEMRI*, "Debate about Normalization of Ties between Gulf States and Israel: Iran Is the Real Enemy; Israel Should Be Part of the Anti-Iranian Alliance", Clip No. 6848, 9 November, 2018.
57 Edy Cohen, "A New Era in Israel-Gulf State Relations?", BESA Center Perspectives Paper No. 1, 22 April 2019, 148.
58 *MEMRI*, "Saudi Researcher Abdelhameed Hakeem: Jerusalem as Israeli Capital with Palestinian Management of Islamic Holy Places Is a Framework for Peace; Arabs Must Change Anti-Jewish Mentality", Clip No. 6324, 15 December 2017.

59 *MEMRI*, "Pro-Houthi Yemeni Politician Muhammad Tahir An'am: Our Hatred of the Jews Comes from the Quran", Clip No. 7034, 17 February 2019.

60 Günther Jikeli, *Antisemitismus und Diskriminierungswahrnehmungen junger Muslime in Europa*, Essen 2012, 117.

61 Ibid., 186–202. The names are pseudonyms.

62 Ibid., 317.

63 Ernst Gombrich, *Myth and Reality in German Wartime Broadcasts*, London 1970, 14, 21, 23.

64 Hamas Covenant, The Avalon Project at Yale Law School, at The Avalon Project: Hamas Covenant 1988 (yale.edu).

65 Jikeli, *Antisemitismus*, 317.

66 Monika Schwarz-Friesel, *Judenhass im Internet. Antisemitismus als kulturelle Konstante und kollektives Gefühl*, Berlin and Leipzig 2019, 154.

67 Mouhanad Khorchide, "Warum Sebastian Kurz kein Islamhasser ist", *Standard*, 6 October 2017.

68 Jikeli, *Antisemitismus*, 205.

69 *MEMRI*, "Saudi Twitter Poll Finds 33% in Favor of Relations with Israel, Versus 47% against", Special Dispatch No. 8125, 18 June 2019.

70 Evelyn Finger, "Tötet sie, bevor sie sich vermehren!", *ZEIT*, 27 September 2017.

71 Cited after Schirmbeck, *Kreuzzug*, 221.

72 Ibid., 231–244.

73 Jikeli, *Antisemitismus*, 252.

74 Theodor W. Adorno, "Zur Bekämpfung des Antisemitismus heute", *Das Argument*, Jg. 6, No. 29, 1964, 88–104, here 91, 102.

75 Michaela Wiegel, "Macron klagt über Islamismus", *FAZ*, 22 February 2019.

76 Alexander Ritzmann, "Fernsehsender verbreiten Antisemitismus", *Tagespiegel*, 7 July 2010.

77 http://en.satexpat.com/tv/palestine/; http://www.tunisvista.com/medias/al-aqsa-tv-live-direct-online-palestine.html.

78 Deutscher Bundestag, Antwort der Bundesregierung auf die Anfrage der […] Fraktion der FDP, Radikalisierungsgefahr in der Bundesrepublik Deutschland durch den islamistischen TV-Sender Al-Manar, DS 16/11544, 5 January 2009.

79 http://english.almanar.com.lb/frequencies; http://www.almanar.com.lb/live/.

80 Thorsten Jungholt, Marcel Leubecher and Uwe Müller, "Was das BND-Papier über die Regierung verrät", *Welt*, 17 August 2016.

81 Dilek Güven, "Der neue Antisemitismus – Kritik an Israel oder Antisemitismus? Das Beispiel Türkei", Wolfgang Benz (ed.), *Jahrbuch für Antisemitismusforschung* 23, Berlin 2014, 50–56, here 52.

82 Aycan Demirel, "Antisemitismus in türkischsprachigen Medien", Wolfgang Benz (ed.), *Jahrbuch für Antisemitismusforschung* 20, Berlin 2011, 213–239, here 215.

83 Ibid., 219.

84 Ibid., 219, 221; Matthias Küntzel, "Antisemitismus als Kinospaß. Warum der Innenminister das türkische Machwerk 'Tal der Wölfe – Palästina', indizieren muss", http://www.matthiaskuentzel.de/contents/antisemitismus-als-kinospass.

85 Karin Brettfeld and Peter Wetzels, *Muslime in Deutschland*, Hamburg 2007, 95.

86 "Zunehmende Judenfeindschaft bei türkischen Einwanderern", *Jüdische Allgemeine*, 19 January 2019.

87 M. Stein, "Fakten zu den in Deutschland lebenden Türken", *heuteplus (TV)*, 27 March 2017.

88 Güven, "Antisemitismus", 53.

89 "Scharfe Kritik an Erdogans Zionismus-Entgleisung", *Spiegel Online*, 1 March 2013; "Turkey's Radical Drift", *Wall Street Journal*, 4 June 2010; Raphael Ahren, "Erdogan Again Likens Israel to Nazi Germany, Says It Commits "Cultural Genocide", *ToI*, 15

December 2018; John Milner, "Netanyahu Responds to Erdogan's Remark That Israel Is a Racist Country Where the Spirit of Adolf Hitler has Re-emerged", *European Jewish Press*, 24 July 2018.

90 ToI staff, "Erdogan Vows to Defend Jerusalem from Israeli 'Invaders'", *ToI*, 24 September 2018.

91 Joseph Croitoru, "Istanbuls Ruf nach Saladin", *FAZ*, 28 August 2018.

92 *MEMRI*, "At Turkey Memorial Service for Mohamed Morsi, Crowd Chants Antisemitic Slogans; Turkish President Erdogan: Morsi Is a martyr; I Doubt His Death Was Natural", Special Dispatch No. 8143, 26 June 2019.

93 https://alqueriaderosales.org/2nd-european-muslims-meeting-in-cologne/.

94 Susanne Güsten and Andrea Dernbach, "Erdogan lässt in Köln eigene Islamkonferenz organisieren", *Tagesspiegel*, 9 January 2019.

95 I address only certain aspects of Islamic antisemitism in Iran here. More comprehensive analyses of the topic can be found on my homepage or in my book *Germany and Iran. From the Aryan Axis to the Nuclear Threshold*, Telos, New York 2014; see also my article, "Tehran's Efforts to Mobilize Antisemitism. The Global Impact", Alvin Rosenfeld (ed.), *Deciphering the New Antisemitism*, Bloomington, IN 2015, 508–532.

96 Institution zur Koordination und Publikation der Werke Imam Khomeinis, Abteilung Internationale Beziehungen, Das Palästinaproblem aus der Sicht Imam Khomeinis, Teheran 1996, 97.

97 Ibid.

98 Moasseseh Pajooheshi Farhangi Enqlab Eslami (ed.), *The Most Important Problem of the Islamic World. Selected Statements by Ayatollah Khamenei about Palestine*, no date, presumably Teheran 2012, 12f., 51, 101.

99 On the Shiite-Iranian origins of suicide-murder attacks, see Matthias Küntzel, "Die Menschheit muss Selbstmordattentate ächten", *Welt*, 24 March 2016, http://www.matthiaskuentzel.de/contents/die-menschheit-muss-selbstmordattentate-aechten.

100 *MEMRI*, "Khamenei's Representative in Qods Force: We Take Pride in Being Killed by Zionists; We Join the IRGC in Order to Sacrifice Our Lives", Clip No. 7189, 12 April 2019.

101 Mahdi Mohammad Nia, "Discourse and Identity in Iran's Foreign Policy", *Iranian Review of Foreign Affairs*, Vol. 3, No. 3, Fall 2012, 53.

102 ToI staff, "Normalizing Ties with 'Zionists' Is against Quran, Iranian Supreme Leader Says", *ToI*, 15 April 2019.

103 Bensoussan, *Die Juden*, 162.

104 Deutscher Bundestag, Antrag der Fraktionen CDU/CSU, SPD, FDP und BÜNDNIS 90/DIE GRÜNEN, Antisemitismus entschlossen bekämpfen, Drucksache 19/444, 16 January 2019, 2. –Benjamin Weinthal, "German Foreign Ministry Celebrates Iran's Islamic Revolution in Berlin", *Jerusalem Post*, 13 February 2019.

105 Deutscher Bundestag, Antrag der Fraktionen CDU/CSU, SPD, FPD und BÜNDNIS 90/DIE GRÜNEN, Der BDS-Bewegung entschlossen entgegentreten – Antisemitismus bekämpfen, Drucksache 19/10191, 15 May 2019; Homepage of the German Embassy in Tehran: https://teheran.diplo.de/ir-de.

106 Antwort der Bundesregierung auf die Kleine Anfrage der Fraktion BÜNDNIS 90/DIE GRÜNEN, "Finanzierung der "Islamischen Gemeinschaft der schiitischen Gemeinden in Deutschland e.V." durch den Bund im Rahmen der Extremismusprävention", DS 19/545, 26 January 2019, 2, 3, 5.

107 Khamenei's speech at his meeting with participants in the international congress on Takfirism was published on 12 February 2014 on the IZH's website. http://www.izhamburg.de/index.aspx?pid=99&articleid=64122.

108 Joachim Wagner, "Imame in Deutschland. Erdogans langer Arm reicht bis Neukölln", *Welt*, 1 March 2018.

109 Antwort der Bundesregierung, DS 19/545.

110 Stephan Grigat, "Gesamte Hisbollah gehört auf Terrorliste", *Die Presse*, 10 April 2019.

111 Benjamin Weinthal, "German Parliament Rejects Ban of Hezbollah, Snubbing US and German Jews", *Jerusalem Post*, 7 June 2019.

112 Benjamin Weinthal, "30 German Mosques and Cultural Centers Tied to Hezbollah: Intel Report", *Fox News*, 11 July 2019.

113 Yossi Lempkowicz, "U.S. House of Representatives Bipartisan Group Urges German Chancellor Merkel to Label Hezbollah a Terror Group", *European Jewish Press*, 17 June 2019.

114 "Niels Annen über Hisbollah: "Wir setzen auf Dialog"", *Spiegel*, 9 March 2019.

115 Bekanntmachung eines Vereinsverbots gegen die Vereinigung Hizb Allah (deutsch: 'Partei Gottes') alias 'Hisbollah' alias 'Hezbollah alias 'Hizbullah' (bund.de).

116 Antwort der Bundesregierung auf die Kleine Anfrage der Fraktion Bündnis90/Die Grünen: Umsetzung und Konsequenzen des Hisbollah-Verbots in Deutschland, auf Drucksache 19/29678 des Deutschen Bundestages, 14 May 2021, 2, 4.

117 Frank Jansen, "Die Revolutionsgarden sind auch in Deutschland aktiv", *Tagesspiegel*, 10 April 2019.

118 Felix Klein, "Vorwort", Bauer, *Antisemitismus*, 1–10, here 4–5.

119 Bauer, *Antisemitismus*, 35.

120 ADL Global. *An Index of Anti-Semitism*, 30, https://global100.adl.org/.

121 *PMW*, "PA Arrests Palestinians for Selling Land to Israelis/Jews, Follows Mufti's Religious Prohibition", 21 September 2018; "Palestinian Shunned for Selling Land to Jews to Be Buried in Jewish Cemetery", *Jewish Telegraphic Agency*, 16 November 2018.

122 *PMW*, "Abbas' Advisor Praises Nazi Collaborator as 'Role Model – Former Mufti of Palestine Haj Amin Al-Husseini", *Bulletin*, 12 July 2019.

123 Arthur Koestler, *Promise and Fulfillment. Palestine 1917–1949*, New York 1949, 79.

124 Matthias Küntzel, "Islamischer Antisemitismus als Forschungsbereich. Über Versäumnisse der Antisemitismusforschung in Deutschland", Marc Grimm and Bodo Kahmann (eds.), *Antisemitismus im 21. Jahrhundert. Virulenz einer alten Feindschaft in Zeiten von Islamismus und Terror*, Berlin and Boston, MA 2018, 135–155, 137.

125 Matthias Gebauer, Ann-Katrin Müller, Sven Röbel, Raniah Salloum, Christoph Schult and Christoph Sydow, "Gezielte Kampagne", *Spiegel*, 29/2019, 13 July 2019, 47.

126 Deutscher Bundestag, 19. Wahlperiode, 104. Sitzung, 6. Juni 2019, 12703.

127 https://legalinsurrection.com/2014/12/a-f-brancos-2014-legal-insurrection-cartoons/.

128 Thomas Mann, *Briefe 1937–1947*, Frankfurt/M. 1963, 176. Emphasis in the original.

DOCUMENT ISLAM–JUDAISM

Appeal of the Grand Mufti to the Islamic World in 1937

Since the beginning of their history, the Jews have always been an oppressed people, and there must surely be a good reason for this. The Egyptian Pharaohs were obliged to take energetic measures of repression against the Jews, who had exploited the Egyptian people and undermined popular morale through usury and various other crimes. In the end, there remained no other choice but to expel the Jews from the country, and under Moses's leadership, they passed across the Red Sea. As the famous Arab theologian Tabari relates, the Jews wanted to kill Moses when he returned from Mount Sinai. As punishment for this crime and for their apostasy from God, God made them wander for 40 years in the desert. Through this penance, the new generation that was born in this period had the opportunity to wipe away the sins of the fathers and return to the path of God. The new generation did indeed spread out across Mecca, Medina, Syria and Iraq, the lands that flowed with milk and honey. However, this generation was even worse than the preceding one, reflecting the Arab saying that "a dog had a puppy, but the puppy was still more dog-like than its begetter."

Those of the Jews who had come to Syria and Palestine then fell under Roman rule. Very soon the Romans recognized the danger the Jews posed to the country and enacted severe measures against them. Moreover, at that time, a serious epidemic, the plague, broke out that was generally believed to have been introduced by the Jews. When even the doctors too had declared that the Jews were the epicenter of the disease – which may well have been true – the people became so angry that many Jews were killed. This event is the reason why to this day the Jews are called "microbes." Because of this, Arabs are especially well placed to understand the fact that in Germany likewise energetic measures have been taken against

DOI: 10.4324/9781003369110-8

the Jews and they have been chased away like mangy dogs. The Arabs, however, are the victims of this, since the Jews, in large part from Germany, have moved to Palestine. There the Jewish scum from every country has assembled in order to take the Arabs' country. They have bought up land from the poorest of the poor and from unscrupulous landowners. They have stolen the bread from the mouth of the poor widow and taken the milk from the children in order to gorge themselves. They have not shrunk even from committing bloody murders when Arabs have opposed Jewish immigration and have robbed many families of their breadwinner and condemned them to poverty. "God will punish them for these foul deeds!"

This struggle of the Jews against the Arabs is nothing new; only the venue has changed in the course of time. The Jews hate Muhammad and Islam and anyone who wants to support his own people and fight against Jewish miserliness and corruption. The struggle between the Jews and Islam began when Muhammad fled from Mecca to Medina, where he laid the foundations for the development of Islam. Even in those days the Jews were great businessmen and immediately sensed that Muhammad's influence was a danger to them in both the spiritual and commercial spheres. They therefore developed a great hatred of Islam, and this hatred increased more and more as Islam grew stronger and mightier. They broke the Khaybar agreement that they had made with Muhammad and their anger reached a peak when the Koran revealed their deepest psychological impulses and exposed their unscrupulousness and lack of conscience and so made these things generally known. And the Jewish methods then were the same as they are today. Their weapon was as always slander, and so they tried to disparage Muhammad in the eyes of his followers. They said that he was a swindler, a magician and a liar. And when that did not succeed, they tried to undermine Muhammad's honor, by spreading the rumor that his wife Aisha had committed adultery. By spreading these rumors and assertions, they wanted to cast doubt into the hearts of Muhammad's followers.

And when this too did not work, they tried to discredit Muhammad's teachings. To that end, some Jews converted to Islam in order on the very next day to return to the Jewish religion. When asked about this sudden reversal, they slyly declared that they had tried out Islam in good will, but had had to conclude that it was all just a lie. In this respect, the Koran says,

> Many of the People of the Book wish they could make you unbelievers again, after you had become believers. The envy in their souls after the truth had become clear to them.
>
> *(2:103)[1]*

When the Jews understood the impossibility of reaching their goal through the means they had hitherto used, they sought a new approach. They began to ask Muhammad senseless and insoluble questions, thereby wishing to show others that Muhammad lacked knowledge and wisdom. But with this method too, just as before, they had no success. So they came to the conclusion that Islam is very firmly anchored in the hearts of the Muslims and thereafter strove to destroy the Muslims. The Jews committed the cowardly crime of paying some non-Muslim Arab tribes to fight against Muhammad. But Almighty God wished otherwise and Muhammad crushed the rebellious tribes with an iron fist and captured their city. The Jews could not bear this defeat and decided to destroy Muhammad at any price and hired murderers for this purpose.

In Medina, the Jews lived in the Banu Nadir district, and after he came to Medina, Muhammad made an agreement with them. One day he made his way to this district with only ten companions in order to talk to the Jews and bring them to Islam. Muhammad laid out the basic principles of Islam to them, and the Jews appeared very interested and approachable. While, therefore, Muhammad was engaged in friendly discussion with some of the Jews, others prepared an attempt on his life. They persuaded a man to hurl a heavy lump of rock at Muhammad's head. Muhammad would very possibly have been lost if God had not given him a warning. An inner voice urged him to leave the place so that the treacherous Jews were unable to carry out their plan. Muhammad sent one of his followers to the Jews to inform them that they must leave the city within ten days, since they had broken their agreement with him by attempting to take his life. Any Jew found to still be in the city after ten days would be punished by death.

But some of the Jews, who had outwardly adopted Islam but had inwardly remained Jews, convinced the other Jews not to leave the city. When therefore the ten-day deadline had passed, Muhammad was compelled to drive the Jews out of the city by force of arms. Some of these Jews fled to Khaybar and others to Syria. The Koran refers to this as follows:

> It was He who has driven these people of the Book who were unbelieving from their dwellings in the first banishment. You do not think that they would leave and they themselves thought their citadels would protect them from God. But God came to them, from where they did not imagine, and cast fear into their hearts, so that they destroyed their houses with their hands and with the hands of the believers. So heed the example, oh you who have eyes.
>
> *(59:2)*

The Jews that had fled to Khaybar did not consider themselves defeated and decided to take their revenge on Muhammad. They approached the other Jews in Khaybar as well as the Jews in Taima and Wadil el-Kura and hatched a plot: With the help of much money, they incited the non-Muslim Arab tribes to attack Medina. When Muhammad learned of this plan, he swiftly armed his people and marched upon Khaybar, the center of the revolutionary plans.

The Muhammadans captured Khaybar and drove out most of the Jews, while Muhammad made an agreement with the remaining Jews and thereby secured peace. Only after this decisive battle could the Islamic Empire develop peacefully. Given the Jewish character, however, it is no surprise that, despite the agreement, the Jews did not give up their evil plans and sought by every means to destroy Muhammad. They invited Muhammad to a banquet, and he unsuspectingly accepted the invitation. Splendidly roasted lamb was set before him and offered him by Zainab, the Jewess, the wife of Sallam ibn Mishkam. The talk was of the agreement and the harmony that now prevailed, and nothing was further from Muhammad's mind than any idea of betrayal. Muhammad and his faithful follower Bishr ibn al-Baraa each took a piece of the lamb; however, Muhammad did not swallow his piece, since he detected an odd taste and said:

> "The bone is telling me that the lamb is poisoned." Muhammad had Zainab, the Jewess, brought to him and asked her whether the meat was in fact poisoned. She replied, "You know that I am held in high regard by the Jews and I confess that I have poisoned the lamb. But in doing so I was thinking that, if you are only a king, I would kill a king; but if you are a true prophet, you would know that the meat was poisoned." Muhammad's companion died from the poison.

However, the little bit of poison that had got onto Muhammad's tongue continued to make itself felt, and some historians attribute his death to this. In doing so, they rely on a hadith narrated by Abu Huraira according to which shortly before his death Muhammad said, "the meal of Khaybar continues to make itself felt, and will do so until I am dead." The Muhammadans must always remain mindful of the meal in Khaybar. If the Jews could betray Muhammad in this way, how may they betray them today.

The Jews were now convinced that Muhammad's person was protected against any attack and therefore decided to sow discord among the tribes in order to break Islam's power. When Muhammad returned to Medina, he succeeded in reconciling the tribes of the Aus and Khasraj, who had been at war with one another for 120 years, and thus enormously strengthen the position of Islam. Under the banner of Islam, these two hostile tribes became true brothers, and peace was brought to the city. This was also the point at which the Jews sought to undermine the Islamic realm. One day, a vengeful old Jew, Shas ibn Qays, was passing with his friend across a square in which a meeting of the two reconciled tribes was taking place. He could not bear to see the two tribes that had fought so many battles with one another peacefully united and hatched a devilish plan. He sent his friend, who was well versed in the war stories of former times, and told him to recite the old songs of hate in the gathering. The Jew, who was a skilled orator, went up to the gathering and began to recite the old battle songs of the two tribes. He succeeded in finding one man from each tribe in whom the old hatred flared up anew. These two began to fight with one another and called their tribal brothers to arms. An incalculable disaster would have occurred if Muhammad, as soon as he received news of this civil strife, had not hurried to the scene. He cried out,

> Oh, my God, must the old times return while I am still with you? After Islam was given to you as a religion, the old tribal feuds were buried and in your hearts you became brothers. Do you want to fall back into unbelief?

By now the two tribes had realized that only through the Jews had the strife between them been sown. They threw down their weapons, begged God for forgiveness, embraced one another and made a new pact of brotherhood. Concerning the Jew Shas ibn Qays, the Koran says, "Oh People of the Book, why do you hold back the one who believes from the path of God, when you yourselves are witnesses? But he does not overlook what you are doing."[2]

And about the two tribes, the Aus and the Khasraj, it is said:

Oh you who believe, you are obeying a part of those who received the scripture, who are making you into infidels again, after you became believers. How can you be unbelieving, when God's verses have been read to you and his Messenger is among you? He who holds fast to God is already on the right path.

(3:94, 95, 96)[3]

But, in spite of all their efforts, the Jews did not succeed in sowing discord among Muhammad's followers and leading them back to unbelief. Although the Jews must have seen the futility of their efforts, they continued to try to implement their diabolical plans. And this time they tried to bring down Muhammad himself through a trick.

Two Jewish tribes were in conflict. The party that was in the wrong held a meeting and sent their leaders to Muhammad. The Jewish leaders said to Muhammad,

You know that we are very influential men. If you judge the dispute in our favor, we will use our influence to convert all the Jews to Islam.

It goes without saying that Muhammad rejected this proposal. In this respect, the Koran says,

That you make your decisions according to that which God reveals and do not follow their desires. Be cautious in their presence, so that they do not divert you from a part of what God reveals to you. If they turn away, know that God will surely strike them for some of their sins. Truly many people are malefactors.[4]

A further example of the subversive activities of the Jews is narrated by Ibn Abbas. At the time when Muhammad went from Mecca to Medina, the direction of prayer was towards Jerusalem. This situation lasted for only 17 months, until Muhammad received a divine revelation changing the direction of prayer henceforth towards Mecca, and since then the prayer has always been said with the face turned towards Mecca. The Koran says in this regard:

We saw you turn your face to heaven, now we want to turn it in a direction agreeable to you. Turn your face in the direction of the holy place of prayer. And wherever you find yourself turn your face in this direction. Behold, those who receive the scripture know that this is the truth from their Lord. And God does not overlook what they do.[5]

When the Jews heard these verses of the Koran, they were very angry and proposed to Muhammad that he restore the original direction of prayer towards Jerusalem. If he were to do so, they promised him, all the Jews would accept Islam. Muhammad, however, did not allow himself to be swayed by this request to repudiate the divine instruction. Thus, we read in the Koran,

We are changing the direction you turn to for prayer only so that we may distinguish him who follows the Messenger from him who turns on his heel. This was surely difficult but not for those whom God guides. And God will not destroy your faith for, behold, God is all-gracious and all-merciful to people.

(2:138)[6]

And here is yet another example of how the Jews did not shrink even from stabbing Muhammad in the back in times of greatest peril. When Muhammad had won the battle of Badr, he sent an emissary on his own camel, because it was the swiftest, to Medina to bring the news of his victory there. But the Jews tried to sow confusion in the ranks of the Muslims and demoralize Muhammad's companions in arms by spreading the lie that Muhammad had fallen in the battle. As proof, they cited the fact that Muhammad's camel had returned to the city with a strange rider upon it.

But when this plan too proved unsuccessful, some of the Jews went to Mecca and tried to incite Muhammad's enemies against him. They even declared themselves ready to support the Meccans in their struggle against Muhammad with an army. When the heathen Meccans asked the Jews whether Muhammad's religion was good, since the Jews even before Muhammad had received a holy scripture, the Jews said, "You know that we are men of science. So believe us when we tell you that your religion is far better."

In the Koran, the following is said about this:

Do you not see those who receive a portion of the scripture? They believe in Jibt and Taghut, but they say of those who do not believe that they are better guided on the path than those who believe. They are the ones whom God has cursed and whomever God curses, you will find no helper for him.[7]

And it can be seen how this curse has been proven true. The Jews are scattered outcast over the whole earth and nowhere do they find true help and support.

There is a further verse in the Koran that quite unmistakably describes the attitude of Islam to Judaism. It reads, "You will certainly find that the Jews and the idolaters harbor the strongest hostility to those who believe" (5:85).[8]

And a remark of Muhammad's expresses this idea even more clearly: "It will never be possible to see a Muslim and a Jew together without the Jew having the secret intention of destroying the Muslim."

Ibn Huraira narrates the following hadith:

The Hour (the Resurrection) will only come when the Muslims have inflicted a
crushing defeat on the Jews. When every stone and every tree behind which a
Jew has hidden says to the Muslim: "There is a Jew hiding behind me, come and
kill him.' Only the Gharqad tree, a little shrub with sharp thorns from the region
of Jerusalem will not take part, for it is a Jewish tree.

(Bukhari-Muslim VIII, p. 188)[9]

The reason for the above discussions is that the Jews are on the verge of reaching
out to take the holy places that are holy for every Muslim and every Christian. The
Islamic world and the friends of the Muslims must be shown what the Jews are
really like in their innermost being; in general we only see Jews with the veneer of
civilization, but the Arabs know best how they really are. And when someone has
come to understand the Jews as they [the Arabs] do, that is, as they are depicted
in the Koran and holy scriptures, then one will understand the torments to which
the Arabs in Palestine have already been subjected and can imagine how these torments will increase immeasurably if the Jews ever take full possession of Palestine.

To my Muslim brothers of the whole world, I present the history and true experience that the Jews cannot deny. The verses from the Koran and the hadiths prove
to you that the Jews have been the most bitter foes of Islam and are still trying to
destroy it. Do not believe them, they know only hypocrisy and guile.

Keep together, fight for the Islamic idea, fight for your religion and existence!
Do not rest until your land is free from the Jews!

Do not tolerate the partition plan, for Palestine has been for centuries an Arab
country and must always remain so.

**Source: Mohamed Sabry, *Islam-Judentum-Bolschewismus*, Berlin 1938,
pp. 22–32.**

Notes

1 The correct Koranic reference is 2:109. Other corrected Koranic references appear in
  footnotes, where appropriate – translator's comment.
2 3:99.
3 3:100–101.
4 5:49.
5 2:144.
6 2:143.
7 4:51–52.
8 5:82.
9 The correct references are Muslim, Vol. 41: 6985; Bukhari, Vol. 52: 177.

BIBLIOGRAPHY

Archival Sources

Bundesarchiv Berlin (BAB)

R 58	Reichssicherheitshauptamt
NS 19	Persönlicher Stab Reichsführer-SS
NS 31	SS-Hauptamt
R 78	Reichsfunkgesellschaft
R 4902	Deutsches Außenwissenschaftliches Institut
R 34	Deutsches Nachrichtenbüro
NS 9	Auslandsorganisation der NSDAP

Institut für Zeitgeschichte Munich (IfZ)

F 44	(Private papers of Felix E.A. Kersten)
ED 113	(Private papers of Werner Otto von Hentig)

Bundesarchiv Militärarchiv Freiburg (BA-MA)

RH 45	Einheiten der Propagandatruppe des Heeres
RH 19-VIII	Panzerarmee Afrika
RW 4	OKW, Wehrmachtführungsstag
RHD 54/3	"Die Oase", 19.3.41–19.3.42
RH 21-5	5. Panzerarmee

Politisches Archiv des Auswärtigen Amts Berlin (PAAA)

R 34	Deutsches Nachrichtenbüro
R 157 III F	The German Consulates in Palestine 1842–1939
R 27192	AA Chef A/O Akten betr.: Ägypten, Afrika 1937–1941
R 104775–104801	Abteilung Pol VII
R 901 58510	Palästina Presseberichte 1927–1940
R 901 58332–58336	Palästina 1939–1942
R 901 58351–58352	Palästina Weißbuch
R 901 73336	Ägypten 1935
Beirut 59	

British National Archive (BNA)

CO 733/326
CO 733/332
CO 733/351
CO 773/352
FO 141/838
FO 371/20807–20815
FO 371/21887
FO 371/21997–21998
FO 371/23342–23343
FO 648/10
WO 208/502
WO 208/560s
WO 208/1701
GFM 33/97
GFM 33/611–618
GFM 33/656

Akten zur Deutschen Auswärtigen Politik
Zentrum Moderner Orient Berlin, Höpp-Archiv
Keesing's Archiv der Gegenwart (AdG)

Books and Articles

Abdel-Samad, Hamed, *Mohamed. Eine Abrechnung*, Munich 2015.
Achcar, Gilbert, *The Arabs and the Holocaust. The Arab-Israeli War of Narratives*, New York 2009.
Adorno, Theodor W., "Zur Bekämpfung des Antisemitismus heute", *Das Argument*, Jg. 6, No. 29, 1964, 88–104.
Ansorge, Dirk (ed.), *Antisemitismus in Europa und in der arabischen Welt*, Paderborn 2006.
Arendt, Hannah, *Eichmann in Jerusalem*, Munich 1986.
Arsenian, Seth, "Wartime Propaganda in the Middle East", *The Middle East Journal*, Vol. II, October 1948, 417–429.

Barbour, Nevill, "Broadcasting to the Arab World. Arabic Transmissions from the B.B.C. and Other Non-Arab Stations", *Middle East Journal*, Vol V, Winter 1951, 57–69.

Barnett, David and Karsh, Efraim, "Azzam's Genocidal Threat", *Middle East Quaterly*, Vol. 18, Nr. 4, Fall 2011, 85–88.

Bauer, Jehuda, *Der Islamische Antisemitismus: Eine aktuelle Bedrohung*, Berlin 2018.

Baumgarten, Helga, *Hamas. Der politische Islam in Palästina*, Kreuzlingen and Munich 2006.

Bensoussan, George, *Die Juden in der arabischen Welt. Die verbotene Frage*, Berlin and Leipzig 2019.

Benz, Wolfgang (ed.), *Handbuch des Antisemitismus. Judenfeindschaft in Geschichte und Gegenwart, Band 1: Länder und Regionen*, Munich 2008.

Benz, Wolfgang (ed.), *Islamfeindschaft und ihr Kontext. Dokumentation der Konferenz "Feindbild Muslim – Feindbild Jude"*, Berlin 2009.

Benz, Wolfgang und Wetzel, Juliane (ed.), *Antisemitismus und radikaler Islamismus*, Essen 2007.

Bergmeier, Horst J.P. und Lotz, Rainer E., *Hitler's Airwaves. The Inside Story of Nazi Radio Broadcasting and Propaganda Swing*, New Haven, CT and London 1997.

Black, Edwin, *The Transfer Agreement. The Dramatic Story of the Pact between the Third Reich and Jewish Palestine*, New York 2001.

Bodansky, Yossef, *Islamic Anti-Semitism as a Political Instrument*, Houston, TX 1999.

Boelcke, Willi A., "Die archivalischen Grundlagen der deutschen Rundfunkgeschichte 1923 bis 1945", *Rundfunk und Fernsehen*, Vol. 16, Nr. 2, 1968, 161–179.

Boelcke, Willi A., *Die Macht des Radios. Weltpolitik und Auslandsrundfunk 1924–1976*, Frankfurt/M. 1977.

Bostom, Andrew G. (ed.), *The Legacy of Islamic Antisemitism*, New York 2008.

Bostom, Andrew G., *The Mufti's Islamic Jew-Hatred. What the Nazis Learned from the "Muslim Pope"*, Washington, D.C. 2014.

Bouman, Johan, *Der Koran und die Juden*, Darmstadt 1990.

Breitman, Richard and Goda, Norman J.W., *Hitler's Shadow: Nazi War Criminals, U.S. Intelligence, and the Cold War*, Washington D.C. 2010.

Brettfeld, Karina and Wetzels, Peter, *Muslime in Deutschland*, Hamburg 2007.

Briggs, Asa, *The War of Words*, London 1970.

Bullard, Reader, *Letters from Tehran*, London 1991.

Bundesamt für Verfassungsschutz, *Antisemitismus im Islamismus*, Cologne 2019.

Caplan, Neil, *Futile Diplomay Vol. II, Arab-Zionist Negotiations and the End of the Mandate*, London 1986.

Chomeini, Ajatollah, *Der Islamische Staat*, Berlin 1983.

Cohen, Hillel, *Army of Shadows. Palestinian Collaboration with Zionism, 1917–1948*, Berkeley, CA 2008.

Demirel, Aycan, "Antisemitismus in türkischsprachigen Medien", in Benz, Wolfgang (ed.), *Jahrbuch für Antisemitismusforschung 20*, Berlin 2011, 213–239.

Deutsche Welle (ed.), *Morgen die ganze Welt. Deutscher Kurzwellensender im Dienste der NS-Propaganda*, Cologne 1970.

Dieterich, Renate, "Germany's Relations with Iraq and Transjordan from the Weimar Republic to the End of the Second World War", *Middle Eastern Studies*, Vol. 41, No. 4, July 2005, 405–419.

Doran, Michael, *Pan-Arabism before Nasser*, New York 1999.

Driesch, Wolfgang, *Islam, Judentum und Israel*, Hamburg 2003.

Ebrami, Hooshang, "The Impure Jew", in Sarshar, Houman (ed.), *Esther's Children. A Portrait of Iranian Jews*, Beverly Hills, CA 2005, 97–102.

El-Awaisi, Abd al-Fattah M., *The Muslim Brothers and the Palestine Question, 1928–1947*, London 1996.

Elpeleg, Zvi, *Through the Eyes of the Mufti. The Essays of Haj Amin, Translated and Annotated*, London 2009.

Flores, Alexander, "Judeophobia in Context: Anti-Semitism among Modern Palestinians", *Die Welt des Islam*, Vol. 46, No. 3, 2006, 307–330.

Finkenberger, Martin, "'Während meines ganzen Lebens habe ich die Juden erforscht, wie ein Bakteriologe einen gefährlichen Bazillus studiert' – Johann von Leers (1902 -1965) als antisemitischer Propagandaexperte bis 1945", *Bulletin Nr. 2 des Deutschen Historischen Instituts*, 2008, 88–99.

Fishman, Joel, "The Postwar Career of Nazi Ideologue Johann von Leers, aka Omar Amin, the 'First-Ranging German' in Nasser's Egypt", *Jewish Political Studies Review*, Vol. 26, No. 3, Fall 2016 & 4, 54–72.

Frantzman, Seth J. und Culibrk, Jovan, "Strange Bedfellows: The Bosnians and Yugoslav Volunteers in the 1948 War in Israel/Palestine", *Istorija*, Vol. 20, No. 1, 2009, 189–200.

Fröhlich, Elke (ed.), *Die Tagebücher von Joseph Goebbels, Teil II, Band 8*, Munich 1987.

Gavison, Ruth (ed.), *The Two-State Solution. The UN Partition Resolution of Mandatory Palestine: Analysis and Sources*, Bloomsbury, New York and London, 2013.

Gelber, Yoav, *Palestine 1948. War, Escape and the Emergence of the Palestinian Refugee Problem*, Brighton and Portland 2006.

Gensicke, *Klaus, Der Mufti von Jerusalem und die Nationalsozialisten. Eine politische Biographie Amin el-Husseinis*, Darmstadt 2007.

Gerges, Fawaz A., "Egypt and the 1948 War", in Rogan, Eugene L. and Shlaim, Avi (eds.), *The War for Palestine. Rewriting the History of 1948*, Cambridge 2001, 151-177.

Gershoni, Israel (ed.), *Arab Responses to Fascism and Nazism. Attraction and Repulsion*, Austin, TX 2014.

Gershoni, Israel, "Demon and Infidel. Egyptian Intellectuals Confronting Hitler and Nazis during World War II", in Nicosia, Francis R. und Ergene, Bogac A. (eds.), *Nazism, the Holocaust and the Middle East*, New York 2018, 77–104.

Gilbert, Martin, *Winston S. Churchill, Vol. IV, Companion Part 2 (Documents July 1919– March 1921)*, London 1977.

Gilman, Sander L. and Katz, Steven T., *Anti-Semitism in Times of Crises*, New York and London, 1991.

Goldenbaum, Hans, "Nationalsozialismus als Antikolonialismus. Die deutsche Rundfunkpropaganda für die arabische Welt", *Vierteljahreszeitschrift für Zeitgeschichte*, Vol. 3, 2016, 449–489.

Gombrich, Ernst, *Myth and Reality in German Wartime Broadcasts*, London 1970.

Graves, Jr., Harold N., *War on the Short Wave*, New York 1973.

Green, David Fati (ed.), *Arab Theologians on Jews and Israel*, Geneva 1971.

Grigat, Stephan, *Die Einsamkeit Israels. Zionismus, die israelische Linke und die iranische Bedrohung*, Hamburg 2014.

Grigat, Stephan, "Zweierlei Vertreibungen, zweierlei Integration", Foreword to Bensoussan, George, *Die Juden der arabischen Welt. Die verbotene Frage*, Berlin and Leipzig 2019.

Grimm, Marc and Kahmann, Bodo (eds.), *Antisemitismus im 21. Jahrhundert. Virulenz einer alten Feindschaft in Zeiten von Islamismus und Terror*, Berlin 2018.

Grobba, Fritz, *Irak*, Berlin 1941, 82.

Grobba, Fritz, *Männer und Mächte im Orient*, Göttingen 1967.

Güven, Dilek, "Der neue Antisemitismus – Kritik an Israel oder Antisemitismus? Das Beispiel Türkei", in Benz, Wolfgang (ed.), *Jahrbuch für Antisemitismusforschung 23*, Berlin 2014, 50–56.

Gutman, Israel (ed.), *Enzyklopädie des Holocaust Band II*, Munich 1995.

Hale, Julian, *Radio Power. Propaganda and International Broadcasting*, London 1975.

Hamli, Mohsen, *Anti-Semitism in Tunisia 1881–1961*, Leipzig 2018.

Harkabi, Yehoshafat, *Arab Attitudes to Israel*, Jerusalem 1972.

Harkabi, Yehoshafat, *The Palestinian Covenant and Its Meaning*, London 1979.

Haurand, Kathrin, "Vom Nazi-Kollaborateur zum Gastland – Iran während des Zweiten Weltkrieges", *Medaon*, Vol. 11, No. 20, 2017.

Havel, Boris, "Haj Amin al-Husseini: Herald of a Religious Anti-Judaism in the Contemporary Islamic World", *The Journal of the Middle East and Africa*, Vol. 5, No. 3, September–December 2014, 221–243.

Heil, Johannes, "'Antijudaismus' und 'Antisemitismus' – Begriffe als Bedeutungsträger", in Benz, Wolfgang (ed.), *Jahrbuch für Antisemitismusforschung 6*, Frankfurt/M. 1997, 92–114.

Herf, Jeffrey, *The Jewish Enemy. Nazi Propaganda during World War II and the Holocaust*, Cambridge, MA 2006.

Herf, Jeffrey, *Nazi Propaganda for the Arab World*, New Haven, CT 2009.

Herf, Jeffrey, "Nazi Germany's Propaganda Aimed at Arabs and Muslims during World War II and the Holocaust: Old Themes, New Archival Findings", *Central European History*, Vol. 42, 2009, 709 – 736.

Herf, Jeffrey, "Hitlers Dschihad. Nationalsozialistische Rundfunkpropaganda für Nordafrika und den Nahen Osten", *Vierteljahreszeitschrift für Zeitgeschichte*, Vol. 58, No. 2, April 2010, 259–286.

Herf, Jeffrey, *Israel's Moment. International Support for and Opposition to Establishing the Jewish State, 1945–1949*, Cambridge 2022.

Hirszowicz, Lukasz, *The Third Reich and the Arab East*, London 1966.

Hitler, Adolf, *Mein Kampf*, München 1934.

Höpp, Gerhard (ed.), *Mufti-Papiere. Briefe, Memoranden, Reden und Aufrufe Amin al-Husainis aus dem Exil, 1940–1945*, Berlin 2001.

Hoff, Klaus, *Kurt Georg Kiesinger. Die Geschichte seines Lebens*, Frankfurt/M. 1969.

Ihrig, Stefan, *Atatürk in the Nazi Imagination*, Cambridge, MA 2014.

Institution zur Koordination und Publikation der Werke Imam Khomeinis, Abteilung Internationale Beziehungen, *Das Palästinaproblem aus der Sicht Imam Khomeinis*, Teheran 1996.

Jikeli, Günther, *Antisemitismus und Diskriminierungswahrnehmungen junger Muslime in Europa*, Essen 2012.

Jikeli, Günther, "Muslimischer Antisemitismus in Europa. Aktuelle Ergebnisse der empirischen Forschung", in Grimm, Marc and Kahmann, Bodo (eds.), *Antisemitismus im 21. Jahrhundert. Virulenz einer alten Feindschaft in Zeiten von Islamismus und Terror*, Berlin 2018, 113–133.

Kabha, Mustafa, "Palestinians and the Partition Plan", in Gavison, Ruth (ed.), *The Two-State Solution. The UN Partition Resolution of Mandatory Palestine: Analysis and Sources*, Bloomsbury, IN, New York and London 2013, 29–37.

Karsh, Efraim, *Palestine Betrayed*, New Haven, CT 2010.

Kedourie, Elie, "The Bludan Congress on Palestine, September 1937", *Middle Eastern Studies*, Vol. 17, No. 1, January 1981, 107–125.

Kedourie, Elie and Haim, Sylvia G., *Zionism and Arabism in Palestine and Israel*, London 1982.

Kedourie, Elie, *Arabic Political Memoirs and Other Studies*, London 1974.

Kempner, Robert, *SS im Kreuzverhör*, Hamburg 1987.

Khalaf, Issa, *Politics in Palestine. Arab Factionalism and Social Disintegration, 1939–1948*, Albany, NY 1991.

Khalidi, Rashid, "The Palestinians and 1948: The Underlying Causes for Failure", in Rogan, Eugene L. and Shlaim, Avi (eds.), *The War for Palestine. Rewriting the History of 1948*, Cambridge 2001, 12–36.

Khalil, Mohammad, *The Arab States and the Arab League, Vol. II, International Affairs*, Beirut 1962.

Kiefer, Michael, "Islamischer, islamistischer oder islamisierter Antisemitismus?", *Die Welt des Islam*, Vol. 46, No. 3, 2006, 277–306.

Kiefer, Michael, "Islamischer oder islamisierter Antisemitismus", in Benz, Wolfgang und Wetzel, Juliane (eds.), *Antisemitismus und radikaler Islamismus*, Essen 2007, 71–84.

Kimche, Jon and Kimche, David, *Both Sides of the Hill. Britain and the Palestine War*, London 1960.

Kisch, Frederick H., *Palestine Diary*, New York 1974.

Klarsfeld, Beate, *Die Geschichte des PG 2 633 930 Kiesinger*, Darmstadt 1969.

Königliche Palästina-Kommission: Bericht über Palästina, Berlin 1937.

Koestler, Arthur, *Promise and Fulfilment. Palestine 1917–1949*, New York 1949.

Kohlstruck, Michael and Ullrich, Peter, *Antisemitismus als Problem und Symbol. Phänomene und Interventionen in Berlin*, Volume 52 of the series *Berliner Forum Gewaltprävention*, Berlin 2014.

Krämer, Gudrun, *Minderheit, Millet, Nation? Die Juden in Ägypten 1914–1952*, Wiesbaden 1982.

Krämer, Gudrun, "Antisemitism in the Muslim World. A Critical Review", *Welt des Islam*, Vol. 46, No. 3, 2006, 243–276.

Kressel, Neil J., *'The Sons of Pigs and Apes'. Muslim Antisemitism and the Conspiracy of Silence*, Washington, D.C. 2012.

Küntzel, Matthias, *Jihad and Jew-Hatred. Islamism, Nazism and the Roots of 9/11*, New York 2007.

Küntzel, Matthias, *Islamischer Antisemitismus und deutsche Politik*, Berlin 2007.

Küntzel, Matthias, *Germany and Iran. From the Aryan Axis to the Nuclear Threshold*, Candor, NY 2014.

Küntzel, Matthias, "The Roots of Antisemitism in the Middle East: New Debates", in Rosenfeld, Alvin (ed.), *Resurgent Antisemitism. Global Perspectives*, Bloomington, IN 2013, 382–401.

Küntzel, Matthias, "Islamischer Antisemitismus als Forschungsbereich. Über Versäumnisse der Antisemitismusforschung in Deutschland", in Grimm, Marc and Kahmann, Bodo (eds.), *Antisemitismus im 21. Jahrhundert. Virulenz einer alten Feindschaft in Zeiten von Islamismus und Terror*, Berlin 2018, 135–155.

Kupferschmidt, Uri M., *The Supreme Muslim Council. Islam under the British Mandate for Palestine*, Leiden and New York, 1987.

Laqueur, Walter, *A History of Zionism*, New York 1972.

Lebel, Jennie, *The Mufti of Jerusalem: Haj-Amin el-Husseini and National-Socialism*, Belgrade 2007.

Leers, Johann von, "Judentum und Islam als Gegensätze", *Die Judenfrage in Politik, Recht, Kultur und Wirtschaft*, Vol. VI, No. 24, 15 December 1942, 275–277.

Lewis, Bernard, *The Emergence of Modern Turkey*, Oxford 1961.

Lewis, Bernard, *Bernard Lewis, Semites & Antisemites. An Inquiry into Conflict and Prejudice*, New York and London 1986.

Lewis, Bernard, *Bernard Lewis, the Jews of Islam*, Princeton, NJ 1984.

Lewis, Bernard, "The Arab World Discovers Anti-Semitism", in Gilman, Sander L. and Katz, Steven T. (eds.), *Anti-Semitism in Times of Crises*, New York and London, 1991, 343–352, here 343.

Lia, Brynjar, *The Society of the Muslim Brothers in Egypt*, Reading, MA 1988.

Litvak, Meir und Webman, Esther, *From Empathy to Denial. Arab Responses to the Holocaust*, London 2009.

Lozowick, Yaacov, *Israels Existenzkampf*, Hamburg 2006.

MacDonald, Callum A., "Radio Bari: Italian Wireless Propaganda in the Middle East and British Countermeasures 1934–38", *Middle Eastern Studies*, Vol. 13, No. 2, May 1977, 195–207.

Maddy-Weitzman, Bruse, *The Crystallization of the Arab State System 1945–1954*, New York 1993.

Magally, Nazier, "The Position of the Arab Leadership vis-à-vis the Partition Plan: The Crime and Its Punishment", in Gavison, Ruth (ed.), *The Two-State Solution. The UN Partition Resolution of Mandatory Palestine: Analysis and Sources*, Bloomsbury, IN, New York and London, 2013, 38–44.

Mallmann, Klaus-Michael and Cüppers, Martin, *Halbmond und Hakenkreuz. Das Dritte Reich, die Araber und Palästina*, Darmstadt 2006.

Mann, Thomas, *Briefe 1937–1947*, Frankfurt/M. 1963.

Marr, Wilhelm, *Der Sieg des Judenthums über das Germanenthum. Vom nicht confessionellen Standpunkt aus betrachtet*, Bern 1879.

Massing, Paul W., *Vorgeschichte des politischen Antisemitismus*, Frankfurt/M. 1959.

Mattar, Philip, *The Mufti of Jerusalem. Al-Hajj Amin al-Husayni and the Palestinian National Movement*, New York 1988.

Mayer, Thomas, "The Military Force of Islam. The Society of the Muslim Brethren and the Palestine Question, 1945–48", in Kedourie, Elie and Haim, Sylvia G. (eds.), *Zionism and Arabism in Palestine and Israel*, London 1982, 100–117.

Mayer, Thomas, *Egypt and the Palestine Question*, Berlin 1983.

Mayer, Thomas, "Egypt's 1948 Invasion of Palestine", *Middle Eastern Studies*, Vol. 22, No. 1, January 1986, 20–36.

Mayer, Thomas, "Arab Unity of Action and the Palestine Question, 1945–48", *Middle East Studies*, Vol. 22, No. 3, July 1986, 331–349.

Mejcher, Helmut (ed.), *Die Palästina-Frage 1917–1948. Historische Ursprünge und internationale Dimension eines Nationenkonflikts*, Paderborn 1993.

Mejcher, Helmut, *Der Nahe Osten im Zweiten Weltkrieg*, Paderborn 2017.

Milstein, Uri, *The Birth of a Palestinian Nation. The Myth of the Deir Yassin Massacre*, Jerusalem and New York, 2012.

Mitchell, Richard P., *The Society of the Muslim Brothers*, London 1969.

Moasseseh Pajooheshi Farhangi Enqlab Eslami (ed.), *The Most Important Problem of the Islamic World. Selected Statements by Ayatollah Khamenei about Palestine*, Teheran 2012.

Morris, Benny, *1948. The First Arab-Israeli War*, New Haven, CT 2008.

Motadel, David, *Islam and Nazi Germany's War*, London 2014.

Motadel, David, *Für Prophet und Führer. Die Islamische Welt und das Dritte Reich*, Stuttgart 2017.

Müller, Jochen, "Zwischen Abgrenzen und Anerkennen. Überlegungen zur pädagogischen Begegnung von antisemitischen Einstellungen bei deutschen Jugendlichen muslimischer/ arabischer Herkunft", in Benz, Wolfgang (ed.), *Jahrbuch für Antisemitismusforschung*, Berlin 2008, 97–103.

Nettler, Ronald L., *Past Trials & Present Tribulations. A Muslim Fundamentalist's View of the Jews*, Oxford 1987.

Nevo, Joseph, "The Arabs of Palestine 1947–48: Military and Political Activity", *Middle Eastern Studies*, Vol. 23, No. 1, January 1987, 3–38.

Nia, Mahdi Mohammad, "Discourse and Identity in Iran's Foreign Policy", *Iranian Review of Foreign Affairs*, Vol. 3, No. 3, Fall 2012, 29–64.

Nicosia, Francis R., *Nazi Germany and the Arab World*, New York 2015.

Nicosia, Francis R. and Ergene, Bogac A. (eds.), *Nazism, the Holocaust and the Middle East*, New York 2018.

Nirenberg, David, *Anti-Judaism. The Western Tradition*, New York and London 2013.

Ourghi, Abdel-Hakim, *Reform des Islam. 40 Thesen*, Munich 2017.

Pappè, Ilan, *The Making of the Arab-Israeli Conflict 1947–1951*, London 2015.

Penkower, Monty Noam, *Palestine to Israel. Mandate to State, 1945–1948, Vol. II: Into the International Arena*, New York 2019.

Picker, Henry, *Hitlers Tischgespräche im Führerhauptquartier 1941–42*, Bonn 1951.

Pink, Johanna, *Geschichte Ägyptens. Von der Spätantike bis zur Gegenwart*, Munich 2014.

Pohle, Heinz, *Der Rundfunk als Instrument der Politik*, Dissertation, Hamburg 1953.

Poliakov, Léon, *Geschichte des Antisemitismus, Band II. Das Zeitalter der Verteufelung und des Ghettos*, Worms 1978.

Porath, Yehoshua, *The Emergence of the Palestinian-Arab National Movement 1918–1929*, London 1974.

Porath, Yehoshua, *The Palestinian Arab National Movement. From Riots to Rebellion, Volume Two 1929–1939*, London 1977.

Qasimiyya, Chairiyya, "Palästina in der Politik der arabischen Staaten 1918–1948", in Mejcher, Helmut (ed.), *Die Palästina-Frage 1917–1948. Historische Ursprünge und internationale Dimension eines Nationenkonflikts*, Paderborn 1993, 123–188.

Ro'i, Yaacov, *From Encroachment to Involvement. A Documentary Study of Soviet Policy in the Middle East, 1945–1973*, New York 1974.

Rolo, Charles J., *Radio Goes to War*, London 1943.

Rosenfeld, Alvin (ed.), *Deciphering the New Antisemitism*, Bloomington, IN 2015.

Rubin, Barry, *The Great Powers in the Middle East 1941–1947. The Road to the Cold War*, London 1980.

Rubin, Barry, *The Arab States and the Palestinian Conflict*, Syracuse, NY 1981.

Rubin, Barry and Schwanitz, Wolfgang G., *Nazis, Islamists, and the Making of the Modern Middle East*, New Haven, CT and London 2014.

Sabry, Mohamed, *Islam-Judentum-Bolschewismus*, Berlin 1938.

Sansal, Boualem, "Avant-Propos", in Küntzel, Matthias (ed.), *Jihad Et Haine Des Juifs. Le lien troublant entre islamisme et nazisme à la racine du terrorisme international*, Paris 2015, 5–6.

Sarshar, Houman (ed.), *Esther's Children. A Portrait of Iranian Jews*, Beverly Hills, CA 2005.

Sartre, Jean-Paul, "Betrachtungen zur Judenfrage", in Sartre, Jean-Paul (ed.), *Drei Essays*, Berlin 1970, 108–190.

Satloff, Robert, *Among the Righteous. Lost Stories from the Holocaust's Long Reach into Arab Lands*, New York 2006.

Schechtman, Joseph B., *The Mufti and the Fuehrer: The Rise and Fall of Haj Amin el-Husseini*, New York 1965.

Schiller, David Th., *Palästinenser zwischen Terrorismus und Diplomatie*, Munich 1982.

Schirmbeck, Samuel, *Der islamische Kreuzzug und der ratlose Westen. Warum wir eine selbstbewusste Islamkritik brauchen*, Zurich 2017.

Schnabel, Reimund, *Mißbrauchte Mikrophone. Deutsche Rundfunkpropaganda im Zweiten Weltkrieg*, Vienna 1967.

Schroeder, Herbert, *Ein Sender erobert die Herzen der Welt*, Essen 1940.

Schwarz-Friesel, Monika, *Judenhass im Internet. Antisemitismus als kulturelle Konstante und kollektives Gefühl*, Berlin and Leipzig 2019.

Schwipps, Werner, *Wortschlacht im Äther. Der deutsche Auslandsrundfunk im Zweiten Weltkrieg*, Berlin 1971.

Shlaim, Avi, *The Politics of Partition. King Abdullah, the Zionists and Palestine 1921–1951*, 1998.

Shragai, Nadav, *The "Al-Aksa Is in Danger" Libel: The History of a Lie*, Jerusalem 2012.

Stav, Arieh, *Peace: The Arabian Caricature. A Study of Anti-Semitic Imagery*, New York, 1999.

Stillman, Norman A., *The Jews of Arab Lands. A History and Source Book*, Philadelphia, PA 1979.

Strawson, John, *Partitioning Palestine. Legal Fundamentalism in the Palestinian-Israeli Conflict*, London 2010.

Taggar, Yehuda, *The Mufti of Jerusalem and Palestine Arab Politics, 1930–1937*, New York 1986.

Taheri, Amir, *The Spirit of Allah. Khomeini & the Islamic Revolution*, Bethesda, MD 1986.

Tal, David, *War in Palestine 1948. Strategy and Diplomacy*, London 2004.

Wawrzyn, Heidemarie, *Nazis in the Holy Land 1933–1948*, Berlin 2013.

Webman, Esther, "From the Damascus Blood Libel to the Arab Spring'. The Evolution of Arab Antisemitism", *Antisemitism Studies*, Vol. 1, No. 1, Spring 2017, 157–206.

Wetzel, Juliane, "Judenfeindschaft unter Muslimen in Europa", in Benz, Wolfgang (ed.), *Islamfeindschaft und ihr Kontext. Dokumentation der Konferenz 'Feindbild Muslim – Feindbild Jude'*, Berlin 2009, 45–61.

Wetzel, Juliane, *Moderner Antisemitismus unter Muslimen in Deutschland*, Wiesbaden 2014.

Wild, Stefan, "'Mein Kampf' in arabischer Übersetzung", *Welt des Islam*, Vol. 9, 1964, 207–211.

Wild, Stefan, "Zum Selbstverständnis palästinensisch-arabischer Nationalität", in Mejcher, Helmut (ed.), *Die Palästina-Frage 1917–1948. Historische Ursprünge und internationale Dimension eines Nationenkonflikts*, Paderborn 1993, 73–88.

Wild, Stefan, "Importierter Antisemitismus? Die Religion des Islam und Rezeption der 'Protokolle der Weisen von Zion' in der arabischen Welt", in Ansorge, Dirk (ed.), *Antisemitismus in Europa und in der arabischen Welt*, Paderborn 2006, 201–216.

Wiesenthal, Simon, *Großmufti: Großagent der Achse*, Salzburg 1947.

Wildangel, René, *Zwischen Achse und Mandatsmacht. Palästina und der Nationalsozialismus*, Berlin 2007.

Wirsing, Giselher, *Engländer Juden Araber in Palästina*, Leipzig 1942.

Zamir, Meir, *The Secret Anglo-French War in the Middle East. Intelligence and Decolonization, 1940–1948*, London and New York 2015.

INDEX

Note: Page numbers followed by "n" denote endnotes.

For Product Safety Concerns and Information please contact our EU
representative GPSR@taylorandfrancis.com Taylor & Francis Verlag GmbH,
Kaufingerstraße 24, 80331 München, Germany

Printed and bound by CPI Group (UK) Ltd, Croydon, CR0 4YY

08/06/2025
01897000-0017